SECURING THE FUTURE

SUCCESSION PLANNING BASICS

AMERICAN INSTITUTE OF CERTIFIED PUBLIC ACCOUNTANTS

10224-356

William L. Reeb, CPA

Sponsored by the Private Companies Practice Section (PCPS)

Notice to Readers

Securing the Future: Succession Planning Basics does not represent an official position of the American Institute of Certified Public Accountants, and it is distributed with the understanding that the author and publisher are not rendering, legal, accounting, or other professional services in the publication. If legal advice or other expert assistance is required, the services of a competent professional should be sought.

Publisher: Linda Prentice Cohen
Senior Managing Editor: Amy M. Stainken
Developmental Editor: Andrew Grow
Project Manager: Amy Sykes
Cover Design Direction: Clay Porter
Interior Designer: David McCradden

Foreword

The AICPA's Private Companies Practice Section (PCPS) is proud to be a part of the *Securing the Future* publication series. When succession planning was identified as a significant profession issue back in 2004, PCPS was there and hired one of the true thought leaders in the profession, Bill Reeb, CPA to gain further insight and to create a publication to address the needs of the profession in this area.

Fast forward four years to 2008, when PCPS again called on Bill to conduct research into this issue and—based on past experience and current issues raised—help PCPS create the PCPS Succession Resource Center. Bill and his partners, Dominic Cingoranelli and Michaelle Cameron, founders of the new organization the Succession Institute, collectively developed the materials and worked in getting the PCPS Succession Resource Center live and content rich on the PCPS Web site (www.pcps.org). The Succession Resource Center is web based learning, and houses both text and video content on succession issues. In addition to it's online offerings, PCPS also wanted to provide a print version for the broader audience. We went back to the Succession Institute team to create a second publication in this *Securing the Future* series.

As part of the succession research, PCPS conducted a survey in 2004 and 2008. The results of the 2008 survey showed slight improvement with 35% of responding multi owner firms and 9% of sole proprietors reporting having a succession plan in place. In 2004, only 25% of multi owner firms and 8% of sole proprietors had a plan. While it appears that some progress has been made, a great deal of work remains to be done in our profession to prepare for succession within firms.

While many firms aren't focused directly on Succession Planning, PCPS has realized that succession issues are more about how you manage your practice than a standard profession rule of thumb on what the multiple may be to calculate value. In this first volume, *Securing the Future: Succession Planning Basics*, does a great job in setting up the reader to start down the proper path of succession by focusing on internal operations. The subsequent volume, *Securing the Future: Taking Succession to the Next Level*, then builds on what is learned in this book and helps apply that learning to the succession strategy you determine for your firm. We believe that the two volumes in this set are "must reads" for anyone in public accounting who is contemplating succession planning or retirement.

However, even if succession or preparing for imminent retirement are not high priorities now, these two volumes are chock full of tools, techniques, ideas, and best practices that can help any professional firm operate more effectively, successfully, and profitability. We would like to thank Bill, Dom and Michaelle for their hard work and tireless contribution to the profession. The *Securing the Future* series is a true gem for the profession. We'd also like to thank the PCPS Executive Committee who, since 2003, have kept a key focus on help-ing the profession with this very important issue. The leadership started with Rich Caturano and continued with David Morgan and we hope to continue to build on the pathway both have set for this committee in recent years.

William Pirolli, CPA
Chair, Private Companies Practice Section Executive Committee

James C. Metzler, CPA_CITP
Vice President, Small Firm Interests, AICPA

Mark Koziel, CPA
Director, Specialized Communities & Firm Practice Management, AICPA

Foreword to the First Edition

The AICPA Private Companies Practice Section (PCPS) is pleased to bring the profession our ongoing series of resources, tools, and guidance for succession in your firm. The mission of the PCPS is to make practicing CPAs and their firms successful. As part of this mission, we have assembled the best resources in the country to help you and your firm chart the proper course to successfully transition to the next generation of leaders. Bill Reeb is truly one of the most renowned and respected experts on firm practice success and is at the top of his fame in his authorship of this practical and insightful book.

We are part of a "graying" America. One Baby Boomer turns 50 every seven seconds. In 1993, almost 47 percent of the AICPA membership was over 40. By the end of 2004, that figure had jumped to more than 68 percent. Members of the accounting profession will retire faster than new CPAs can replace them; today, a substantial number of firms do not survive the founding partner. Firm succession discussions at Managing a Practice (MAP) conferences a few years ago were only about maximizing value. Now, the most pressing issue is to enable firms to continue successfully after key partners retire or move on.

This series of AICPA/PCPS succession resources are all under one tent: To build a firm that can be transitioned successfully in the future, the firm must be built to be strong and successful *today*.

Current and future success go hand in hand. Even if succession is not a focus of your attention at the moment, there are many powerful lesions in this book from Bill Reeb that will enable your firm to indeed be stronger and more profitable right now.

Many thanks to the members of the PCPS Executive Committee Succession Task Force, who devoted countless volunteer hours to the development of this book. Special thanks to the Chair, Wayne Berson, CPA.

Richard Caturano, CPA
Chair, Private Companies Practice Section Executive Committee

James C. Metzler, CPA
Vice President, Small Firm Interests, AICPA

Sheryl Martin, CPA
Director, Firm Practice Management, AICPA

Acknowledgments

First, I would like to thank my wife and associate, Michaelle Cameron, Ph.D., for her help writing this book. As a marketing professor for Saint Edwards University in Austin Texas, her experience and insight added significant value to the Business Development Chapter (chapter 4). Michaelle also supplied an essential perspective and clarity as to how to best develop the materials in each chapter.

Next, I want to thank the PCPS Executive Committee for engaging me to do this project and the PCPS Succession Task Force, Sheryl Martin, Mark Koziel and Jim Metzler for working with me throughout this process. Sheryl provided the necessary management and oversight for this work and supported me during its development, Jim's and Mark's vision never wavered as to how he wanted this product to support our public practitioner members.

I want to thank everyone who has worked with me, offered feedback, and provided support materials for this venture. One of my close friends, Michael Harnish, an associate with Plante & Moran, spent a great deal of time discussing CPA firm management issues with me. I have had the benefit of the support of all of my friends and clients, as well as the many firms that participated in the PCPS Succession Survey. I would like to give a special accolade to those firms that additionally contributed time by granting me personal interviews regarding various topics in the book.

I want to express my gratitude to the firms that contributed the many exhibits now found on the Web site accompanying this book and *Securing the Future: Taking Succession to the Next Level*. Some firms wanted to remain anonymous while others allowed me to give their attributions:

- Mathis, West, Huffines & Co., P.C., Wichita Falls, Texas
    - Sample New Client and New Work Acceptance Policy
    - Sample Client Acceptance Form for Projects of $7,500 or More
- Horovitz, Rudoy & Roteman, Pittsburgh, Pennsylvania
    - Sample Billing and Collection Policy
    - Sample Owner Retirement Policy
- Brady, Ware & Schoenfeld, Inc., Dayton, Ohio
    - Compensation Plan (adapted for publication)
- Miller Grossbard & Associates, P.C., Houston, Texas
    - Compensation Plan (adapted for publication)
- Walter & Shuffain, P.C., Norwood, Massachusetts
    - Sample Point System Tracker

Finally, I would like to thank Laura Inge, Editor; and Marie Bareille, Manager of Specialized Publications, and Rich Grant, Product Development Manger, all of the AICPA. Marie and Laura have been improving my writing since they worked with me on my first book in 1988, and with numerous publications since then. Laura has a special ability to organize, simplify, and improve my work, a rare talent. And without Marie mentoring, guiding, and supporting me throughout the years, I believe I would never have written this book. Rich made numerous project management contributions throughout the development of this work and orchestrated the creation of content for the accompanying Web site.

The following are members of the PCPS Executive Committee Succession Planning Task Force who provided direction for and reviews of this book.

Wayne Berson, CPA, Task Force Chair
BDO Seidman, LLP
Bethesda, Maryland

David K. Morgan, CPA/PFS
Lattimore, Black, Morgan & Cain, P.C.
Brentwood, Tennessee

Norman L. Myers, II, CPA
Rotz & Stonefifer
Chambersburg, Pennsylvania

William Pirolli, CPA
Pirolli, Deller & Conaty, PC
Warwick, Rhode Island

Roy J. Russell, CPA
Roy & O'Connor, CPAs, Inc.
Paso Robles, California

Gorden E. Scherer, CPA
Horovitz, Rudoy & Roteman
Pittsburgh, Pennsylvania

John Welch, CPA
Doshier, Pickens & Francis, PC
Amarillo, Texas

About the Author

Bill Reeb, *CPA, CITP*

Bill is CEO and co-founder of the consulting firm Succession Institute, LLC. He has been consulting for three decades to all sizes of businesses, from Mom and Pop operations to Fortune 100 companies, primarily in the areas of organization, automation, and revenue generation. He decided to add the credentials of CPA behind his advisory work and became a CPA in 1986. Prior to his life as a consultant, he worked for IBM in sales back in the late 70's. As an entrepreneur, Bill has founded eight small businesses in the retail, software development, and services sectors.

As an award-winning public speaker, Bill lectures throughout the U.S. and Canada to thousands of executives and CPAs each year. In addition, he has been featured on numerous video-taped and live television programs. As an award-winning author, Bill is internationally published with hundreds of articles and columns to his credit. He currently authors a bi-monthly column called "In the Bill-iverse" which at the time of this printing is distributed by 15 State CPA Societies as part of their Practice Management e-newsletter. Besides being published by various magazines, journals and newspapers, Bill has written a number of books, including the fourth edition of his consulting book. Bill also authored the second volume of *Securing the Future: Taking Succession to the Next Level.* And as you can see, this book is a sequel to his first book on succession with this material covering Succession Planning as well as a number of best practice CPA Firm Management topics. Finally, Bill co-authored the Succession Resource Center Web site materials for PCPS in 2008.

Bill is an active volunteer within his profession, having served in many leadership roles in the AICPA such as being a current commissioner of the National Accreditation Commission (NAC). He has also served in numerous other roles including being a member of AICPA Council several times, a member of Strategic Planning and Chair of the Consulting Services Committees. On a local level, Bill has been a member of the Executive Board, Strategic Planning, and Chaired several Technology Committees for the Texas Society of CPAs. Additionally, he has been honored by being named as a CPA Ambassador, was presented the Pathfinder Award and served as the Texas Vision Delegate. *Accounting Today* has recognized his efforts by listing him as one of the Top 100 Most Influential CPAs, CPA Magazine has named him as one of the Top 100 Most Influential Practitioners, and Inside Public Accounting listed him several times as one of the most recommended CPA firm consultants.

Table of Contents

Introduction

Chapter 1: The Environment and Strategy: Managing Resources, Maximizing Reward

Chapter 2: Structure and Leadership: Establishing a Foundation and Consistency

Chapter 3: Management and Operations: Extending the Life and Culture of the Firm

Chapter 4: Growth and Transition: Increasing the Value of the Firm

Chapter 5: Succession Strategies: Passing the Torch

Introduction

The objectives of this introduction are to:

- Introduce and impart an understanding of the concepts behind the superstar and operator models.
- Recognize how planning can help you avoid the common spinning motion many CPA firms encounter when setting sail towards a destination.
- Outline how to use this book.

For many who first pick up this text, they will expect the first chapter to get right into the meat of this book. Suggestions provided include:

- Terms for creating a retirement or practice continuation agreement
- What should be put in place so that the retiring owners have confidence that they will receive their full payout
- What a client transition plan and timetable should look like for retiring owners
- How to get senior owners to timely transition their clients
- What behaviors firms should expect from retiring owners at the time of retirement and after
- What kinds of arrangements make sense for retired owners who still want to contribute to the firm

- How the outgoing owners can gain confidence in the incoming leadership
- What a firm should look for in a merger or buyer candidate
- Some common pricing models for selling or merging your firm, and so on

I will get to all of this and much more, but, in order for this book to be helpful, succession must be put into a much broader context. By analogy, think of succession as the roof of a house. To serve its purpose and provide value, it has to be supported by a strong foundation and load-bearing walls. Similarly, it is difficult to put succession into perspective without considering the strengths and weaknesses of a firm's foundation and supporting infrastructure.

Based on my experience with CPA firms, I can tell you that, although addressing the questions above is essential, the first step is to understand the root causes of the problems and critical success factors. For example, having confidence in the incoming leadership is less about finding the right people and more about the structure these new leaders will inhabit. Another example is the danger of overemphasizing the terms of the retirement agreement and the agreed-to payout rather than building a strong foundation that can endure the stress of transition. Although the terms and conditions are critical, if the firm splits up and every owner goes his or her separate way as a result of disagreements about strategic direction or core values, the retired owners are likely going to have to work hard to get their full payout.

Based on what I have seen, a successful firm succession is less about the legal agreements and more about the entire business strategy. Think of it this way … the more dependent a firm is on individuals rather than infrastructure, the more likely the transition will fail. For example, if you are sitting on the board of a public company, you would take hiring a new chief executive officer (CEO) very seriously. At the same time, you would not assume that the company was totally dependent on this person's personal performance. A CEO's poor performance might result in less than the desired success, but the board would assume that the real assets of the business, such as its customer base, employees, products or services, marketing programs, and quality control processes, would drive the company's future.

So, if you are serious about succession planning, please read this book from cover to cover to get the most out of it. Give me a chance to make my case if I take a position that is controversial or antagonistic to your view. I am just trying to share my experiences and those of many firms around the country. I am not guaranteeing that the approaches I cover will work for you, just as I am not telling you that your approach—if it is different—will not work. I am suggesting that if you read the entire book, I am confident that the discussions will spark ideas that will help you and your firm operate more successfully and profitably.

I want you to take one more point under consideration. As I introduce stories of how other firms work through these situations, as well as survey data, keep an open mind. When working with firms, I frequently hear comments like, "Our firm is different because we operate in a small community," or "The norms don't apply to us because of our firm size," or "Our problems are unique because of the part of the country we're in." Generally speaking, most CPA firms, regardless of where they are located, are facing the same problems. Yes, a firm in a small town might be able to pay a CPA with five years of experience $40,000 a year, while an accountant with the same skills might cost $65,000 in a metropolitan area, but the issues are still the same. Yes, the average owner's billing rate in a Midwestern firm might be $150 per hour, while an owner with similar skills might bill at $225 per hour on the West Coast. However, in the final analysis, all firms share big picture issues, such as:

- Getting a fair return on payroll investment
- Maximizing personal income within the parameters of firm members' desired work/life balance
- Increasing the value of the largest asset most owners have-their interest in the firm
- Attracting the best and brightest people in order to develop the firm's future leaders
- Feeling that they are making a difference to the clients they serve
- Enjoying the people they work with while building a firm that they are proud to be a part of
- Being able to decide how they want to spend their limited time

So, as you consider the experiences of other firms and read my recommendations, please start your analysis from the assumption that CPA firms, regardless of their locations, and in all shapes and sizes, are far more similar than they are different.

Two concepts are fundamental to this book. First, there are two basic models used to build a firm, namely, the superstar model and the operator model. Second, there is the concept of planning for firm succession. These concepts are discussed below and are followed by a guide on how to use this book.

Superstar Model Versus Operator Model

CPA firms, generally speaking, look to one of two strategies to build and operate their firm. The first of these is what I call the *superstar* model, and the second is the *operator* model. CPA firms usually start out using the superstar model, which can be defined as a model that places a premium on the "extraordinary capability, commitment, aggressiveness, entrepreneurship, and stamina of a few people for its success." When you are just starting out, or if you are a small operation, this model not only makes sense, but it is very efficient, effective, and profitable.

The second model, the operator model, is the opposite. It can be defined as a model that places a premium on "the extraordinary systems, processes, procedures, and methodology (the infrastructure) of a firm to maximize the potential of the people that work within it." Here are a couple differences I see between the two:

- Superstars look for extraordinary employees to leverage the firm's processes. Operators look to extraordinary processes to leverage its employees.
- Superstars believe that the perpetuation of the firm and its future success is heavily dependent on having a natural leader at the helm. Operators believe the firm's future success is less about the leader and much more about a strong infrastructure with clearly defined roles and responsibilities.
- Superstars place a premium on adding strong personalities (like business developers and entrepreneurs) to sustain the growth of a business. Operators look for more

processes, support, and methodology (like enhancing the firmwide marketing or compensation systems) to place emphasis and capability throughout the organization to grow the business.

- Superstars believe that those that are worthy must go through an "eat-what-you-kill" rite of passage. It is a mentality that assumes that *cream will rise to the top on its own* or *only the strong will survive*. Operators believe that almost anyone can develop into a technically competent project manager with client relationship responsibility; therefore, career management that provides clear career paths becomes critical to the firm's success.
- Superstars thrive on creating, changing, inventing, experimenting, and taking risks. Operators thrive on consistency, controls, setting standards, compliance with standards, continuous improvement, and low risk.

Both profiles are important to building and developing a successful service operation, but the optimum profile differs depending on the maturity of the firm. Consider a continuum, with the left-most point being a superstar and the right-most point being an operator. Start-up CPA firms are usually founded on the superstar philosophy, which relies on an individual or two to find the clients, service them, bill and collect, and, in their spare time, run the business. Without these entrepreneurs, there would be no business to transition. But because the superstar strategy is so dependent on these individuals, successful transition is tricky. As a firm matures and the demand for services shifts from exponential growth to a more methodical and predictable level, firms usually shift to an operator strategy of management, in order to build a firm that can continue through generations of leaders. This operator mentality shifts the firm's philosophies away from catering to irreplaceable people to developing an infrastructure that creates irreplaceable positions (that a variety of people can successfully fill). A few basic principles of an operator model are:

- Developing leadership that can successfully function within the existing structure so that the firm's success will continue.
- Creating a viable and enduring chain of command with clearly understood and adhered-to roles and responsibilities. This allows a structure that supports new people filling important positions functioning within a range of known flexibilities and limitations.
- Operating like a firm rather than like a group of individual owners. The firm controls who serves the clients, what services are offered, and what processes and procedures are followed—not the individual CPAs managing the relationships.
- Transitioning of clients occurs any time the firm decides a client could be better served by other resources (e.g., the skill set of an individual more closely matches the services utilized by that client) or in order to balance the distribution of demand among resources (owners with huge differences in books managed).
- Developing systems to reward desired behavior and discourage undesired behavior. These systems are built to reflect the current firm strategy, are usually based on objective criteria, reward overachievement, put a spotlight on underachievement, and are put in place to raise the firm's minimum standard of performance.

- Developing a staffing model that leverages realization and utilization, while balancing the need for business development, technical competence, project management, client service, and the management of client relationships.

First of all, I want to clarify one point ... both models work, and there are successful examples of each all over the country. But, as you can tell from the above narrative, far more money is invested in the firm's infrastructure in the operator model than in the superstar model. However, that tends to be a short-term difference because I find that, over the long term, the operator-driven firms deliver higher incomes to owners than the superstar-driven firms. Also, my experience shows that the easiest path for successful succession is in the operator model. Although success may flourish in the superstar model, its succession strategy is dependent on finding incoming superstars to take over. This model can be very limiting. It is hard for a firm to grow beyond about $5 million to $8 million in revenues because firms in this size range grow to the point that there are too many superstars. Inevitably, each superstar:

- Has a very definite opinion about how the firm should operate.
- Is unwilling to give up certain privileges of ownership.
- Believes that the success of the firm is less important than the personal relationships he or she maintains with clients.
- Believes he or she is entitled to have a say in every aspect of the way the business is run.
- Is convinced that any compromise to his or her personal strategy of running the firm is doomed to failure.
- Inwardly (and sometimes vocally) threatens to take his or her clients and leave the next time a compromise is required. This constant posturing often holds the firm hostage.

It shouldn't surprise anyone by now that this book is about how to bridge the gaps between the superstar and operator models.

Planning Is the First Step

One of the goals of this book is to motivate you to start thinking about where you want to go. Theodore Roosevelt said, "When you aim at nothing, you'll hit it every time." A great many firms right now are *aiming and firing everyday without agreement as to the target*. The best image that describes the typical CPA firm is a sailboat hundreds of miles from any shore, with several equally desired destinations under consideration. Although this firm would be happy to land on any of a multitude of shores, they remain offshore because there is no consensus about the firm's strategy. Typically, part of the owner group vocalizes a desired destination and the firm starts heading toward it, only to find an owner or two on the back of the boat throwing anchors overboard to impede progress. Then, the group gets together and someone bullies the others into changing course. This results in the sailboat turning toward a different shore, only to find another owner hoisting the sails, while others are at work, again, with the anchors. In reality, the owners would be happier at *any* of the various destinations than where they are—stranded in the water. But since each owner is entitled to choose a destination, the firm rarely makes significant progress in any direction. Just as the sailboat picks up speed in one direction, it is forced to change course again, causing the boat to spin rather than consistently moving ahead.

This section considers the following issues when planning, namely, when to plan, the time frame for a plan, monitoring a plan, and the purpose of a plan.

When to Create the Plan

A number of firms take the position that they do not want to spend time planning until they can identify near-term addressable obstacles. Well, simply put, a great deal of the time, those "addressable obstacles" are actually behaviors (or lack thereof) of members of the owner group. The most expedient way to overcome these obstacles is to face the issues directly. Although most owner groups are very good at addressing general business matters, they struggle when it comes to conflict among themselves. Therefore, if you can frame a problem area or behavior in a larger context, as a broad owner-agreed-to strategic objective, the alternatives are much less personal and therefore far easier to resolve.

For example, let me give you a common "near-term addressable obstacle." Consider a senior owner who is ready to retire. The retiring owner often wants nothing to really change during his or her last few years ... and, often, these same people want to put restrictions on the firm regarding the changes allowed through their payoff. Since these owners often control a significant block of voting rights, they are able to strong-arm younger owners. For instance, older owners can argue, "If you don't agree, I will sell the firm," or, "If you don't accept my offer, I won't retire." It should come as no surprise that the younger owners often feel that they have been backed into a corner with no alternative but to agree because both options, i.e., selling the firm or the retiring owner deciding not to retire, are even more unacceptable. If these conversations turn from the issues at hand, and become matters of principle to the owners, the situation can unravel very quickly, leading to the fragmenting of the firm. The point is that the extreme positions taken in these situations may be in the best interests of an individual, but are rarely in the best interests of the firm. In reality, although a majority owner might be able to sell or merge the firm without the other owners' consent, he or she will probably not be better off for doing this. The buying or merging firm will lose interest quickly if they see a fragmenting of the owner group. Typically, existing owners are almost always willing to pay the highest market price for a firm when it is time for an owner to retire. Over and over, I see situations in which everyone has something to gain by sitting down and *airing* critical and sensitive issues. Through planning, the focus is shifted away from personalities and placed instead on creating a path for the future.

Time Frame for the Plan

Most people think that you conduct firm planning sessions when everything is running smoothly and you want to figure out a five-year plan. However, most planning starts when the firm is in chaos and evolves from there. The first plan, when chaos is the driver, will likely cover a six-month period. The second plan might cover an 18-month period. By the third planning session, the firm might actually get around to considering the horizon for the organization rather than just reacting to tactical issues. Planning is dynamic. Today's plans affect tomorrow's reality; tomorrow's reality influences tomorrow's plans; tomorrow's plans affect the future's reality, and so on.

Monitor the Plan

In a perfect world, planning and reality pictorially could be illustrated as two straight lines overlapping each other. But in our world, which is mostly out of control, both plans and reality are moving targets. So, our expectations need to be put into perspective. First, don't expect reality to emulate the plan. The best we can hope for is that the two begin to parallel each other at some point in the future.

> **O—ᴄ Key Point**
>
> Plans continually need to be monitored and adjusted so that they are consistent with the resources available. Operations need to be continually monitored and adjusted so that outcomes approximate the plan.

In the absence of planning and plan monitoring, your firm is likely to zig and zag too often … and for too long … wasting resources and losing competitive advantage by missing market opportunities. The purpose of planning is not to eliminate missteps (as they will always occur in any business), but to minimize the duration and extent of those deviations. Consider the sailboat analogy earlier. Sailboats do not travel in a straight line towards their designated target. The key is to keep adjusting the boats' path so that the variations from the straight line are kept to a minimum. All too often, scarce resources such as money and owner time are wasted on efforts that do not contribute to the organization's long-term survival and profitability.

So, the question of success often boils down to whether management can remain focused on its goals. Every time your firm veers off course, it can take months and even years to reverse the momentum. Long recovery cycles (like services that never should have been launched or mergers that never should have been approved), in many circumstances, are too much for an operation to support. Therefore, by planning, and planning often, although you may not avoid making bad decisions, you can see the misdirections earlier and make course corrections more often. This minimizes the mistake and recovery cycle, the zigzag effect, thereby making a significant contribution to your bottom line.

Purpose of the Plan

In order for an operation to continuously improve performance, workers need to have a clear sense of direction or mission. The theory is simple:

> **O—ᴄ Key Point**
>
> The more people working towards a common goal, the greater the likelihood of its achievement.

By formalizing the planning process, you can more easily create synergy among the owner group. The plan in turn drives the development of targets and the actions required to reach them. With this definition in place, roles and responsibilities can be better developed to support the attainment of the overall strategy. This understanding can be used to develop and communicate *individual expectations* that *synchronize with the firm's objectives*, culminating in the accomplishment of the firm's goals. Planning is the foundation on which firms define and build their future success. And, given our profession's landscape, there has never been more at stake (either to win or to lose).

How To Use This Book

The preceding introduces two concepts on which the following chapters will be based: Chapter 1, "The Environment and Strategy: Managing Resources, Maximizing Reward," outlines the present business environment and includes insights gathered from two recent surveys. Chapter 2, "Structure and Leadership: Establishing a Foundation and Consistency;" Chapter 3, "Management and Operations: Extending the Life and Culture of the Firm;" and Chapter 4, "Growth and Transition: Increasing the Value of the Firm," reveal underlying support systems, foundation principles, and processes that firms should consider to develop and enhance the performance of their employees at all levels of the organization. Then, once this framework has been constructed, Chapter 5, "Succession Strategies: Passing the Torch," addresses succession. Chapter 5 will also offer anecdotal evidence about how firms have approached succession, both successfully and unsuccessfully, connecting those experiences to the fundamentals covered in the earlier chapters.

But if you just skip to Chapter 5 now, be warned that the principles covered in the earlier chapters will constantly be used to tie concepts together by describing either options to consider or pitfalls to avoid.

A variety of firms have generously shared materials that were used in the preparation of this book. These samples have not been reviewed for legal acceptability or viability. Should your firm decide to use any of this material, you do so at your own risk; it is up to you to get proper legal assistance and advice to ensure that all documents are adequate and suited to your needs. Given the equally wide range of firms for whom this book is intended, readers are urged not to focus on the specific details of the samples described herein. The best focus is on the intent and general guidance provided. Each firm is well advised to hammer out its own best approaches.

But before you get together for your next planning retreat, have every owner and manager in your firm read this book. If you do, I can assure you that your dialogue will change forever because this book can impart:
- A broader understanding of the interconnectivity of many of the core issues facing your firm, and
- An awareness of the various strategies that can help your firm bridge the gaps between these interconnected issues.

Note to Sole Proprietors

As you can tell, this book will dedicate a great deal of its subject matter to how to create an infrastructure that allows a firm to organize its processes and policies in order to increase its value and ability to smoothly transition to new owners. A firm with one employee has a far simpler road to travel than one with 50 employees. Obviously, the higher the number of people affected by the process, the higher the number of exceptions that will have to be addressed and the more difficult the implementation will be. Take, for example, a compensation plan. If your firm has two employees in addition to you, a fair, objective incentive plan might take you an hour to devise, and a monitoring system might take an extra couple of hours to put in place. For a 50-person firm, a similar system is likely to take two weeks to devise and months to implement. When we discuss this in Chapter 3, I go into detail about the issues that should be considered so that, regardless of the size of the firm, enough information has been provided to construct a foundation for moving forward. However, if you look at the fundamentals addressed (billing rates, fair multiples for performance, rewarding exceptional service, monitoring performance objectively, and reporting), it becomes clear that those same principles apply to everyone. Thus, I am suggesting that if you wade through the more complex multiemployee discussions, the dialogue will likely spark ideas that should be valuable as you design your less complicated versions.

Second, being a sole owner or running a small firm does not stop you from applying the kind of infrastructure (albeit far more simplified) typically found in larger firms. For example, in Chapter 2, I refer to the value of delineating the oversight roles of management and a board of directors. Although these are one-and-the-same for a small firm, setting up an advisory board to generate a broader discussion regarding strategy might be a viable substitute. Once again, I am asking that you look at the underlying philosophy to determine ways to improve the value and operating effectiveness of your firm.

If your strategy is to sell or merge your practice, this book should give you insight into the attitudes and obstacles of firms a little larger than yours, which are potential suitors. By understanding their priorities, it is far easier for you to take steps in the coming years to position your firm to integrate more seamlessly with theirs. This might include looking for ways to make yourself less indispensable (so that someone can more easily step in) as well as establishing client relationships that would be deemed valuable to them. For example, if you charge rates that are so low that a purchasing firm could not service your clients profitably without raising fees to the point of losing those clients, then you are not positioning your firm to have value. If you are the only person in your firm who has a relationship with your clients, then it will be more difficult to transition them.

O—ᴄ **Key Point**
Knowing more about your likely buyer helps you identify steps to drive up the value of your firm.

So, as you go through the book, many of the sections may describe solutions that exceed your needs. Nevertheless, I am confident that the time spent with this material will pay large dividends if your outlook is, "How can I apply the concepts to my situation?" I can assure you that I have consulted with practices as small as $200,000 to larger than $50 million and have successfully applied versions of the concepts in this book to all of them. I can also tell you, as an owner of my own small firm, the effort to codify these ideas has helped me make different decisions about how I plan to operate my firm in the future. So, as one small firm owner to another, if you feel mired in the detail, keep in mind that there is "a pony in there somewhere."

Conclusion

As I stated in the beginning, succession is about business strategy. What you will find is that almost every aspect of succession is influenced by multiple areas within the business. For example, firms often cannot address simple changes in a retirement agreement without having to revisit the compensation formula, which cannot be adjusted without considering ownership percentages, which then have to consider the impact on management and voting privileges. This kind of integration continues until it comes full circle, back to the issue that started the conversation. In order to successfully address succession, you have to holistically look at the firm and its processes to find a viable solution. For example, rather than the firm needing to find an entrepreneurial business developer to take over as managing partner, maybe a strong firmwide budgeted marketing plan and foundation will create a path for a variety of other personalities to be successful in that key position. Or, rather than trying to promote everyone to an owner position in order to keep key people happy, maybe a compensation system and a career path for nonowners will take the heat out of this transition. Because of the holistic, integrated nature of many of the problems succession reveals, your firm is only as strong as its weakest link. Hopefully, this text will not only help you identify what those areas might be within your firm, but also describe integrated solutions to address them.

Chapter 1

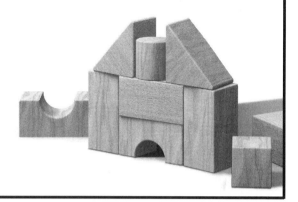

The Environment and Strategy: Managing Resources, Maximizing Reward

The objectives of this chapter are to:
- Introduce the legislative and demographic forces that affect our profession.
- Consider marketplace and CPA firm practice forces that firms either have encountered or will encounter.
- Review data from national surveys that support the conclusions of this chapter.

Many issues are affecting our profession and the strategies we engage for survival. Probably, the best place to start is to state the obvious: "Change is the only constant that describes our current professional landscape." This chapter covers the many forces influencing the accounting landscape, including legislative, demographic, marketplace, and CPA firm practice issues. This chapter also outlines the results of two recent surveys.

Legislative Forces

In the past 25 years, the environment for the CPA profession has continually evolved. The many developments include allowing firms to advertise, the impact of consolidators, and an almost exponential growth in the range of services offered by CPAs. In addition, more

CPAs now work in industry than for public firms, and most states allow non-CPA owner-ship of firms. Ever-changing technology and the global economy have changed how and where we work. The Sarbanes-Oxley Act of 2002 had a significant impact on the demand for CPA services, while the recession that began in 2008 diminished some of that demand as clients struggled to cope with an uncertain economy.

Working in this profession is like riding a series of waves in the ocean, with the one behind you even bigger than the one you are trying to stay on. Each wave seems to present at least two very different choices. We can try to ride the wave and experience its power and forward momentum, or we can try to stop it (or ignore it).

> **O━ Key Point**
>
> You cannot legislate the market-place.

Although we can buy some time by restrict-ing marketplace activity, in the end, it is like the "blob" in the old 1950s movie; it will just find an alternative path to go where it wants to go. For example, if the rules and restrictions placed on auditing become so stringent that the street price becomes too high for nonpublic companies, other less costly services will be offered to take its place. We have seen the beginnings of this as banks offer monitoring services to their customers as an alternative to an external audit.

Alternatively, consider the financial statement. As it drifts further and further away from being a timely management tool and/or depicting "a point in time snapshot of the value of a company," it may be replaced by a series of performance statistics compared to industry benchmarks.

The first decade of the 21st Century presented a series of sharp highs and lows for the economy. The CPA profession, as well, has gone from a time of robust demand for services to one of economic uncertainty. After some of the corporate scandals early in the decade, the audit shifted from being a commodity service to one of unique distinction. As a result of the increasing scrutiny of the work performed, new independence rules, and expanding standards, CPA firms could charge more for their work and take on fewer clients because the increased scope of work tapped out their resources. This created a trickle-down op-portunity for firms of all sizes, throughout the country, and great prosperity at many firms. The recession has changed much of that situation, however. Clients and the marketplace still understand the value of what CPAs have to offer, but when the businesses that use our services are in trouble, we can't help but be affected. It is a time of great challenge—and opportunity—for the profession.

Demographic Forces

Now, here is a quick comment or two on the demographic changes affecting our profes-sional landscape. We will look at age, gender, and retirement trends and conclude with a few predictions based on this information.

Age Trends

Take a look at this table:

Aging of AICPA Membership			
Age	1993	2004	2008
31–54	73.81%	71.24	65.5%
40-under	53.01%	31.76%	23.8%
Over 40	46.99%	68.24%	76.2%

Add to this that, in 1990, the number of AICPA members in public practice was about 131,500, and now, nearly 20 years later, that number has declined by about one percent. Our profession is not growing in size, but is advancing in age. Figure 1-1 shows the relationship between numbers of CPAs and age demographics since 1993. When you consider the economic growth over this time, it is clear that the profession has not attracted enough young people. Ideally, our profession should have each new generation of people being larger in population than those in the previous generation. Instead, we have fewer people in each new generation than in the previous generation. Although the efforts of the AICPA, the state CPA societies, and many volunteers have helped increase the number of young people entering accounting programs in college, we have yet to see any substantial shift in the percentage of those graduates who earn CPA certificates.

Figure 1-1: *CPA Age Demographics*

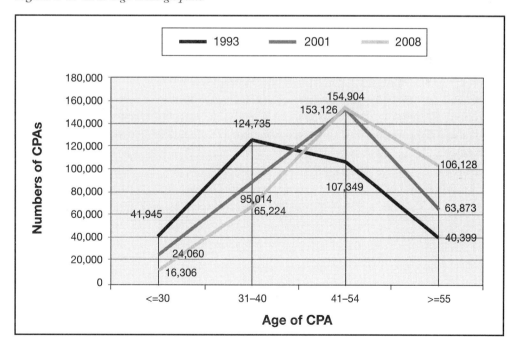

Gender Trends

The hope, supported by a concerted national effort, is that the accounting profession will attract many new entrants in the next decade, but there is another demographic that will have an impact. That demographic is the number of women entering the profession. In

1993, about 45 percent of new entrants were women, and 55 percent were men. In 2009, that split was about 50/50.[1] Clearly, our profession is becoming more and more appealing to women. But, of the women that enter the profession, historically, a small percentage of them have either dropped out or moved to a part-time status, driven by lifestyle choices, later in their career. Although there are few hard statistics about the rate of fallout, the best anecdotal evidence suggests that it occurs frequently. For instance, almost all of the firms I have worked with over the past 20 years have at least one woman who works part time in order to meet family commitments. Only one of those firms, to the best of my recollection, had a man filling a similar part-time role. It has become commonplace for firms to increase the size of their work force by tapping into a talented group of part-time workers, almost entirely made up of women, either during tax season or part time throughout the year. If the current recruiting efforts result in an increasing number of CPAs, it appears that the demographic shape will begin to look like an hour glass (measured by a higher rate of new entrants' certification than that of the previous generation of CPAs). Nevertheless, over time, that shape might actually continue to more closely resemble a funnel, depending on the rate of experienced CPAs who continue to opt for part-time responsibilities.

Retirement Trends

The current demographic funnel is likely to continue for at least several decades. Moreover, given the number of CPAs in leadership positions who plan to retire in the next 10 to 15 years, an almost revolutionary reshuffling of ownership is about to take place. The historical model for CPA firm continuation by most firms has been to find at least one owner (often two) to replace each retiring owner. As you can see from the graphic, this model cannot be sustained because the CPAs about to retire outnumber the younger group that is available to replace them. This means fewer leaders will likely be running the evolving public practice marketplace.

Also, if we fast forward a decade, it is predictable (assuming the reliability of some succession planning survey results that are discussed later in this chapter) that a significant percentage of our firms' soon-to-be-retiring-owners will anticipate that selling or merging their firms is their exit strategy. Because a higher than normal number of firms will likely pursue selling or merging at a time when the number of CPA firm leaders will be shrinking, it stands to reason that we can expect the coming decade to gradually become a buyers' marketplace. With this oversupply of sellers, the buyers will be in a position to dramatically reduce the purchase or merger price (below what you might expect today), negotiate to buy only parts of a firm (specific clients or a couple of industry niches), thus creating for themselves very favorable deal points.

Consolidation Trends

It is my belief, based on the convergence of these demographics, that public accounting will be poised to embrace a great deal of consolidation of firms during the next decade. Logically, firms with strong leadership and well-defined processes and procedures will be well positioned to consume the excess demand from both firms (trying to sell) and clients (looking for a new CPA firm because their CPAs appear lost in transition).

---

[1] AICPA. 2009 Trends In the Supply of Accounting Graduates and the Demand for Public Accounting Recruits. New York, AICPA. 2009.

A couple of other trends that are likely to continue or emerge due to this demographic shift are:

- As the oversupply of CPA firms up for sale is in clear view of our profession, it will become increasingly more difficult to find owners who will want to take on the full burden of buying out their predecessors, especially given the unfunded nature of these buyouts. Because of this shortage, younger people who are interested in stepping up to the challenge will be in a position to cut very lucrative deals for themselves.
- The consolidation that will likely occur will create a much wider chasm, in the firms under $10 million in size. Right now, there are about 42,000 firms with 10 or fewer owners, with the vast majority of that number being firms around $2 million in revenues or less. It is in this smaller size firm range that, I believe, most of the consolidation will occur, resulting in many firms that will remain under $1 million in size, while many consolidated firms will exceed $4 million. In other words, 15 years from now, instead of 42,000 firms, there will likely be half as many, or about 21,000 firms.
- Even after consolidation is well on its way, the marketplace will not roll up into just a few firms because the limiting factor will be service pricing. As firms approach $10 million in revenues, their fee structures and preferred client profile move them away from being able to profitably deliver services to the true small-business marketplace. So, the prospects for the sole practitioner to become the lifeline for small business clients look strong, assuming these small firms position themselves correctly.

Marketplace Forces

Besides the formidable marketplace and demographic forces that are in play, there are also three trends that are or will have a noteworthy impact on "the size of the marketplace waves" that we either are or will be encountering.

Trend 1. An Uncertain Market

Legislative changes early in the decade created a market surge anomaly because they expanded the need for services and required many organizations to hire multiple professional firms to perform the services traditionally done by one firm. This definitely created additional opportunity. However, based on my experience working with CPA firms, I believe that for the vast number of businesses (which include those that have not been affected by legislation), regarding compliance services, if one firm picks up a new tax, audit, or financial statement client, it is most likely because another firm lost that same client. This means that CPA firms, in order to survive, have to become more aware of:

- Developing client loyalty.
- Satisfying their clients' needs (rather than just providing them with the services you have always provided them).
- Building a wall of services around them to protect them from poaching by other CPA firms.

Trend 2. Reshaping Services

Because of the legislative environment and increased focus on independence, during the next decade, many firms will drastically reshape the services they offer. A number of firms will surround all of their offerings with a cloak of independence, while others move to the other end of the spectrum (becoming management advocates), with room along the continuum for everyone in between. I am pointing this out because those firms that rethink the synergy of their services and develop their service strategy early will be able to:

- Create alliances with other firms quickly to minimize service gaps in their offerings,
- Attract clients from firms that discontinue services that you offer that those clients still need, and
- Create a culture that understands that the greater the number of different services a client purchases from your firm, the greater their loyalty to the firm.

Trend 3. Milking the Cash Cow

Many firms are behaving as if they were selling declining-demand services within a dying industry (i.e., they do not want to invest any more than necessary so they can take out as much cash as possible each year). This strategy is commonly referred to as "milking the cash cow," and it is going to hurt many small to medium-sized firm owners in the coming decade because their firms will have been stripped bare of much of the value other firms look for in a purchase or merger, namely, that the firms are well run, have a diversity of skills, highly trained people, and/or are technically savvy.

CPA Firm Practice Forces

We have looked at our professional landscape from 30,000 feet. Now, I would like to highlight four universal issues that I have encountered over and over again in working closely with firms. They are foundation and consistency; management, staffing and operations; growth; and succession strategies. These issues coincidentally also outline how the book is organized.

Issue 1. Foundation and Consistency

Most CPA firms, especially those under $15 million in size, operate more like a local real estate office than a single firm. In other words, owners share operating costs but, for the most part, they practice and manage independently. However, with a *corporate* model of governance:

- The firm owns the clients.
- The actions of the owners are in lock step with firm goals.
- There is clear delineation between being an owner versus having a say in every decision.
- There are established roles and responsibilities, identified limitations and powers for those positions (board of directors, CEO/MP, firm administrator) so that everyone can be effective at their jobs.

Most firms have not adequately groomed, mentored, or grown their replacement owners or new managers.

Issue 2. Management, Staffing, and Operations

Firms have relied too long on specific people for their success rather than developing consistent process and methodology that will allow the organization to flourish as people come and go, and leadership changes take place. Also, firms are not addressing the reverse pyramid. This is the reversal that results when owners do too much manager work, managers do too much staff work, and the staff is underutilized. Underperforming staff, management, and owners are the results of this career-directionless model that does not force people to live up to their respective roles.

Most firms rarely hold anyone accountable, especially the owners. This can be readily ascertained in the absence of any documentation of organization-wide processes and procedures. Accountability is not possible unless there is clarity as to what actions are expected (desirable), along with consistently enforced consequences for inappropriate behavior.

Too many firms underpay their best performers and overpay their marginal employees. The salary system no longer works because so many employees elect to be career professionals rather than aspiring owners. The traditional systems have not changed to fit today's environment and are, therefore, shrinking profits. Compensation systems for the typical firm have not changed much in the past 20 years (a percentage change here or there is about all). At the same time, the strategies that drive the firms have changed significantly during this same period. Yet, firms are always surprised that their staffs do not follow the organizations' communicated priorities.

Issue 3. Growth

The smaller the firm, the more the marketing rests on an individual (or a small group of individuals). The larger the firm, the more the marketing relies on a process (a marketing engine that runs all the time). As you would guess, business development skills are at a premium in small to medium-sized firms, and technical competence and project management skills are at a premium in the largest firms. Until the small to medium-sized firms begin treating marketing as a foundation process that drives the firm's future, their long-term viability is extremely suspect.

Historically, a firm's new services have been driven by an owner's or manager's desire to specialize rather than what was best strategically for either the firm or the clients being served. This model has lost a lot of firms a great deal of money for a variety of reasons over the past decade.

Issue 4. Succession Strategies

Because of the age of our professionals, it is becoming a higher priority for firms everywhere to establish a plan for the senior owners to "cash out" of their practices. This might come in the form of:
- Owners being able to retire and be paid their ownership value over time
- Selling to another firm
- Merging with another firm
- Owners running their firms long past retirement age, maximizing their income with diminishing workload and client attrition coinciding throughout this period

Regardless of the strategy, the transition and retention of clients by either the existing firm or the buying or merging firm is a key to maximizing value. And there are numerous other issues, from agreements to compensation adjustments, that have to be considered to ensure the success of this process.

Survey Results

In the paragraphs below and throughout the remainder of the book, I refer to two different surveys. The first is the 2008 PCPS/TSCPA National Management of an Accounting Practice Survey (MAP Survey). That survey had over 2,700 respondents, with over 2,200 of those firms having less than $2 million in gross revenues. The second survey is the 2008 PCPS Succession Survey (Succession Survey). Almost 500 firms responded with overall average revenue per multiowner firm of $5.9 million and about $500,000 at sole owner firms. Both surveys are reporting on 2007 year-end revenues.

This discussion will focus on the following highlights from the surveys-growth and changes in revenue, operations, and succession.

Growth and Changes in Revenue

As the 21st Century began, the demand for CPA services seemed to have reached a saturation point. The growth of one firm was often due to the loss of clients at another. That changed dramatically, however, after the passage of the Sarbanes-Oxley Act of 2002, and the renewed emphasis on better governance and objective assurance. For several years afterward, firms enjoyed strong revenue growth. That growth surge slowed in 2008, however, after the global banking crisis and steep declines in stock market and real estate values. Figure 1-2 depicts 2008 firm growth rate statistics.

CPA firms have held their own in these uncertain times, but the heady growth of past years has slowed. The 2008 MAP Survey found that CPAs were continuing to experience high income

Figure 1-2: *Firm Growth Rates (+ or –) 2008 MAP Survey*

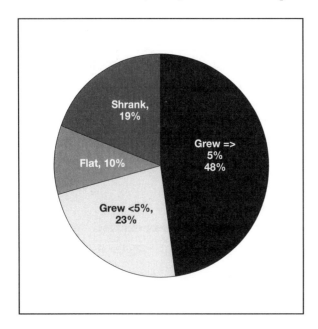

levels and billing rates as the recession was poised to begin, but the results raised questions about the future economic outlook for firms.

Figure 1-3 shows that a total of 26 percent of firms grew between 10 percent and 19 percent, while another 8 percent expanded by 20 percent to 29 percent and 5 percent grew by 30 percent or more. Only 10 percent saw no change, and fewer than 10 percent decreased in size. Those numbers were little changed from the 2006 survey, attesting

Figure 1-3: *Self Reported Firm Growth for 2008*

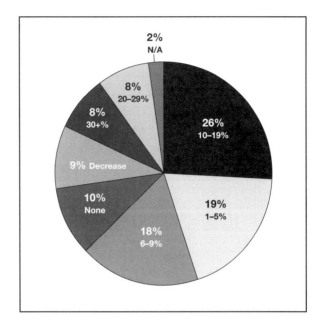

to the success many firms were seeing before the recession began. In terms of services performed, CPA firms generally earned most of their money through traditional services, with more than 50 percent on average coming from tax clients and about 23 percent from write-ups, compilations and reviews. The survey results, although generally positive, still raise questions about the prospects for continued strong growth in the midst of a persistent recession. And even before the downturn began, CPA firms were reporting some plateaus in demand. It seems safe to say that it will become increasingly more important for firms to do some basic competitive analysis as part of their planning process.

Operations

Operational spending issues have already been addressed, including, "milking the cash cow" as a cash maximization strategy, or relying on the firm superstars instead of investing in the firm's foundation processes and procedures. Here are some statistics that support the idea that accounting firms are not making the necessary long-term investments in infrastructure or in developing their people. We will look at marketing, information technology (IT), training, and net revenues and then offer a concluding observation.

Marketing

If marketing and business development is such an important foundation for firms to embrace, why is the average marketing-expense-to-net-client-revenues ratio across all sizes of firms so low? The MAP Survey showed the average percentage of revenue spent on marketing was 1.2 percent. If a firm wants to safeguard its future, it must stop relying on its superstar model and begin developing a firm-wide marketing engine and marketing culture so that the organization has a chance of long-term continued success.

Information Technology

If firms are short staffed, why are personnel allowed to waste one second of their scarce time doing anything that technology can do for them? The MAP Survey found an average IT-expenses-to-net-client-revenue ratio of 2.1 percent, even though IT spending is a number that can truly affect efficiency. I have found that the larger the firm, the greater the realization that technology costs (while high) are far less than salaries. Since salaries (exclusive of owners) typically represent over 30 percent of overall firm costs, it seems that leveraging this investment would be high on the list of priorities for firms of all sizes.

Training

Even though it is not surprising that CPA firms are not investing in their people, as noted in the preceding discussion, the statistics are shocking. The 2008 MAP Survey showed a .8-percent training expense to net client revenue, little changed from the percentage in past surveys. As a profession, this level of training budget supports my earlier claim that, despite staff shortages, not enough is done to develop the available staff or move them along defined career paths. The recession only reinforces the need to make the most of the staff you have and to equip your people to deal with changing circumstances.

Net Revenue per Full-Time Equivalent

In the MAP Survey, overall net revenue per employee, i.e., full-time equivalents (FTEs), averaged almost $200,000 with top performing firms averaging over $240,000, as illustrated in figure 1-4. However, the larger firms (above $10 million) really skew that average upward. When you consider firms less than $2 million in size, the overall average falls below $152,000 and a little over $144,000 for those ranked as top performers. If your firm is producing at a rate of less than $144,000 per FTE, you probably are encountering both an upside-down pyramid and an organizational model that needs some attention.

Figure 1-4: *Net Revenue Per Employee (FTE)*

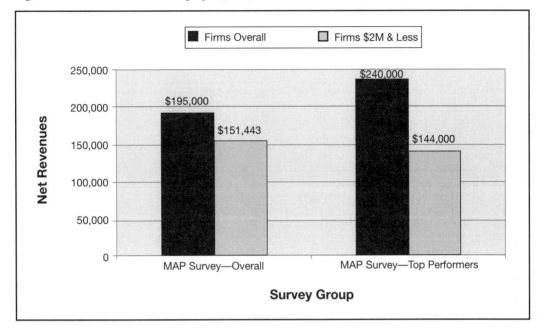

A Final Word on Operations

In summary, the analysis of the two surveys relative to operations uncovers obvious hand-writing on the wall. There are a number of firms (probably about 10 to 15 percent) that are, right now, investing heavily in marketing, technology, and training. In the short term, this money will fall out in the form of lower profits for the owner group. In the next five years, these firms will start developing a real strategic competitive advantage over other firms as their enhanced infrastructure, processes, and methodologies become foundational for their firm.

Succession

Succession is the area in which all of the issues mentioned above, or the failure to address them, intersect. For example, your ability to develop young leaders within your firm directly correlates to the likelihood that your firm will attract owners who want to buy you out. The more the infrastructure supporting your organization is based on consistent, repeatable processes that are uniformly applied and built on objective accountability, the easier it is to change leadership without negatively affecting profitability or viability. The more it is a function of the firm to serve its clients, rather than an individual serving his or her clients, the greater chance that the firm can efficiently manage its scarce resources by balancing the workload, developing necessary skills within the firm, creating the right breadth and depth of scope of services, and transitioning clients. Succession is the light that shines brightly, revealing our aptitude at working on our business rather than just *in it*.

A few PCPS Succession Survey highlights to consider are discussed below. Let's start with the question of whether firms have a written succession plan in place. In the 2008 survey, 35 percent of multiowner firms did, along with only 9 percent of solo proprietors.

Sole Practitioner

Firms in the sole proprietor group were also asked whether they had practice continuation agreements in place. These agreements, by definition, create a plan for another firm to take over the practice and pay the sole proprietor's estate a specified value. They also outline what happens in the event of the sole proprietor's temporary or permanent disability. They are critical because a firm's value can diminish at an exponential rate starting as early as three or four months after the death or disability of the practitioner, and even faster during the tax season. This rapid loss in value occurs because a number of clients will scramble to find another CPA to assist them as soon as they grasp the situation. By the time the survivor finds a firm to take over (even if it is only a few months later), 50 percent or more of the clients may have already gone elsewhere.

Given the clear negative financial implications of *not* having a practice continuation agreement in place, it should come as a surprise that only 9 percent of sole proprietors said that they had an existing written practice continuation agreement with another firm. That's an increase of only one percentage point from the 2004 survey.

Retirements on the Horizon

No matter how conscientious firms are about beginning their succession plans, it's difficult to create a concrete process or strategy if owners can't set a concrete date for retirement. In small and medium-sized firms, owners typically do not want to set the date of their departure, for economic reasons and because of the desire to continue working. In contrast, senior owners in large firms set departure dates because their retirement is mandatory, not negotiable. During a series of phone interviews with past survey respondents, senior owners, whether they were 55 or 75, all said the same thing, namely, "I think I will work another 5 to 10 years." This lack of clarity regarding the change in ownership and voting privileges has many repercussions on the transition and viability of the firm.

Figure 1-5 shows the percentage of partners retiring in the next five years. Sixty-three percent of the firms in the survey noted that at least one owner would retire within that time; 32 percent anticipated the retirement of more than one owner. Regarding ownership, 52 percent of those in the most senior owner category were 60 or older.

Figure 1-5: *5 Year Horizon re: Retiring Partners*

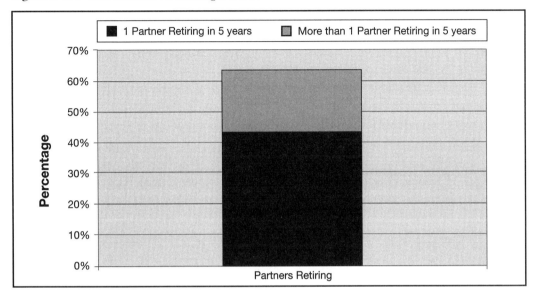

Succession Plans

The responses to a follow-up question regarding status of the succession plan (only asked of those respondents who did not have a written succession plan), the responses were:

- 42 percent of multiowner firms and 66 percent of sole proprietors said they would start the process within the next five years.
- 35 percent of multiowner firms and 17 percent of sole proprietors have started their plan and soon hope to complete it.
- 10 percent of the respondents stated that they "did not feel the need to have a succession plan, written or otherwise."
- 9 percent of multiowners and 3 percent of sole proprietors have a plan that has not yet been approved.

A quality-enduring succession process takes years to put in place. Thus, if you have a senior owner five years from retirement, you have little time to waste. A troubling statistic is that 10 percent of those without a succession plan believe they do not need one. Follow-up interviews, as well as my personal consulting experience, reveal that a significant part of this group believes a plan is not necessary because either:

1. They are going to sell or merge their firms, or

2. They have an owner agreement in place that addresses buyout.

Item 1, the assumption that the firm is going to be sold or merged, is a viable strategy to consider, though it is a very risky and short-sighted, singular-option. Item 2, owner agreements, is problematical because I have seen too many firms miscalculate that succession is just a legal issue. Young owner candidates may sign almost anything to be allowed to join the owner club. But once they are in, they know full well what their options are. The single biggest card they are holding is the timing of their departure.

Timing of Succession

Most firms appear to be aware of the need to plan. A total of 20 percent of multiowner firms—and 14 percent of sole proprietors—had current succession planning challenges. Another 30 percent of multiowner firms and 33 percent of sole proprietors expected to have them in the next three to five years.

Regarding the timing of succession challenges, roughly half of the firms surveyed are expecting to be confronted with succession challenges in the next five years. Another 3 percent of multiowner firms and 5 percent of sole proprietors do not expect to address this issue in the next ten years.

Funding of Retirement

As to whether retirement programs are funded, 67 percent do not plan to fund, another 12 percent do plan to fund but have not gotten started and the rest are in various stages of funding, with only 7 percent funded by 61 percent or more. However, even this number may be overly optimistic. In follow-up interviews conducted in the past, it became apparent that many people who said their plans were funded were commenting on whether the owners' 401(k) accounts were being funded each year—not the buyout retirement amounts.

I had an interesting dialogue with the owners of one firm about fully funding retirement. They had funded their firm's retirement program at a 50 percent rate and did not plan on ever increasing that percentage. Naturally, I asked why, and the answer was revealing: "We have found that as individuals' retirement funds approach 100-percent funding, which means that their payout is not at risk, these people lose interest in:
- Doing the right thing for the firm,
- Making the necessary investments to secure the future success; and
- Taking on roles and responsibilities that push them out of their comfort zone."

I did not expect this response, but I can certainly see the logic.

Form of Transition

One question asked what the likely transition of the firm would be when the current senior owner(s) retire. The responses were as follows:
- 11 percent noted said the firm would most likely be sold so that the senior owners can maximize the value of their investment.
- 8 percent answered that the firm would most likely look for a merger candidate due to the senior owners' lack of confidence in the firm's continuation, to the surprise or displeasure of the junior owners.
- 7 percent said the firm owners would run the firm long past typical retirement age, maximizing the income of the firm, with diminishing workload and client attrition coinciding throughout this period.
- 6 percent stated that the firm would most likely look for a merger candidate in order to fund the retirement of the senior owners, which is fully supported by the junior owners.
- 4 percent responded that the firm would most likely be sold because the remaining leadership would not be strong enough for the retiring owners to feel confident that the firm could succeed through the retirement payout period.

- 2 percent said the firm would likely be split up because the remaining owner group does not share a vision of where the firm should be going.

The percentages above can be misleading because this question asked for a "select all that apply" response. Seventy-nine percent of the respondents *also* selected the choice that "their firm's clients would be transitioned to the remaining owners or incoming owners." But the 79-percent response does not change my observation: Many senior owners, especially those controlling the majority interest of the firm, while they are considering following the owner agreement and allowing the remaining owners to buy them out, are also quietly considering the options of selling or merging the practice when it comes time for their last day of work.

Conclusion

Additional survey data will be discussed in subsequent chapters. However, the data addressed in the preceding provides a broad overview of the current landscape, as well as perspective on how firms are positioning themselves in the marketplace.

Chapter 2

Structure and Leadership: Establishing a Foundation and Consistency

The objectives of this chapter are to:
- Outline operational structures that enable change; specifically, decision-making authority and a standard operating procedure foundation.
- Demonstrate how these operational structures operate in different sized firms.
- Give guidance on implementing powers, administrative, and accountability policies.
- Discuss leadership traits that can mean the difference between a dysfunctional firm and an effective firm.

The superstar and the operator models both tend to follow different paths when creating operational structure. Regardless of the approach, planning has to be the catalyst to develop any enduring, holistically integrated support infrastructure. With planning comes change. And change without a clearly communicated long-range purpose just creates unnecessary stress, confusion, and frustration.

Early in my career, I conducted retreats for CPA firms. Often, three to five years later, I would be asked to return to facilitate follow-up sessions. For most firms, I observed that nothing had really changed. The list of issues and their order of priority had changed very little; the same old "sacred cows" were still points of contention. This baffled me, given the contrast with most of my planning clients, who were corporate clients that invariably experienced significant changes during comparable intervals. I asked myself, "Why is real progress in achieving identified strategic initiatives so rare among CPA firms?"

I found myself hypothesizing that CPA firm retreats were meant to be more catharsis than catalyst, and that the spirit of many of the firms' strategic objectives were "it-would-sure-be-nice-if-we-could" rather than "this-is-what-we-need-to-accomplish." As I began investigating further, I found that the vast majority of the owners were truly committed to achieving their stated strategic direction. Their excuse for their shortfall was always that the day-to-day routine of serving clients seemed to keep getting in the way. As time went on, I paid closer attention to what was happening between retreats. I found some firms made significant progress, but most did not. My hypothesis changed; I believed that some firms are just better managed, and that management is the critical success factor driving change.

Once again, my theory was not supported by the statistics for firm profitability and success. Then it dawned on me ... there are two distinct enablers that are always discernible when major change is embraced.

The first enabler is the presence of decision-making authority, and the second is the presence of a standard operating procedure (SOP) foundation. Without both, there is only directionless spinning.

This chapter discusses decision-making authority and SOP foundation as well as leadership issues that can significantly affect a firm's ability to effectively implement these critical enablers. Although an SOP foundation is introduced, the real focus of this chapter is on developing the necessary decision-making authority with supportive leadership that can confidently and efficiently navigate the turbulent waters of succession.

Enabler 1. Decision-Making Authority

Decision-making authority is simple to ascertain. Could the chief executive officer/managing partner (CEO/MP) or a small executive committee *force the acceptance of change through mandate*? Commonly, this authority is one of two variations. The first authority is voting control. When I look at my small business clients, they have no trouble implementing plans because one or two owners, with voting control, make the decisions and everyone else has to either (1) go along or (2) find a new job. With my larger corporate clients, the CEO rarely has voting control, yet implementation is rarely a problem there either. This led me to the second authority variation—organizational infrastructure, which I define as:

> Defined organizational hierarchy, roles, and responsibilities that are put in place to distribute the necessary individual authority, powers, and limitations to support attaining operational compliance with strategic direction.

The CEO/MP's ability to mandate change rests in the *distributed individual authority, powers, and limitations* component of this definition. As you know, midsized and larger for-profit companies are typically organized with both a board of directors (board) and a management team. The board's role is to establish the strategic direction of the organization. The management team, headed by the CEO, is charged with the implementation of the board's plan within the authorized limits and powers (with the broadest authorization of both limits and powers usually coming from the approved budget).

The Problem

Normally, when a CPA firm is first formed, voting control is not an issue. This is partially because most are sole proprietors. For instance, over half of the more than 40,000 CPA firms registered with the AICPA are sole proprietors. Even startup and small firms having more than one owner do not struggle with voting control because, often, more than 50 percent of the firm is owned by one person. As the firms grow, more owners are usually added. At the point of redistributing ownership, voting is spread throughout the group so that one or two people cannot easily mandate firm strategy and tactics. It is at this time that the firm often enters a "no man's land" regarding decision-making authority wherein decisions are often made by committee. Typically, when firms are operating by committee in this "no man's land," the CEO/MPs are consensus builders with little to no authority to implement change.

The Solution

For those firms that continue to incrementally grow and prosper while in this desert, it becomes clear that the vacuum of management and implementation authority has to be filled in order to sustain long-term success. An organizational infrastructure is created to establish the authority needed to manage the firm. This organizational infrastructure mimics limited voting control by defining the powers and limitations of the management team. Depending on the size of the firm and the distribution of ownership, decision-making authority exists if there is voting control or if the organizational infrastructure is established to mimic some level of voting control (i.e., the CEO/MP's authority is defined by the position, not the actual individual's ownership).

Decision-making authority provides management, when necessary, with the powers to make significant changes to the way the organization competes. This ability is indispensable to keep it from becoming the spinning sailboat discussed earlier. Someone has to have the authority to maintain the strategic course, regardless of the territorial storms brewing within the firm.

Enabler 2. Standard Operating Procedures Foundation

The second enabler—SOP foundation—is put in place to raise the minimum standards for performance, generate consistency, and leverage overall firm capabilities. I define this as:

> Those processes, procedures, systems, and methodologies that create the foundation for the firm's operations and are built to generate the highest level of performance by the team rather than by individuals.

An organization's SOP manual details most of this, from collection to investment policies, from client acceptance to client firing guidelines, from performance expectations to compensation systems, from client management to client marketing processes, from staff training to partner development programs. This enabler creates a framework for the organization within which everyone is expected to work.

Here is the anecdotal evidence and exercise I ask my clients to work with to resolve conflict regarding this point. Sit down and list all of the companies your firm services that are successfully run by committee or by a weak management team without robust SOP foundation. Then, start a new list of those clients you serve that are successfully run by a strong management team, and a visionary board, with SOP foundation at its foundation. Every time we have gone through this exercise, there are few clients in the first column ... while most of the firm's top clients are in the second.

A firm can embrace SOP foundation regardless of size, from a one-person shop to a firm that employs thousands of people. SOP foundation is strongest when decision-making authority is robust enough to hold everyone accountable. In contrast, if there is SOP foundation but no decision-making authority, the firm will likely be successful, but that success will hinge on the firm's ability to make incremental changes to its current course. When major course adjustments have to be made for either competitive advantage or strategy failure, the firm will have *little ability* to quickly right the ship.

Enablers And Synergy

Although having either decision-making authority or SOP foundation is better for the firm than having neither, a firm's best chance for success lies in having both. The former creates the ability to make efficient course corrections; the latter provides the foundation for consistent and high levels of performance.

The following are examples of each of these enablers.

⇄ Sample Scenario: Voting Control

A sole proprietor (who owns 100 percent of the firm) decides to launch a forensic accounting service and establishes an educational program for one of his top audit managers. The manager objects to his new assignment. The sole proprietor responds by pointing to the door as a viable option. In this situation, the owner has control and can make these kinds of demands at will.

⇄ Sample Scenario: Organizational Infrastructure

The CEO/MP (who owns 15 percent of the firm) decides that one of the senior owners has client responsibility for too many clients and therefore is underserving many of them. Therefore, it is time to reassign and transfer some of those clients to owners who have both better skills and more time to serve them. The senior owner is given a schedule as to which clients will be moved to which owners in what time frame. In this situation, the CEO/MP is granted the authority through organizational infrastructure.

> ### ⇅ Sample Scenario: SOP Foundation
>
> Given the facts of the preceding examples, the CEO/MP, seeking to align compliance and directives, makes a proposal to the board requesting modifications to the compensation system. This proposed adjustment not only takes into account the reshuffling of client responsibility, but outlines the penalties for transitions not made timely (for the senior owner) and for clients lost after transition because of lack of scheduled contact (for the newly assigned owner). Changing the compensation system to immediately align and support the desired behavior requested by management is an example of properly utilizing SOP foundation.

The evolution, strengths, and weaknesses of these enablers require additional clarification. For example, voting control and organizational infrastructure have been lumped together as if they were exactly the same, but that is not quite true. On one hand, voting control typically grants more authority than does organizational infrastructure. This can be either good or bad, depending on the circumstances. On the other hand, voting control does not have the natural built-in checks and balances, as well as the consistency of performance, that can be expected within an organizational infrastructure. Reflect on the following:

> ### ⇅ Sample Scenario
>
> Consider a firm run under a dictatorship in which control is held by a person, maybe two with similar perspectives. Regardless of whether that dictator is benevolent (leads through influence) or not (manages through command and control), the firm's future potential is directly proportional to the abilities, vision, and philosophies of those controlling owners. Since there is no requirement to operate within a planning framework (such as a vision, and goals and objectives) or within a financial framework (such as a budget), and because these owners are not accountable to anyone, they can revise the direction, priorities, and resources of the organization as often as they desire without any necessity to defend their actions. This tends to create an operating environment in which the owners are rarely challenged by anything outside their own personal desire to minimize their weaknesses or develop their strengths.

So, the good news is that while voting control allows the instant implementation of ideas because no one but the owner has to sign off, the bad news is that voting control allows the instant implementation of ideas because no one but the owner has to sign off. Let me be clear. I am not telling you that a one- or two-owner firm cannot be incredibly successful. Nor am I proposing that a one-owner firm cannot create an SOP foundation that would compare well with the best in the country. I am saying that there is no requirement to justify why actions are or are not taken, or why best practices are or are not followed. The resulting flexibility can be both the reason for a firm's successes as well as its Achilles' heel of future evolution.

Enablers And Firm Size

It may be that the attitudes and aptitudes required to grow a firm from nothing to $2 million in revenues (throughout this book, millions of dollars in revenue refers to annual revenues) are significantly different than those required to grow a firm from $2 million to $10 million. We talked about this in the "Introduction." As an organization grows, a critical success factor influencing its future is its ability to shift from being a firm driven by the strengths and personalities of various individuals to an organization that is driven by strategy, structure, process, defined expectation, and monitored performance. Below is a discussion of how enablers operate in various sized firms.

Enablers and Up to $2-Million Firms

In small firms (with annual revenues of between less than $1 million and about $2 million), voting control is the norm. Because these owners like the flexibility of making up the rules as they go, an SOP foundation is rarely put in place. The interesting point about this is that most small businesses, regardless of the industry, love the flexibility of a "no-rules," "we-are-all-part-of-the-same-team" structure. This philosophy permeates every aspect of the business, from defining sick time and vacation days to performance pay. Apparently, the theory is that, by formalizing expectations, you are establishing an acceptable minimum level of performance. There is a general belief among owners that once you have set a minimum level of performance, no one will ever make any effort to exceed that level. For example, if the firm announces that its employees have a total of five paid sick days, they believe it amounts to telling each employee to take at least five sick days. The hope is to get more out of the firm's average employees by not setting the minimum standard bar. However, what usually happens is that the marginal employees get a free ride on the backs of the young, developing superstars. Consider this commonly observed scenario:

> ### ⇵ Sample Scenario
>
> Assume for a moment that there is no policy regarding sick time or sick pay. Also assume that there has never been a problem in this area. The firm continues to grow and prosper from 2 to 12 people. In order to meet the ever-expanding workload, employee number 13, Michele, is hired. Michele works well for the first six months, but by month seven, she starts calling in sick fairly often on Monday. By the eighth month, Michele is occasionally calling in sick on Friday, too. After several counseling sessions, and about six months of elapsed time, a meeting is called to establish a sick time policy. The need for such policy becomes especially clear after the management team learns how hard it is to fire someone for excessive sick leave in the absence of a well-defined policy. The firm creates a policy that allows each employee to earn one-half day paid sick leave for every month worked, up to a maximum of six days.

Based on this scenario, who won as a result of the lack of a sick time policy? Was it the employees who had to continually perform Michele's work while she was absent? Was it the employees who never abused the policy, but now are limited to six days? Was it Michele, who now gets one-half day for every month worked up to six … plus … the 20 days she has already taken? Small businesses too often believe that setting clear expectations though an SOP foundation places stifling limits and restrictions on their valued employees. Nevertheless, what most frequently happens is that, in the absence of clear expectations, your marginal employees will continually take advantage of your good employees; the wrong groups are satisfied and burdened, respectively. In the end, the consequences of the "no-rules" philosophy are the exact opposite of what was intended. I believe it is far more important to establish systems that take care of and reward good employees than to squeeze a little extra out of bad ones. I would take this point a step further and say that I believe it is important to build an SOP foundation that drives off the marginal employees … hopefully, into the employ of our competitors. So, for this size firm (sole proprietor and two-owner firms), even though voting control is not an issue, the lack of an SOP foundation becomes a bigger and bigger burden as the firm grows.

Enablers and $2-Million to $8-Million Firms

Now, let's take a look at firms in the range of $2 million to $8 million. In this size range, you often *don't find any of the enablers* strong enough to drive the firm, which is why this is the most difficult sized firm to manage. As firms surpass a couple million dollars in revenue, new owners are added and voting control begins to disappear. By the time these firms grow to the $3- to $6-million-dollar range, they either have to find a way to embrace organizational infrastructure or they are likely to split and break up into several smaller sized firms. Firms that embrace organizational infrastructure have a good chance of growing through this difficult period (especially if they also embrace an SOP foundation). For those that do not, the good news is that, after breaking up, the remaining firms are small enough to reinstate voting control, and the preferred superstar model is effective again. Firms that enjoy substantial growth after breaking up but do not embrace an organizational infrastructure will most likely follow the same path … adding more owners, losing voting control, spinning, and then deciding that the only solution is to split up, and start again as smaller firms. Obviously, not all such firms break up. A number of them simply get stuck in this gap. A firm in this situation cannot go anywhere fast, so it slowly but surely loses its competitive advantage as the wind in its sails is wasted by the countervailing weight of its anchors. Over time, the firm will probably stagnate in terms of growth, but even if it is enjoys continued success, the likelihood that the owners will further diverge in philosophy and values with each passing year sets the firm on a course for eventual disaster.

Why are strong enablers so rare among firms in this size range? The following are likely explanations:
- There are too many owners, which precludes voting control.
- The firm has evolved through merger, resulting in a firm that is large in terms of gross revenues, but really functions as several smaller firms that are no more than loosely connected. The firm is most likely trying to operate under the superstar model, and every owner believes that he or she is entitled to steer the sailboat (or drop an anchor whenever he or she chooses).

• With the retirement of one of the owners, the firm lost voting control because the retiree held dictatorial command and control (and probably was a bullying personality). In other words, the remaining owners each have fairly equal voting rights but no one has the control once held by the dictatorial owner. The response of the remaining owners regarding authority will tend to swing 180 degrees in the other extreme; the result is a kinder, gentler, but ineffective "we-are-all-in-this-together" management by consensus.

The more owners in a firm, the more the need to rely on both organizational infrastructure and an SOP foundation to keep the firm heading toward a preferred destination. Because a firm in this group typically lacks an established organizational infrastructure, the CEO/MP rarely has a chance to be as effective as a typical industry CEO. Based on my personal experience, the vast majority of CEO/MPs that do not have voting control are consensus builders, with little to no ability to mandate change. The CEO/MP's job is to keep the firm moving forward by taking the path of least resistance, which is apt to be the path that no one really wants, but no one really hates, either. To make a bad situation worse, typically, no one has the authority to hold people accountable to existing policies regarding management processes. Therefore, rules and procedures are applied inconsistently. Moreover, each owner can override policy by simply asserting, "That is not acceptable to my client, so I am not going to comply." This situation does not get better with time … it only gets worse. As firms grow, it becomes more and more imperative to profitability and long-term survival that they shift from a superstar model to an operator model, which means there is a fundamental requirement to address both decision-making authority and SOP foundation.

Enablers and Firms of $8-Million and More

Most firms larger than $8 million realize that it is necessary to embrace an organizational infrastructure in order to build the equivalent of voting control. Such firms also start to grasp the need for an holistically integrated SOP foundation as well. Among the larger firms, around $15 million or more in revenue, both organizational infrastructure and an SOP foundation are usually at the heart of their operating strategies.

> **⊙ⁿ Key Point**
>
> I am proposing that a natural evolution is observable among successful firms as they grow and prosper, namely that they mature as follows:
>
> • From the superstar to the operator model
>
> • From voting control to organizational infrastructure
>
> • From "no-rules" to an SOP foundation

This is not to say that firms are wrong or unsuccessful, or headed for failure if they follow a different strategy. A given firm may be one of the best in the country as long as a superstar is at the helm. The point is that, for the same firm, the ideas in this book may resonate more significantly when contemplating how the firm will operate when the superstar is no longer there. Here's the real question: "When the current senior management team retires, do the owners feel secure about the long-term viability of the firm?" If they don't, it is likely that your firm is built around individuals (the superstar model) rather than process and structure (the operator model).

Enablers And Their Properties in CPA Firms

Decision-Making Authority—Voting Control Properties

Voting control is typically manifested by the following:

- One owner owns more than 50 percent of the firm.
- Two owners that own more than 50 percent of the firm have a long-lived special relationship of trust, have the same basic personal goals for the firm, and rely on each other for perspective.
- Any decision, other than those expressly identified as needing more than 50.01 percent of the votes through the charter or owner agreement, can be mandated to everyone in the firm, including the hiring and firing of owners, setting retirement formulas, buyout formulas, compensation, and process and procedure.

Decision-Making Authority—Organization Infrastructure Properties

Organizational infrastructure is typically manifested through:[1]

- Creation of a board of directors, which, throughout this book, refers to the role played by this group, not the legal definition of a corporation's board of directors
- Understanding that the role of the board is to establish the firm's vision, create policy, authorize powers, and set limitations as a framework for the CEO/MP to operate
- Understanding that the board does not get involved in the minutia of day-to-day operations except through the setting and approval of budgets, compensation plans, marketing objectives, and training policies
- Structure in which staff reports to management, management reports to executive management, executive management reports to the CEO/MP, and the CEO/MP reports to the board (If there are multiple offices, those office partners-in-charge [PIC] are accountable to the CEO/MP and the staff in those offices is accountable to the office PIC.)
- Accountability of the CEO/MP for the firm meeting its goals and objectives, which is why his or her compensation objectives should be different than the other owners
- Owners' understanding that they serve on the board in one capacity, but also report to the CEO/MP in another. (The distinction is that, as a board group, they direct the CEO/MP. As individuals, they report to the CEO/MP.)
- Firing of the CEO/MP if he or she fails to perform up to the defined objective expectations of the board or within the powers allowed (However, the board does not have the right to occasionally drop down and take on management responsibilities just because it does not like how the CEO/MP is performing. If this violation ever occurs, then all accountability is lost, the CEO/MP becomes a figurehead, and the board takes on the roles of CEO/MP.)

---

[1] Many of the concepts mentioned below can be found in *Boards That Make a Difference: A New Design for Leadership in Nonprofit and Public Organizations* by John Carver, published by Josey-Bass Inc., San Francisco, 1997.

Other requirements for clarity of organizational infrastructure include job duties for all key roles in the firm (board, CEO/MP, chief operating officer [COO]/office manager, partners, managers), power policies, and having a firm organizational chart that reflects how the firm should actually operate. A discussion of each requirement follows.

Job Responsibilities

One of the most basic steps to making a firm's organization concrete is to outline job duties. This is true at all levels in a firm.

Power Policies

Power policies are those policies established by the board of directors that outline the authority, including its limits, for various positions within the company. A simple example of a *powers policy* might be an outline of what positions the CEO/MP can hire and fire without board approval (i.e., it might include all staff and managers, but stipulate that board approval is required for directors or owners). Another example of a powers policy is to empower the chair to vote rather than just break ties.

Organizational Chart

If you are like many people, the mention of the need for an organizational chart would evoke a smirk; an organizational chart seems like a theoretical nicety that could not be less relevant to the practical reality of creating organizational infrastructure. Seven or eight years ago, I would have agreed.

At that time, I decided to add an additional question to the confidential employee surveys that I typically send out as part of the CPA firm retreat planning process. The question is, "Please draw your firm's organizational structure the way it actually works and e-mail or fax it to me." Generally, from 50 to 75 percent of the respondents from any given firm draw different charts. Let me be clear, if there are 20 respondents, I am likely to receive 10 to 15 different versions of the organizational chart. Obviously, this magnitude of deviation would not apply to a smaller firm (e.g., three people) or larger ones (in excess of 80 people). In the smaller firms, organizational structure is very simple and clear. In the larger firms, because the structure tends to be expressed through both organizational infrastructure and SOP foundation firmwide communication, it is widely understood how the firm works. But even in those larger firms, when you request a drawing depicting how that organization *actually* runs, you would be surprised at the variation. Interestingly, the variation is rarely at the very top in large organizations, but a layer or two down, where there can be many disconnects. Although the formal company hierarchy may be widely announced, many of the rank-and-file will perceive that power is actually wielded quite differently.

SOP Foundation Properties

The most basic properties of an SOP foundation are what I call *administrative policies, accountability policies*, and *processes*. These are practices, processes, and procedures that apply to everyone in the organization with the expectation that they will be followed. These policies and processes create the framework for actions.

A word of warning: Do not spend a lot of time trying to draw black and white distinctions among these terms. They are used only to provide a better explanation of what constitutes decision-making authority and an SOP foundation. In reality, they all go in the same policy manual and need to be reviewed and updated on a regular basis.

This section will discuss administrative policies, accountability policies, and processes and methods for codifying your policies.

Administrative Policies

Consider something as routine as *client acceptance*. An administrative policy addressing this should help an owner decide whether he or she can serve a new client on his or her own or must get approval from the CEO/MP. An owner might be limited in any number of ways, including the following:

- Project size (because the organization-wide availability of resources has to be considered for large projects)
- Discount factor (meaning that the estimated earnings of the project be at least a minimum percentage of the firm's standard rates)
- Competence (to assess whether the work being requested is outside the scope of this owner's personal expertise)

Another example of an administrative policy might be in the handling of accounts receivables. This policy might address the timing of the following steps:

- The firm will send out delinquency statements.
- The owner or manager has to follow up personally to collect.
- The owner's compensation is affected by nonpayment.
- Future work is stopped because of the delinquency.
- The account is turned over for collection.

These questions may sound trivial or seem to be an exercise in documenting minutia, but an unbelievable number of owners get involved in very serious conflicts over such issues.

⇄ Sample Scenario

Consider Steve, an owner with the firm's second largest book of business. One of his good clients has exceeded the collection limits to the point that the policy dictates cutting off current work. Also consider that Steve takes offense every time anyone tells him how to run his client practice. Without an accounts receivables policy, odds are that no action would be taken until it was too late, i.e., the client declares bankruptcy or goes out of business. In other words, the client would take advantage of the firm as long as possible in a manner similar to the example given earlier, specifically, the employee abuse of an undefined sick time policy. In this instance, the owners, in order to avoid confrontation, would probably ignore the delinquency, hoping that the situation will take care of itself.

In a firm with a clear accounts receivables policy, a collections issue sees the light of day much earlier and it is either addressed according to the policy or the owner has to convince the owner group why a given instance should be treated as an exception; the existence of the receivables policy makes the latter a much more difficult pitch to sell.

At this point, the CEO/MP first has to decide whether this situation is a legitimate exception to the policy; no policy should be enforced without this level of scrutiny because policies are guidelines, not laws. For example, what if the account is a seasonal business, and the firm knew from the beginning that it was performing work during the client's down time, with the understanding that payment would be delayed for several months. If so, the CEO/MP should extend the date to cut off work to conform to the original agreement.

However, assume there are no legitimate excuses for delinquency. The CEO/MP should tell the owner that work cannot be continued until some or all of the outstanding balance is collected. Because this condition is based on a known policy (one that Steve, a board member, probably approved) rather than just an arbitrary decision by the CEO/MP, Steve is likely to comply, rather than resist by tying up firm resources or playing politics. Moreover, even if Steve does decide to play politics over this issue, he has to defend why he thinks his owners should subsidize his bad client practices. This kind of dialogue, grounded by the firm's established policies, is completely different and more beneficial to the firm than the veiled threats and ultimatums that commonly result in the absence of policies.

Accountability Policies

Accountability policies can be illustrated by outlining the responsibilities of employees in managing the firm's top clients. For instance, you could put together a policy that requires face-to-face meetings at least three times a year (outside of tax season) for all clients in the firm's top-tier category. This policy might also detail the minimum amount of specific information that must be collected during those visits.

Many accountability policies are incorporated in owner agreements. Consider the following responses to a question on the Succession Survey. They sketch the issues that would stimulate an accountability policy:

"Which of the following are addressed in your firm's agreements?"
- Mandatory retirement age   48%
- Acceptable arrangements and situations allowing retired owners owners
  to continue working for the firm   46%
- Allowable activity with clients after retirement to ensure client retention   32%
- Personal liability of the remaining owners for retired owners' full payout   27%
- Specific recourse or cures should a retired owner not be paid in full   20%
- Ability of existing partners to change the retirement benefit of retiring
  partners due to improper client transition   18%
- Ability of retired owners to block mergers or total sale of the business
  unless the retirement obligations are paid in full prior to the transaction   11%
- Ability of retired owners to block the sale of a line of business unless
  the retirement obligation is paid in full prior to the transaction   6%
- Key-person insurance to cover the outstanding obligations of retirement
  payment obligations   54%
- Acts that can trigger the forced retirement of an owner (illegal activities)   62%
- Acts that can trigger the forced retirement of an owner (misconduct like
  sexual harassment or public embarrassment of the firm)   57%

- Acts that can trigger the forced retirement of an owner (lack of performance)   31%
- Acts that can trigger the forced retirement of an owner owner disability)   52%

The survey asked other questions regarding retirement, payout, and expectations. In addressing the involvement of retired owners in the firm, it found that:

- 36 percent of firms, the largest group, did not allow retired owners to have influence or involvement in firm operations.
- 23 percent allowed them to work with former clients, but as a manager while another partner handled the relationship.
- 17 percent allowed retired owners to handle the same responsibilities they had always had, with fewer hours.
- 16 percent allowed retired owners to continue to manage client relationships, while the same number of firms had retired owners who were still active in the community and had a formal role as ambassador for the firm.

Which components are utilized in current owner retirement payout calculation? According to the survey, they can be summarized into three general categories: multiples of ownership, book or salary.

Which occurrences will force a change in the payment duration, monthly payment amount, and/or total payout amount of standard calculated retirement pay? The 2008 survey found that almost one-third of firms will penalize a retired partner for the loss of his or her clients. Early retirement and competing against the firm after retirement also trigger a reduction in benefits.

When owners are two or three years out from retirement, those retiring owners are:

- Asked to start transferring their clients to other owners or managers.   49%
- Not asked to do anything unique until about one year away from retirement.   25%
- Subject to a new compensation structure that allows him or her to focus on transition activities.   7%

These questions quickly lead one to think of a number of other policies that would appropriately address issues such as retirement age, sale of interest age (and if mandatory, when), what functions and duties retired owners can continue to perform, and what approval is required to authorize them, and under what conditions would early retirement, if any, be allowed. These are all examples of policies you may wish to address.

Processes

Processes are systems put in place by firms to create consistency in performance and relieve superstars of the sole burden of creating and maintaining success. Not that every firm does not want their superstars to perform at the highest level possible, but there is a difference between superstars who are top producers and superstars who are the main producers.

Consider a sports team. When superstars join a team, whether it is Michael Jordon joining the Chicago Bulls, John Elway joining the Denver Broncos, or any of the other hundreds of similar examples, the teams can lose, even though the superstars set all kinds of personal records. The team does not begin to win until the performance improvement gap is closed between the average player and the superstar. That gap is predominantly closed by the development of defensive schemes and offensive plays that capitalize on the strengths of the group, creating incentive systems to reward people to focus their talent on how it can best support the team. Put another way, why is it that certain teams can, with little negative impact, substitute key players with lesser known talent? Once again, this is the result of a support infrastructure that puts people in positions with clear duties and roles that allow them to be valuable almost instantaneously.

Process can counterbalance superstars as well as enabling organizations to maximize the talents of their employees quickly. Consider the firm with one or two owners who are excellent rainmakers. Because these owners successfully go out and socialize, network, and interact with their clients and referral sources to bring in new business, they are called into action whenever the firm is short of work. So, the rainmaker superstars are expected to drum up new business every time it is necessary … and they do this well. Therefore, the firm grows comfortable with the extraordinary skills of a few people and never develops these areas from an organizational perspective. As I have stated before, the superstar model relies on the natural instincts, capabilities, and sense of urgency of individuals. The operator model sets processes in place to consistently maximize everyone's ability to bring in business. The point is that the exceptional ability of an individual or two (in this case, the rainmakers) will likely result in a firmwide weakness in process (in this case, marketing). A similar story can be outlined for the owner who is the firm's walking tax library. The question is, "Why develop additional capability when the firm has all it needs?" As we discussed earlier, the typical answer is to do nothing … at least until those key people decide to do something else (like retire or start a new firm). So, for many firms, building a strong SOP foundation in critical business areas is a far better long-term solution than relying on a few specific people.

The process component of SOP foundation is all about creating systems and methodologies that support and augment personnel performance so that the firm can rely on systems that support people rather than just relying on people.

Codifying Policies

I want to make a suggestion about how to approach memorializing your policy decisions. As you can tell from the foregoing survey responses, some of the firm's foundational policies are contained in owner agreements. By using the following technique, you are likely to save tens of thousands of dollars. A very small savings comes from a reduction in the attorneys' fees paid to modify your legal agreements. But the most significant savings results from avoiding ugly owner disputes arising from the *unintended consequences* of those agreements. The adage, "out of sight, out of mind" has validity; the firm's legal agreements all too often only see the light of day about once every 10 years, or once a dispute is under way. No matter how you look at it, these important agreements should be given regular scrutiny.

One way to effect this scrutiny is to scan your owner agreements and extract every reference to a formula or value and place these references in an SOP manual. Draft the clauses of the agreements, which are legally binding so that they refer to policy numbers or titles spelled out in the manual. Furthermore, lay out the details of all this in a section of the SOP manual entitled "Board Policy." For example, if your owner agreement addresses the value of the firm, then the text of the agreement should introduce the topic and refer to the manual for the definition of *Firm Value SOP*. If the owner agreement specifies the retirement formula, then refer to that formula as the "*Retirement Formula SOP*, which can be found in the manual," and so on. This is a simple process. Anything in your owner agreements that is subject to evaluation and change should be recreated as part of the board's policies.

A board policy could be in the form of a memo and as simple as the following:

Firm Value

Board Policy

Date created:	12/15/2007
Last date revised:	04/30/2009
Vote required to update policy:	A quorum of the shareholders, 66.66% of the outstanding shares
Next Scheduled Review Date:	04/30/2010

Policy Details

This policy sets the agreed-to value of all of the entities affiliated with the shareholder group for purposes outlined in any of the legal agreements, between the shareholders. Any time Firm Value is referred to in our agreements, any legal action, dispute, or question regarding this topic is to be interpreted and/or resolved based solely on the most current board-approved version of this policy.

For the CPA firm:	The value of the firm is set at 90 cents on the dollar for firm net revenues
For the Technology firm:	Book value of assets plus 1 times earnings
For the Bookkeeping firm:	75 cents on the dollar of firm net revenues

---

The following are the steps that should be taken to establish and fully document policies:

Step 1. Identify and remove every formula that appears in owner agreements. Instead, substitute correct and current references to the SOP manual.

Step 2. Identify and remove every issue that appears in owner agreements that is likely to need regular scrutiny. Instead, substitute current and correct references to the SOP manual.

Step 3. Confirm that all existing and fully enacted board policies are included or referred to in the SOP manual.

Step 4. Regularly, every year or every other year, schedule a board review and approval of all board policies.

Usually, the CEO/MP is responsible for bringing a group of SOPs before the board on a scheduled basis. Sometimes, various committees are responsible for certain SOPs, like the compensation committee making recommendations on compensation-related policies. It doesn't matter who does it as long as all of the policies are scrutinized on a scheduled basis. Whoever is assigned to bring them forward is also charged with recommending changes. Even if no changes are recommended, the fact that a policy is before the board for approval will stimulate important conversations about how to incorporate best practices or how to best maintain the intended consequences.

Benefits of Separating Policies and Owner Agreements

There are two reasons to consider the benefits of separating policies and owner agreements. All too often, owners get "caught" between relationships and legal agreements. Most legal agreements are put together when everyone is excited about working together. However, the agreements are not really tested until someone has lost enthusiasm. Only the most commonly violated issues are addressed initially because people are overly optimistic in formulating agreements, and because best practices evolve over time. With that in mind, the following is a scenario that can be generically applied to hundreds of situations:

⇄ Sample Scenario

An owner agreement has just been updated for a five-owner firm in order to address how to compensate owners who retire early. Currently, no one is approaching retirement so it is really not a major issue. Consequently, a section is added to the owner agreement that reflects how to calculate the retirement payout should someone decide to retire up to five years early.

Now, fast forward ten years. The most senior owner is retiring as expected and on schedule. Three months later, the other senior owner opts for an early retirement to begin six months from that date of declaration. As a result, an incredible burden is placed on the remaining three owners with regard to both payout requirements and the transition of the clients to ensure their retention. Because the early retirement issue was agreed to 10 years ago, no one has really taken a close look at this issue since then, especially since the early retirement declaration was a surprise to the three youngest owners. Therefore, those owners get caught having to comply with an outdated agreement that, in the interim since it was first entered into, should have been updated several times.

Complexity is the second reason to remove these significant issues from the legal agreements and reflect them in a board policy SOP manual. Consider the following, typical example of one owner responding to the concerns of another:

> Yes, I agree that we need to change that formula in the owner agreement. However, if we are going to do this, let's look at everything and redo whatever else needs to be done so that we only have to involve the attorney once.

The result is that owner agreement updates are infrequent because a quick change that everyone agrees to quickly turns into a tortuous, six-month (or longer) review. In the end, if the issues were all adequately addressed after six months, the effort could be justified. But the reality is that the project becomes unmanageably large. Areas of conflict are abandoned and left unresolved. A number of issues are interwoven with other formulas and assumptions, and these more complex topics are also tabled.

In short, the results are as follows:
- Ill will arises among the owners about the policy revisions because there are so many issues and everyone has one or two that are very personal to them.
- The task cannot be completed because the review effort takes up entirely too much time and resources to accomplish.
- Often, there are too many issues that need to evolve through lengthy discussion, and cannot adequately be addressed by one round of revisions.

Thus, the common perception is that updating owner/firm agreements is an exercise to be avoided if possible. However, if these issues are part of an SOP manual, updating one stand-alone policy is very easy. At least the discussion has been narrowed down to policies that affect each other (for example, compensation, retirement pay, and the valuation of the firm, which might be intertwined). The conversation has not, however, been opened up to include everything in the agreements. Finally, and most important, you want people to look at the essential policies and formulas regularly to make sure they are withstanding the test of time. Every year, we learn more about best practices. The firm's future is managed best by changing your legal agreements to refer to policies that you can amend at any time without creating a legal nightmare. It allows a flexibility that is hard to achieve by embedding formulas and issues in a document that only gets dusted off when there is a crisis.

What Policies Should Be in the SOP Manual

How many policies should you create? As few, and as many, as necessary to document areas of performance and compliance you expect from owners and staff alike. A general rule of thumb is that a policy is called for if the subject matter is important enough to take up 30 minutes or more in an owner meeting, or there are diverging opinions about how something should be done. Once there is agreement or understanding about how the firm should approach such issues in the future, the consensus will normally drive the creation of operating policies and processes.

Implementing Organizational Structures

To review, we have talked about the requirement to have decision-making authority in place to keep the firm from constantly spinning. As part of that, organizational infrastructure was introduced, which included the creation of powers policies. SOP foundation was also discussed as fundamental to creating consistency and elevating employee performance. *Administrative and accountability policies*, along with the development of processes, were at the core of this strategy. So, given all of this, the logical next question is, "Where do we go from here?" There are four simple steps to moving forward:

Step 1. Choose a strategy for your firm.

Step 2. Choose who you want to manage the firm and give him or her the directives, authority, and powers necessary to achieve your goals. Then, get out of the way!

Step 3. Choose the style of governance.

Step 4. Implement SOP foundation wherever it supports strategy to create consistency, improve performance, and close the gap between the average employee and your superstars.

Steps 1, 2, and 3 are discussed in detail below. Step 4 will be discussed in the next two chapters, which focus on several top-rated areas as examples. Chapter 3, "Management and Operations: Extending the Life and Culture of the Firm," discusses management and operational issues, and Chapter 4, "Growth and Transition: Increasing the Value of the Firm," spotlights business development.

Step 1. Choose a strategy for your firm.

I know this will surprise you, but the implementation starts with strategy. This means asking, "What areas of the business are the most important to address?" Your answer will determine the right place for your firm to start.

To get my clients to consider the big picture, I ask them to answer the following questions as they imagine themselves four years into the future:[2]

- What would you most like to see happen?
- What should the organization look like?
- How should the organization operate?
- What should the client experience be? (Moreover, what should clients say about us?)
- How should employees feel about the organization?
- What should the organization have achieved between now and then?

However, so that we have a starting place to continue this discussion, here are four very common questions (in no particular order) that rise to the top at almost every CPA firm planning session. They are:

1. How do we create and implement a fair system of accountability?
2. How do we become a firm instead of a group of individual practices?
3. How do we develop a fair system that will pay for performance not only today, but all the way through retirement?
4. How do we ensure that everyone knows his or her role, that there are clear limitations and powers within those roles, and that we have created an operating foundation that is designed to give us the best chance for success?

If voting control is in place, then the first three questions are only discussed openly if the dictator is benevolent and is looking for solutions that will work long after he or she is gone. Otherwise, these questions are not an issue because the dictator will likely institute

---

[2] Adapted from *Built to Last: Successful Habits of Visionary Companies* by Jim Collins and Jerry I. Porras, published by HarperBusiness, New York, 1994.

accountability however he or she chooses, make all the decisions for the firm, and decide what everyone should be paid (mostly based on very subjective criteria). This may sound like a criticism of the style of the dictating owner, but it is merely what I commonly observe.

For those firms without voting control in place, the answers to the first three questions hinge on the answer to the fourth. Question four is all about setting up the structure to enable decision-making authority in a way that is palatable to all of the owners and shareholders. For a reminder, please review the delineation of duties between the board of directors and the CEO/MP outlined above under the previous section entitled "Decision-Making Authority—Organizational Infrastructure Properties."

Step 2. Choose who you want to manage the firm and give them the authority to do it.

Let me share with you how I answer the question, "How do we go forward from here?" The first step is to name an MP or CEO, which means finding someone who is sufficiently trusted by the owner group to fill this role. Every firm has an MP or CEO, but many in this position are just figureheads without much power. So the question is, "To whom are you willing to actually give some power?" Once that decision has been made, the next question is, "What are the limits of his or her authority?" The answer is simple—the limits are whatever the owner group wants them to be. However, I will put this caveat on my statement: Wherever the lines are drawn, they must be drawn in a way that keeps the remaining owners focused on strategy, budgets, policy, and oversight at the board level; and out of the daily management and implementation of operations.

A key question that should always be in everyone's mind when attending board meetings is, "As the issues are being discussed, is the focus on personal preferences as to how the firm operates, or on modifying strategy, updating policy, and reflecting values?" Sometimes the subject matter is very unclear. For example, let's revisit the earlier discussion between an owner and the CEO/MP about accounts receivable delinquency. If the owner does not accept how this matter was resolved, he or she will likely bring it before the board—and this is the point at which the system most often breaks down. If the board believes the policy should be modified, that belief defines the function of the board. The board's solution is an updated policy that applies to everyone. If the board overrules the CEO/MP in order to accommodate personal preferences, the decision-making authority of the CEO/MP is undermined, no matter how insignificant the issue. Moreover, the lesson taught to everyone is that accountability is not about following the rules, but about playing politics. How do you expect the CEO/MP to hold anyone accountable if every issue goes before the board and the CEO/MP's decisions are often overturned? If the board regularly distrusts or disrespects the day-to-day decisions and interpretations of the CEO/MP, it is time to find a new CEO/MP. Otherwise, by leaving the CEO/MP in place and constantly overriding his or her decisions, the board of directors is assuming the management responsibilities of the organization.

Thus, it is necessary to walk a fine line or the system starts to fall apart. The balancing act has two dimensions. Any time the CEO/MP starts acting like he or she has the powers of the board, or anytime the board starts acting like it has the powers of the CEO/MP, the failure of the system is imminent.

Once everyone understands how this model is supposed to work, it starts to fall into place fairly quickly. You will always have at least one major violator who constantly wants to impose his or her personal preferences on the way situations are handled. However, because all the owners understand the delineation of responsibilities, the micromanager can quickly and easily be put in check.

Avoiding Common Traps

Some common traps that should be avoided are the following:

- Firms adopt a new organizational infrastructure but key individuals do not change the way they operate. It becomes clear that decisions are more about politics than policy.
- Micromanaging is a danger because it is easy. Macromanaging is often avoided because it is very difficult. Focusing on the root causes and trying to ease the chaos long term is much more difficult than solving the problem in front of you.
- Boards need to constantly be reminded to manage authority and responsibility through budgeting, performance measurement, and policy.
- Boards try to do too much at one time, which results in achieving very little. Picture implementation as being all about the turtle, not the rabbit. Slow methodical progress, consistently applied, is far more valuable than quick starts that are apt to fizzle out and be followed by inactivity.
- Boards are willing to turn over the responsibility of maintaining certain performance levels to the CEO/MP, but not the authority that is required for the CEO/MP's success.

Supporting the CEO/MP

The most contradictory directive given to the CEO/MP by the board goes something like the following:

> We charge you to implement the above (or current strategy) with three caveats. They are:
>
> - Do not spend much money.
> - Do not reduce your billable time by more than a couple hundred hours over the rest of the owner group.
> - Do not ask the owner group to change, in any way, how they want to individually service their clients.

Obviously, the board is not taking the CEO/MP position very seriously if it does not immediately reduce the number of client billable hours expected of this person. My rule of thumb is that a CEO/MP should spend about 40 percent of his or her time managing a firm of up to about $2 million in revenues, about 60 percent of his or her time managing a firm with about $6 million in revenues, and 80 percent or more of his or her time managing firms of $10 million or more in revenues. The point is that managing the firm is a job, not an assignment to do once the real client work has been done. In a $2-million firm, an extra 400 billable hours by the CEO/MP might generate an additional $80,000 to $100,000 dollars. However, if that same 400 hours is focused on firmwide realization, it might enhance processes, understanding, and training, generating an additional $100,000 or more every year. There is a great deal of money to be made by improving systems, support, and processes. But it takes time to:

- Understand what is actually going on.
- Determine where (and who) the hurdles are.
- Decide what the best approach should be.
- Develop the support to ensure that the necessary changes are adopted.

As I have said before, if you take your firm's future seriously, you need to dedicate someone to spend more time focusing "on your business rather than just working in it." And, just as important, the CEO/MP role is not a personality contest; it is a difficult job for which not everyone is suited. So, if the person you first select does not have the ability to operate the firm profitably by carrying out the directives of the board, put someone else in the job. Understand, however, that the better you define the role and its powers and limitations, the easier it will be for someone to successfully fill the role.

Step 3. Choose the style of governance.

Now that you have taken the biggest step forward and decided that you are going to give someone the authority to run your firm like a business, the next decision is, "What kind of business do you want to run?" The answer to this question creates the foundation for the job description, powers policies, and an SOP foundation that should be put in place. There are two options discussed below—a silo model and a one-firm concept.

Silo Model

If you are like most firms under $8 to $10 million in size, your business probably operates as if made up of individual sole proprietorships sharing office space, administration, and systems. Although this model works nicely with an "eat-what-you-kill" philosophy, and it allows owners to customize their work/life/income balance any way they want, it has some organizational drawbacks. It is hard to implement accountability through firmwide processes or systems in this type of structure. Why? Because in this model, owners handle their clients the way they want, which is confusing for staff since they often work with multiple owners and on multiple projects. It is also difficult to rate performance or create compensation systems that pay for performance because the criteria for performance vary so much between owners. For example, one group of owners cares about work/life balance, the second is looking for more income (efficiency, growth), and the third is anticipating retirement and is ultra conservative in order to protect existing assets.

A final drawback, one that is currently generating the greatest interest and provided an incentive for writing this book, is business succession and continuation. The more indispensable a person is to a firm's success, the less value that firm has to someone else. So, if you have five owners acting as if they are all running their own sole proprietorships, and those proprietors have not been involving anyone else in their client relationships, then there is no one to take over and seamlessly continue your firm. Therefore, you are left with a client list to sell or merge. If you position your practice so that your only exit alternative is to sell or merge it, you are picking a weak strategy.

> **⊙━ Key Point**
>
> The more your organization is run by process, and the more interchangeable people are in serving your clients, the more value you are adding to your firm.

This idea is neither novel nor new. In John Maxwell's best selling book, *The 21 Irrefutable Laws of Leadership*, law number 21 is the Law of Legacy, which is "A leader's lasting value is measured by succession." This value is realized when someone can step into a leader's place and never miss a beat.

One-Firm Concept

The most commonly touted solution to the "Multiple Firms Under One Roof Concept" is logically called "The One-Firm Concept." Interestingly enough, it is the model used by corporate clients. Although this model is widely discussed in CPA/CA firms throughout the United States and Canada, the record for its implementation is marginal. Why? Because, for this model to work, decision-making authority has to be in place with a strong SOP foundation. Most firms are not willing to invest the required money, time, and resources to create this model, for a number of reasons. Owners tend to be reluctant to give up the privileges they have grown accustomed to receiving. An investment is required to close the competence gap between average employees and superstars (even though, currently, the superstars' performance may be adequate to sustain the firm). Finally, an unprecedented level of accountability to the firm is required. Specifically, in the one-firm concept:

- The firm owns the clients rather than the owners owning the clients.
- The actions of the owners must always be in lock step with the firm's goals, not with personal agendas (i.e., the firm comes first).
- There is clear distinction between being an owner and having autonomy to do as you please.
- Strategy drives the budget process, and compensation is tied to budget achievement; the notion of pay-for-performance should be part of the firm's foundation. This approach creates a direct link between compensation and strategy achievement.
- All members of the firm must be accountable, not just nonowners. Standard operating procedures and firm methodologies should be formalized and followed by everyone, with consequences for noncompliance.
- The firm must make necessary investments to support long-term success, such as technology integration, more formalized marketing procedures, and defined career paths.
- The firm—rather than individual owners—should control decisions on client acceptance and assignment of owners or managers or staff to those clients.
- The firm should shift clients between owners and managers to create a balance of work and expectations instead of allowing personal empire building.

In the following subsections, I would like to talk a little bit more about owner accountability and balancing of clients.

Owner Accountability

Owners have been incredibly accountable to their clients for decades. Typically, firm hierarchy is apt to be owner first, client second, and firm third. For the One Firm Concept to work, the firm has to be first, the owner second, and the client third.

No doubt, the last two sentences are alarming and outrageous to many CPAs. The idea that an owner or a firm would put themselves ahead of their clients seems ludicrous. It also sounds unethical, but is not to be confused with seeking to benefit from clients in ways that are detrimental to clients. Consider the following examples. A client is terrible to work with. Or, a client wants you to work for 25 percent of your rates. Or, you think a client is unethical. If you choose not to work with these clients, you are placing the best interests of the owners (or the firm for that matter) ahead of the clients' demands. Over and over, I hear owners say, "I won't do that because it is not how my client wants to be treated." This is an example of putting clients ahead of the firm. Or, I hear comments like, "I know that we offer other services my client needs, but I am afraid that we might not do a good job and that will affect my long-term relationship with the client." Here, the owner is putting him- or herself ahead of the firm. Clearly, a different argument could be made, but in the end, the owner is protecting turf—specifically, his or her relationship with the client—even though the client is in need of a specific service that the firm might provide. Too many clients are underserved because of this protective philosophy. A number of CPAs will insist that it is better to provide one service than to lose the client. However, this is just a rationalization to defend inaction. To the contrary, I cite the findings of one internal study by one of the 10 largest CPA firms. It was found that clients' loyalty and satisfaction with the firm was directly proportional to the number of services they bought. For example, a client who only purchased an audit was more likely to eventually walk away and find a new firm than a client who bought both audit and tax services. Similarly, a client who bought audit and tax services was found to be more likely to find a new firm than a client who bought audit, tax, and consulting services.

Balancing of Clients

CPAs may find that balancing clients is more important than they think. First, balancing clients is necessary to balance resources. It is silly to have one owner underserving clients because he or she is covering too many, while another owner scrambles to find something to do. (By the way, that something, when he or she finds it, is often work below his or her current ability level.)

Second, balance also ensures that the firm's top clients are being adequately taken care of by owners. The owners can spend the needed time with these clients and stay abreast of their needs.

Third, and potentially the most important, the bigger the gap in books of business, the more those with the large books will hold everyone else hostage to their demands. This story is so common it is almost folklore among CPA firms and it goes like this:

> **⤴ Sample Scenario**
>
> The firm has four owners, namely, Bob, Jon, and Sue, who each has books of business of around $500,000, and Stan, who has a million-dollar-plus book. Although their ownership shares are equal, Stan always wants everything to be run his way. The minutia in dispute literally include the cotton content and color of the firm's letterhead. Every time Stan does not get his way, he threatens to quit. Moreover, although Stan is great at bringing in business and doing the work, he is a Tasmanian devil about managing people. The other three owners spend an enormous amount of time working with staff to keep them from walking out.
>
> The three owners have continually rationalized their decision to put up with Stan's micromanagement because they do not want to lose the volume of business that he brings in. They have grown comfortable with their salaries and having access to their current level of support staff, which depends on the $2.5-million-dollar volume. Finally one day, Stan goes too far. The other three owners take him up on his offer and ask him to leave.
>
> Two years later, the three-owner firm has revenues in excess of $2.5 million, and the owners are ecstatic. Stan has a small office, still manages his million-plus business, and couldn't be happier being the sole decision maker.

The point of the story is how remarkably often these splits occur, and everyone ends up winning. Stan was better off because he could do exactly as he pleased. And the three owners who had similar views and values as to how to operate the firm flourished once Stan was out of their way. If there is consensus except for one person, who always wants a different solution, it may be time to part company with that person. If there is continual dispute, the bottom line is that the two groups are not seeing value in the same place. It doesn't matter who is right or wrong; the chasm will just continue to grow. The surprise is that, whatever the owners feared would be lost is quickly regained as a result of owner synergy and the willingness to be mutually accountable.

As regards implementing change, the moral of the story is that owner disconnects can sometimes keep a firm from moving forward. Those disconnects might be around strategy, philosophy, personal goals, risk, or whatever. It may be that too many personalities like Stan are standing in the way, preventing the firm from finding a way to turn around.

It just may be that the current group of owners cannot find happiness on the path favored by the majority. If this is the case, you not only have to decide where you are going, but who is going with you and who will be left behind. Sometimes, taking a firm to the next level requires that you let go of an owner or two.

A Final Word on Implementing Organizational Structures

Regardless of the style of governance or the size of the firm (sole proprietor to large firm), firms should consider operating within the general framework outlined in this chapter as much as is practical. Sole proprietors and small firms might set up an advisory board to obtain a broader perspective and balance.

Take this slowly, like the turtle. Culture is difficult to change. In your first year, try to work out the kinks in decision-making authority so that everyone truly works inside the new framework. Implement one project that has been difficult to complete in the past using the concepts of creating process to support it.

Leadership

In the final section of this chapter, I want to spend some time considering how CPA firm leadership can create disconnects and/or synergies that are critical to establishing a culture that can embrace changes you might be contemplating.

This section is not about how to become a leader or what qualities and characteristics make up a great leader. If this is what you are looking for, there are plenty of great books on this subject, including my personal favorite from Dr. Paul Hersey called *The Situational Leader*. John Maxwell wrote an insightful book as well called *The 21 Irrefutable Laws of Leadership*.

Instead, I want to discuss a number of leadership issues that affect our ability to effectively run and manage our firms, which makes this not about staff, but about the owner group. In order to implement decision-making authority in an effective way, we have to address the dysfunction that runs rampant in professional service organizations like ours.

This section will address various aspects of the dysfunctional firm including the Peter Principle, the lack of organizational infrastructure, and behavior traits.

Dysfunction and the Peter Principle

Some dysfunction is attributable to the Peter Principle, a theory of occupational incompetence formulated by Lawrence Peter, which, simply put, is that we often rise to our level of incompetence, and then we plateau there. This is easy to imagine for professionals such as CPAs if you consider that what initiates our rise to the top is our technical ability and our capacity to produce. Yet, with each promotion, our focus is supposed to shift from getting work out ourselves to getting more work done through others. Our efforts are expected to shift from doing client work to managing client relationships. By the time we are asked to be an owner, our jobs are often defined as providing high-level client advisory support, the oversight and management of projects, and the management of client relationships. The journey we are expected to make throughout this promotional path is to abandon the natural tendencies and skills, one by one, which propelled our success in the first place. And we are expected to replace those time-proven abilities with skills that are entirely different and foreign to us.

The Peter Principle is not an insult to those who are rising in position; it may be the highest compliment. Such employees have been so good at what they do that superiors put them in positions for which they have little experience in the belief that these are professionals who will rise to any occasion. The criticism is not aimed at the ascent to one's level of incompetence (which is a sign of success), but rather in one's decision that one does not need to develop new skills required by the new position. Unfortunately, once people decide that they know everything they need to know, they have put themselves on the plateau where they stagnate (until they are finally pushed out of the organization, or terminated). Many owners can be described as living the Peter Principle because the only real change between their current managerial roles and their former roles is a higher billing rate. So, unless you want examples of the Peter Principle running rampant, it is important to develop job descriptions that spell out the different expectations of various positions in your firm. This way, although employees may continue to rise to their level of incompetence, they will know what they need to do next to make sure they do not remain incompetent.

Dysfunction and Organizational Infrastructure

The bulk of the remaining dysfunction comes from the natural evolution from voting control to the installation, or the lack of installation, of organizational infrastructure. Whenever you have a service organization like a CPA firm (law firms and consulting firms would fall into the same category for example), ease of entry and the cost of startup are low. Therefore, the barriers to starting your own firm are minimal. This fact creates a general attitude, namely, "if the going gets tough, then I will get going … and split off to form my own firm." Among owners, this becomes a false level of security; everyone feels that he or she can go out on their own tomorrow and do as well or better as in the firm. Generally speaking, this is not true from a financial perspective given that, the larger the firm, the higher the average pay per owner. Spinning off into a very small firm will probably reduce an owner's personal income. Nevertheless, if you consider the factors of quality of life, work/play balance, flexibility, or pay, most people, on their own, would probably find a compromise that works equally well for them. But in order for these spinning-off owners to be successful, they will likely have to take on the exact roles that drove them off in the first place. It surprises me how many people draw a line in the sand about what they will or will not do, cause a rift in the firm, find themselves leaving the firm, and thereafter go on to happily fulfill the same roles they refused to accept in the first place.

So, believing that your top professionals, especially those who are the most marketing oriented, will at least conceptually keep the option of staying or leaving in play, how do you keep the scale tipped toward making them stay? Start with strategy. I keep repeating this directive because it is true. Most dysfunction in owner groups is not because of work or character, but rather because of the disconnects between owners' personal strategies and the dynamic driving the firm. Consider the following story:

↯ Sample Scenario

A firm of about $2 million in revenues has developed a strategy to grow the firm to $4 million in revenues in five years (about 15 percent growth per year). This means that the firm is planning to add about 17 people (currently, there are 18 people and the belief is that 35 will be enough). This also means that the firm will probably add several new owners, from the current three to five or six.

Of the three owners, Tom is three years from retirement (and owns 45 percent of the firm), Craig is 53 (and owns 35 percent of the firm), and Ralph is 44 (a fairly new owner who owns 20 percent of the firm). The senior owner's strategy is to retire soon and he is taking a very risk-averse posture because he wants to protect his biggest personal asset—the firm. The two younger owners are the ones with the strategy to double the business (the vote came down 55 percent to 45 percent in favor of growth). However, Craig's and Ralph's reasons for wanting to achieve this growth are totally different. Ralph wants to add more owners to help carry the burden of paying out Tom and later Craig. Craig has made it clear that he wants to retire early, but in order to do that, he needs a lot more growth in order to significantly leverage his current income and later retirement payout.

Right now, the dysfunction in this firm is on the brink of running rampant and problem owners soon will be cropping up everywhere. For example, Craig and Ralph would likely see Tom as a problem owner trying to sabotage the firm's growth plan. Tom fears that growing the firm as fast as planned will consume resources and, therefore, minimize his personal take-home pay during his final three-year period. This reduction in pay is important not only because he does not want his income to shrink, but because his retirement payout is based on the average of the last five years of his income.

However, the coalition on the home front of 55 percent is not a bed of roses either. Craig and Ralph's strategies are going to disconnect soon because Ralph is going to want to add owners faster than Craig. Although Ralph has not yet made it clear to Craig, because they have similar initial objectives, Ralph does not want Craig to have a controlling interest in the firm. If only one owner is added by the time Tom retires, based on the natural reallocation of shares, Craig will end up with just over 50-percent ownership. If two owners are added by that time, no one person will have a controlling interest. Nevertheless, the quick addition of too many owners will shrink Craig's planned growth in personal income to the point that early retirement may not be feasible for him.

Soon, in all likelihood, all the owners will begin to demonstrate dysfunctional behavior to support their privately held positions. As expected, Tom will probably passive-aggressively sabotage the firm's growth by failing to support the initiatives. Craig possibly will hold Ralph hostage, demanding special accommodations and concessions in return for voting in new owners. And Ralph may form a coalition with Tom to restrict early retirement options. Everyone has a great deal to gain through cooperation, but even more to lose through dissension. By sitting the owners down and discussing their points of view, a strategy can be created that will avoid all of the issues before anyone gets rooted in principles and positions. Craig and Ralph can set a retirement payout for Tom based on an agreed-to formula that does not penalize him for the investment in growth that is about to be made. Craig can agree that, regardless of when the new owners join the firm, his interest will not climb above 49 percent (but that his interest will be re-adjusted back at some point in the future). And Ralph can agree to provisions for early retirement for Craig, assuming Craig agrees to changes regarding the number of owners, and the transition of clients before he leaves.

Although there can easily be a happy ending to this story, there is a far greater chance that the owners will quietly sabotage the others' objectives just to avoid the confrontation of hurting each other's feelings by speaking openly.

Dysfunctional Behavior Traits

The following sections address some of the most common issues and traits that generate dysfunctional behavior among owners.

Trait 1. Conflicting Personal Goals (Work/Life Balance)

Conflicting personal goals usually revolve around the amount of work an owner is expected to perform. Some owners feel you should dedicate your life to the firm to make more money, and other owners feel like the firm's role is to allow them the flexibility to spend more time with their families.

Neither of these is wrong, nor are any of the variations in between. But if minimum acceptable owner standards are not agreed to, the differences will constantly be an active battleground.

Trait 2. Different Personal Goals

Different personal goals among owners create a strategy problem. Once the personal agendas are out in the open, you can usually find a strategy everyone will support. However, if you can't, then it is time to separate—everyone will be better off instead of each person dragging the others down.

Trait 3. Need for Special Accommodation

The need for special accommodation includes owners wanting resources to fund their special interests (services, outings) or an unwillingness to be accountable to the firm. It is the outcome of living in "no man's land" for too long. Owners actually start believing that the firm belongs in the third position on the list, that their wants and desires come first, the client's needs second, and the firm is last.

The solution to this disconnect usually lies in accountability, operational budgets, and performance systems.

Trait 4. Relentless Advocacy of One's Own Ideas

The person proceeds on the premise that he or she knows more than everyone else. He or she may treat the firm like a personal business, take the attitude that no one else has any right to interfere, or insist on having a say in every firm decision, regardless of the insignificance of the issue.

Such a person is best suited to being spun off on his or her own. If a person truly believes he or she is smarter than everyone else, is only happy when his or her ideas are being implemented, or cannot or will not pick his or her battles by distinguishing important decisions from unimportant minutia, this person should be on his or her own. This personality profile will probably be very successful as a sole proprietor. Nevertheless, if this individual remains in the larger firm, he or she is likely to hold the entire firm back from achieving the success it should be experiencing.

Trait 5. Voting Rights in Excess of Contribution

If an owner has voting rights in excess of his or her contribution or business acumen, or if he or she never should have been made owner, you must "put out a fire" that should never have been allowed to start in the first place. If the firm has a partner-in-training program with identified objective hurdles, then whoever makes "owner" is qualified to be one. But this isn't what always happens. Here are some typical anomalies:

- A person's book of business is allowed to grow without the oversight of making sure his or her key clients have multiple contacts and loyalties within the firm.
- A person with account management responsibilities is not tied to an employment contract that requires them to make payment for any clients that they take with them if he or she leaves the firm.
- The firm launches a service and allows a person to be the only one that can manage or service those clients.
- My personal favorite is the senior owners who are concerned that there will be too-few owners to do their work after they retire. To protect against not receiving their full retirement payout, they quickly waive whatever owner requirements were in place and several of the most senior people are voted in as owners.

In the scenarios described by the first three bullets, it is predictable that the firm will be held hostage and forced to add an owner to salvage a bad situation. The last situation, which might seem more benign at first than the others, can actually have a far more damaging result. Although the senior owners may give themselves a better chance of being paid out in the short term, the long-term viability of the firm may be at a much higher risk because people who, perhaps, never should have been made owners will, over time, gain more control over the firm.

All of the preceding anomalies are symptoms of not having infrastructure in place to develop owners. And, by the way, under the superstar model, you need to have at least one new superstar, or maybe two, to replace every retiring owner. In the operator model, because of the reliance on infrastructure as the firm's foundation (like pay for performance, or marketing) and defined roles and duties, a firm can continue to grow with a reduced number of owners because more work is being passed down to managers and staff. Being able to increase the size of the firm with a declining number of owners will become exceedingly more important, given our profession's current demographics and the probable buyer's market discussed in Chapter 1.

Trait 6. Disorganization and Lack of Planning

Disorganization and lack of planning by one owner, often becomes everyone else's crisis. This is a common characteristic within superstar firms. Superstars need to be involved in everything. They want to help, but they also want to keep their finger in every pot.

Therefore, they become bottlenecks to getting work out. Work completed by staff sits on their desks for days or even weeks. And then, at the last minute, the owner pitches a fit so that everyone will put down whatever they are doing at the moment and jump through whatever hoops are necessary to get the project out on time. This person's inability to let go of some control, delegate more effectively, and focus on what is really important also allows the disorganized owner's chaos to infect the entire firm. This situation creates a great deal of ill will and destroys the motivation of the staff.

The solution rests with accountability and process. The owner's first job is to plan and manage projects. If there are no consequences for this lack of organization, then the firm is ensuring that it will continue.

Trait 7. Manipulating and Undermining the Process

Rather than address issues head-on with everyone involved, this owner starts by putting together side deals and bringing ideas forward only after backroom private meetings. Or, this person will not let go of anything by bringing up the same previously resolved topics at every meeting. You cannot focus enough time on going forward because he or she keeps reliving every decision in order to get his or her way. This person is unwilling to accept the decisions and policies of the group to guide how he or she operates within the firm.

Owners are always caught by surprise with this one. In public, the dissenting owner keeps a low profile. But that owner is always shooting flares to find out who is dissatisfied with the decisions being made. Once a weakness in the armor is discovered, one owner approaches another to build an alliance. These alliances are formed with many different personal agendas, as illustrated in the example given previously. These short-term synergies help each owner in the alliance because none of their agendas have a chance to succeed unless the current agenda is derailed.

As discussed previously, open discussions are essential if this dilemma is to be resolved; the owner group will be crippled with dysfunction if this kind of manipulation becomes part of the operating norm. Just as we have discussed above, the solution may also rest in separating an owner or two from the herd.

Trait 8. Passive-Aggressive Behavior

Public agreement to support ideas and initiatives, followed by passive-aggressive attempts to kill those same decisions, is probably the most disabling of all traits because it takes so long to uncover. You have all seen it. At the owner meeting, there is an animated discussion that generates excitement, and a solution is identified. Assignments are handed out, and owners readily accept them. However, a key owner is not willing to follow the agreed-to decision. Therefore, every time the project needs to move forward, this owner finds a different logical and defensible boat anchor to throw in the water. Finally, the project dies due to lack of momentum, which was always the intent.

Someone must be held accountable. Project rewards must be developed to motivate appropriate behavior and penalties must be created to demotivate inaction.

Trait 9. Refusal to Participate or Attend Important Firm Meetings

Generally, the owner with a nonattendance problem is the first to second-guess all decisions made without his or her input.

The solution to this problem is pretty straightforward and by now, you already know what I am going to say. However, my first comment might shock you: Do not ask for compliance if it is not needed. As accountants, we sometimes want to dot all of our *i*'s and cross all of our *t*'s, even though that may be a personal preference, not a necessity. If you are frustrated because someone will not do what they are told to do, make sure you are not telling them to waste their time. Many times, people do not need to be at meetings and should not be asked to participate in the first place. Many times, the people would come if the meetings were not so poorly run. Sometimes, we ask people to come to meetings when it really is not the best use of their time for the firm, but it is convenient for someone else. So, start by not asking people to come to meetings when it is not truly necessary.

Now to the part you expected. If the meeting is required, and someone does not have a legitimate reason for being absent, then he or she just forfeits his or her say in the decisions made during that meeting. This is a policy that is simple and represents accountability at its best. It boils down to saying, "If you don't want to pay, then you can't play."

Trait 10. Obliviousness to the Needs of Others

Obliviousness to the needs of others also includes being oblivious as to how he or she comes across, or being given to constant outbursts of temper, which require others to follow up by regularly making the rounds to mend fences with critical staff and management. This describes a great number of accountants. We are very good at what we do. We often consider that our technical prowess is what really demonstrates our value, not our interpersonal skills. In psychological terms, we are *low self-monitors*. This means that we are often unaware how our actions or emotions might affect others. Consider the temper tantrum thrown by an owner in reaction to this situation: The deadline for a submission has come, and the project is being reviewed at the last minute. During the review, it comes to light that there are errors. As you know from the examples given previously, it is likely that the basic problem is that the work should have been reviewed earlier. The owner would do well to be rational and recognize his or her own responsibility. Nevertheless, several employees are publicly chastised over the incident. Moreover, the owner proceeds to tyrannize everyone until the project is correct and out the door to the client. Once the dust has settled, another owner has to make the rounds, doing damage control and calming the employees so that they do not quit.

If the owner who habitually loses his or her temper has a controlling interest in the firm, this issue will be difficult to resolve because its solution lies in accountability. Controlling owners rarely submit themselves to being accountable. Nevertheless, every time an owner indulges in this kind of behavior, it costs the firm all the time that is spent on damage control, and lost productivity (including the time wasted by employees gossiping about the incident). A simple remedy is to total all that lost time and bill it to the owner whose destructive behavior is the root cause. On the other hand, if the individual is not critical to your operations, he or she should be given a warning. If the behavior is repeated, he or she should be let go. No productivity level, however high, can justify the negative consequences of tolerating a personality that can and will wreak havoc on your firm at any given moment (and usually at the worst possible times).

A Final Word about Leadership

In the end, if you cannot agree on the foundation principles, values, and attitudes required by the firm from all the owners, managers, and staff, then you do not have much to build a firm around. Once you decide what you expect, then violations have to have consequences. That is why it is extremely important to keep from making up rules that you do not plan to enforce. If something is not important enough to warrant imposing serious consequences for noncompliance, then do not bother trying to get compliance. Moreover, remember that any number of solutions can be found by creatively utilizing your compensation system so that people's choices can be accommodated in a way that benefits the firm.

So, now we are about to go full circle with this discussion. Most commonly, dysfunction flourishes in CPA firms that lack the following:

- Defined and agreed-to strategy (with an open and honest communication driving that strategy)
- Decision-making authority (because someone has to hold everyone accountable)
- Agreed-to organizational chart (which clearly communicates the hierarchy of authority)
- Defined job duties and responsibilities (which provides important insight as to expectation of each role)
- Standard operating processes, procedures, and policies (which help support and raise the minimum standards bar for performance)
- Clear objective accountability (because people do what they are rewarded and motivated to do)
- Willingness to:
  - Quickly address issues (because time does not make problems go away, it makes them fester)
  - Address the conflict in a timely manner (to prevent small, but neglected conflicts from turning into "time bombs" that do serious damage)
  - Enforce consequences (because accountability cannot work if there are no consequences for inappropriate action or behavior)
  - Take a step backward in order to move forward (e.g., be willing to let an owner go even if he or she has the largest book of business, or fire a bad client even if it is one of your biggest; invest in foundation systems even if it reduces owner income; every day, consider steps that might hurt in the short term but are the right thing to do to protect the long-term viability of the firm)

Often, if the discussion turns to moving a firm to a more corporate model with process and procedure based modes of operations, there is a concern about the potential damage to the culture that the new model may bring. Preserving the individuality of the members and the firm's culture is seen as part-and-parcel of protecting the future success of the organization. My response when this is brought up is simple.

I am not suggesting the creation of a bureaucracy. I am not proposing the cessation of creativity and entrepreneurialism. I am not recommending a prison to house your employees. I am not advising that your values, ethics, or principles be compromised in any way. I am, to name a few ideas, describing a business model in which:

- You ask everyone to practice what they preach.
- Desired behavior is appreciated, reported, and rewarded.
- Unacceptable behavior is defined and penalized quickly to minimize the damage to the firm and its people.
- Authority and limits to that authority are openly outlined and shared.
- Roles and responsibilities are identified and followed.
- Expectations are clearly communicated and embraced.

The fact that a firm operates under more defined processes and procedures does not have to change the culture. As a matter of fact, these steps can just as easily strengthen it because people (1) feel more secure in their positions, (2) have less ambiguity about the direction of the firm and their role within it, and (3) can avoid conflict by staying within the known unacceptable boundaries of acceptable behavior and performance. Additionally, just because someone has the authority to dictate a solution does not mean that he or she should stop listening to others or be inconsiderate to those around them. Just because a policy is in place doesn't mean that it shouldn't be rewritten, or that an exception shouldn't be made when the situation justifies such action.

Good leadership requires inclusiveness, building consensus, having empathy, being flexible, caring about people, and so much more. Nothing within the corporate or operator models precludes these from blossoming. It is only through abuses of power and privileges, like authority and leadership, that a firm's culture is likely to change in a negative way. And quite frankly, it is far more likely that these abuses will flourish in a superstar than an operator model. It is far more likely that the firm's overall culture will suffer more under the individual practice model (in which employees are put at odds with each other based on turf protection and personal loyalties) rather than under the corporate model (in which the firm has to come first and everyone's loyalties should be more synergistic).

It is critical that leadership understands that processes, procedures, and policies are a way to empower people to fully leverage their situation and appropriately respond to their responsibilities rather than assuming they are mechanisms of restraint. For most of us, being privy to this kind of organizational intelligence is not a way to clip our wings, but a way to better understand the freedom we have to succeed in the roles we fill.

Conclusion

I would like to end this chapter with one final suggestion. As you decide how your firm will address the various issues raised in this book, you will not all be on the same page. There will be many heated arguments before everyone gets to the point at which the board has a vision that it is ready to implement. There will be many missteps as people convey more authority than allowed, dive into deeper minutia than appropriate, put themselves before the firm, violate procedures, and shirk their responsibilities. This is all part of an evolution—a "growing-up" process in your firm. If you want to reach your final destination, you have to agree to disagree in the boardroom. You have to be willing to share your thoughts without worrying about being judged. You have to be open and honest about what you want and need. But once all of this has been aired, you have to understand two critical success factors:

1. What happens and is said in the boardroom stays in the boardroom.
2. Whatever decisions are made, everyone must agree to support them as if they were his or her own ideas.

If the firm cannot accomplish these two goals, then you will find the firm behaving like Don Quixote, spending too much time tilting at windmills.

Chapter 3

Management and Operations: Extending the Life and Culture of the Firm

The objectives of this chapter are to:
- Take a look at today's workforce and the tools being used by firms to motivate this force.
- Present the "upside-down" pyramid concept and outline ways to reverse it.
- Discuss how enforcement of accountability can take a firm to the next level.
- Outline the role and responsibilities of a manager in a firm.
- Consider various standard operating procedure (SOP) foundation programs to implement in your firm.
- Demonstrate how to align a firm's compensation system with its strategy.

Developing an SOP foundation is about putting in support (systems, procedures, policies, and processes) that will help your employees, overall, produce at a higher level. It is about creating an environment that motivates your employees to "do what they enjoy and enjoy what they do." Standard operating procedures refer to creating bridges that tie together seemingly unrelated issues, fairness, culture, and principles to make "doing what is best for the firm" the easiest choice to make. It concerns management and the various techniques that help synergize the needs of your people and their personal evolutions to the objectives of the firm.

Creating an SOP foundation is about moving from a superstar model, in which people create systems to leverage their personal capabilities, to an operator model in which firm-wide systems are put in place to leverage the overall group's performance. Systems such as these are paramount to the success and seamlessness of succession because of the clarity and consistency they provide to roles, responsibilities, expectations, evaluations, and rewards. People are the single largest cost of a service business. Consequently, it only makes sense that creating an infrastructure that motivates and leverages employee performance not only adds significant value to the firm, but also allows leadership to change with minimal disruption of service delivery.

So, to kick off this chapter, the following discussion outlines the current situation between the workforce and firms, followed by discussions on a variety of the key principles and values that form the foundation of a firm's culture and working environment, which then can be translated into policies, processes, and procedures that support the organization. These key principles are the upside-down pyramid, accountability, the role of managers, staff reporting models, SOP foundation programs, and effective compensation systems.

Today's Workforce and Firm Culture

Discussion of the management of a service organization often brings to mind the mammoth hurdles that must be overcome. The discussion below is in two parts. First, I want to talk about the generational gap and its effect on how we address younger employees (generally speaking, this includes CPAs in their late thirties and younger). Second, I will outline motivation issues, meaning, what really motivates staff and what firms do to provide that motivation.

The Generation Gap

In an article called "Management and the Generation Gap,"[1] author Robert Reed discusses some important characteristic differences in the younger generation, including:
- They want "everything now."
- They want to be independent.
- They have "never had to do without."
- "Instant gratification is what they are accustomed to."
- "This generation has no respect for authority."
- "They are rude, impatient, spoiled, stubborn, and unreasonable."

A popular, often-quoted passage describes today's youth this way: "They love luxury, hate authority, they are bored and ill-mannered, and lack respect for adults." The problem is that Robert Reed's article was published in 1971. The second quote, from a 1966 speech reported by the New York Times, was attributed to Socrates.[2] Clearly, every generation has made the same kinds of observations, not just about today's youth, but about baby boomers, their parents, their grandparents. The current young generation is always lacking in the eyes of the older generation that is currently in power.

---

[1] Robert Reed, "Management and the Generation Gap," *S.A.M. Advanced Management Journal*, January 1971, pages 16-18.

[2] *The New York Times* quoted Gijsbert van Hall, the Mayor of Amsterdam, when he reminded the people of Socrates' quote in his speech following a street demonstration in 1966 (*The New York Times*, April 3, 1966, page 16).

To see beyond the generation gap, we must make an effort to close the chasm. The three aspects of this chasm are issues arising from environment, revisionism, and realism. Each is discussed below.

The Environmental Gap

First, we have to consider how the environment has changed. Much of the baby boom generation grew up in households in which one person worked to make money, and the other ran the home. Baby boomers were often able to meet or exceed their own parents' standard of living before reaching the age of 30. This was partially due to parental support, better education, and better opportunities, including the chance to leverage the income from two wage earners. Boomers got support from all angles. They could enjoy the luxuries of having two incomes while counting on the women in the preceding generation (who didn't work) to become grandmothers who were available whenever they were needed to help with the kids or assist with family matters.

In contrast, excluding the wealth that may be passed down to them, today's youth is the first generation in a long time, in my opinion, that could be very successful, yet on average unable to easily duplicate the wealth of their parents (especially if both parents were professionals).

Today, immediate families often provide a flimsier support structure; younger people are likely to be on their own more, because both parents work and are less available to assist.

Moreover, because it normally takes two incomes to make ends meet in today's households, the balance between work and play has tipped toward work. The typical day of a young professional starts at 6:30 a.m. and goes until 6:30 p.m. (including commuting time), and family and household issues consume the hours between 6:30 and 9:30 p.m. This gives our young generation about 30 minutes to decompress from the day before they go to sleep and start all over again. My point is … it's certainly not that our young people are not willing to work; it is that there is little excess capacity for the firm, or them, to pull from.

The Revisionist Gap

Another chasm stems from the rewriting of our past. Simply put … we forget how we were viewed when we were young. I dare to say that there is not an owner in our profession today that wasn't viewed by his or her supervisors years ago as having a "questionable" ability to earn their current position. I bring this up often with firms and occasionally I see shock on a face or two in an owner group. Their responses are predictable, "Your comment is not true about me. I was always considered owner material." Yet, in every case, when I have had the chance to talk with that owner's mentor or sponsor, the debriefing was always the same. "Yes, we saw a great deal of promise. But we were concerned about … and didn't know if they could make the cut." In some cases, a person's technical ability was not in question, but their ability to bring in business was. In others, although their business development acumen was superior, project management skills fell short. In a few situations, even though a person was perceived as having a great balance of skills, their work commitment to the firm was substandard. The point is … I have yet to find anyone who has said, "Yes, that person was always owner material and had the full package we were looking for." In other words—we, the current owners in power—were just like those who report to us ... *"to some degree, there were question marks next to our names."*

The Realist Gap

A final chasm comes from the rewriting of our current job descriptions to match our comfort zones and strengths. Rather than looking at what the marketplace is expecting from owners, or what our fiercest competitors are demanding, we begin to assume that the strengths we already possess are the only ones that matter and our weaknesses are not relevant. Many owners have stagnated in their own personal growth, are suffering from the consequences of the Peter Principle, and are trying to sustain the next evolution of their firm's operating model on foundations that get weaker with every regeneration of them. As owners, it is irrelevant what our senior generation did before us to be successful. The environment is different today; it is more competitive and, in order to remain an owner, we need to embrace an evolving role that needs to keep pace with market expectation.

A Final Word on the Generation Gap

To summarize, today's youth are operating at maximum capacity; we were as questionable as owner material as our young people are today; and we are probably falling just as short of realizing our "marketplace-adjusted-roles-and-responsibilities" as they are at living up to our expectations.

So, given my premise that we all have some growing to do, how can we motivate people to want to step up to this challenge?

> **O━ Key Point**
>
> Our younger people aren't much different than we were.

Motivating Staff

Based on several surveys I have seen over the past 15 years, most managers rank money as their number one carrot for motivating their employees. Employees, however, rarely rank money even in the top five motivators. What do employees usually rank first, second, or third? Their choices, paraphrased, are "Feeling good about the work they perform," "Feeling that their work makes a difference," or "Feeling that they did a good day's work."

The Problem

So, how can management be so wrong about something so important? It's easy. The reality is that we don't pay much attention to the people who work for us. To most managers, managing (addressing the issues of employees) is an inconvenient, low-reward function. We value technical not managerial expertise. Using the superstar ideology, management is something you have to do to leverage your poor performers because superstars don't need guidance ... they just need more rope. So we rarely take the time to adequately communicate our expectations up front (partially because we want the flexibility to make up the rules as we go along). Instead, we create environments in which we ask people to take initiative, and then we mistreat them when they fall short. Consider this example.

⇄ Sample Scenario

The receptionist, Sue, has many duties, from having the responsibility of giving a good first impression of the firm to handling a variety of overflow work from other administrative positions. She does a great job. The orders from management are "take initiative and do what is necessary. Don't expect people to hold your hand." So, the time comes when a group of marketing mailers to clients needs to go out with the deadline of that day. Without much instruction or anyone around to ask (because there is an all-day office-wide meeting going on), Sue figures out how to print the labels, puts them on the materials, stamps them, and drops them off at the post office on her way home. She believes she really accomplished something special that day. A couple days later, a client calls about an unrelated matter, but while on the phone, comments that they had received multiple marketing pieces. After investigation, it turns out that Sue selected the wrong label list. Rather than using the marketing list, she used the master list (so people with multiple companies received a marketing piece for each entity). One of the owners, embarrassed by the client's comment and frustrated by the mistake, marched to the front of the office and publicly scolded Sue for what he called "her brainless error."

While this might sound insignificant, I am using it as an example because it happens—in some version—all the time, across all levels of jobs in accounting firms. First of all, given this scenario, everyone has to remember that it is difficult to find people with personalities that can handle the chaos of the front desk, maintain their poise, and be willing to work for what that position pays. So when you find someone good, you need to take good care of him or her. In this situation, Sue is comfortable making decisions and taking action when she needs to. But given the public reprimand by the owner, especially if this kind of assault happens multiple times, Sue will quickly be trained to never take initiative again because the price of being wrong is too high. The next time she has to make a call in the field, even if she is fairly confident about what she should do, she will sit on the decision and wait for someone to tell her specifically what to do.

⊶ Key Point

We have to keep a perspective. If our people are not making some mistakes, it is because they are *only* doing what they know how to do rather than what they can do.

People should be rewarded—not punished—when they are willing to venture outside their comfort zone and take action. The idea that we reward correct answers and punish mistakes means that you are creating an environment that will stifle the overall production of your firm. No one will push very hard to expand their capability because the risk and reward system makes that learning experience too painful. The owner may be frustrated that money was wasted in postal costs and more marketing pieces than were necessary. However, Sue's diminished inclination to take initiative in the future will cost the firm 20 times over those costs, and is a price that will be paid every year from now on.

When mistakes are made, we want to correct the action to prevent a repetition, but we want to also maintain the dignity and respect of the person doing the work. If you want your employees to be motivated to go into battle with you every day, you need to support their mistakes and respect their learning curves. Do not tolerate managers who cannot control their emotions and constantly burden the firm with the temperamental chaos they create.

The Solution

In the most recent PCPS Top Talent Study, firms were asked about staff policies that help to motivate and retain staff. Here is a summary of their responses in descending order of frequency:

• Open door/accessible management style	96%
• Frequent client contact	96%
• Paid personal/vacation time	96%
• Comfortable office atmosphere	95%
• Medical benefits	92%
• Interesting/challenging projects	90%
• Paid sick days	90%
• Retirement savings plans	89%
• Respect for work/life balance issues	88%
• Training/professional development	87%
• CPE credit reimbursement	83%
• Flexible work schedule	81%
• Career growth opportunities	79%
• Casual dress code	78%
• Regular performance reviews/feedback	77%
• On-site/in-house CPE	76%
• Access to the latest, cutting-edge technology	74%
• Paid time off to take CPA exam	73%
• Life insurance	73%
• Team orientation of firm	72%

Firms have become very creative in looking for ways to motivate their employees and respond to their needs. Because of the pressure on young people to spend time addressing family matters during the day, job flexibility is becoming a cornerstone of our profession. Consider that 81 percent of the survey respondents offer flexible work schedules for employees and 88 percent say they respect work/life balance issues. It is clear that firms recognize the need to release capacity pressure through the benefits they can bestow. This extra time becomes motivational because employees can more readily "feel like they are making a difference" because they are better equipped to successfully meet the demands of both their professional and personal lives.

The Upside-Down Pyramid

During the last few decades, public accounting firms have dramatically expanded the scope of services they offer. Many of these services have been in specialty areas, aligned with industries like auto dealers or health care, or services like business valuation or fraud detection. When these services are launched, they are typically championed by an owner, principal, or someone highly respected in the organization. Because some of these areas have sporadic demand or require a high level of expertise, firms have often relied on the same senior people to manage and do the bulk of the work. This has supported a trend in small to mid-sized firms, based on my personal observation, to build a *work-flow process* that looks like an upside-down pyramid. This operating environment, for many firms, functions as follows:

> The lion's share of the firm's income is generated by the owners and managers. The owners and managers are very hands on and involved in the details of most client projects. The work-flow hierarchy trickles down; partners do the technical work until they have worked all the hours they can stand, and then the excess trickles down to the managers. The managers do the technical work until they have labored all they can stomach, and then the remains trickle down to the staff pool. At each level, keeping the workers in the level below busy is almost an afterthought.

This section is in two parts. First it will discuss the problems caused by *the upside-down pyramid* (see figure 3-1) and, second, it will outline how to reverse it.

Figure 3-1: *The Upside Down Pyramid Workflow Process*

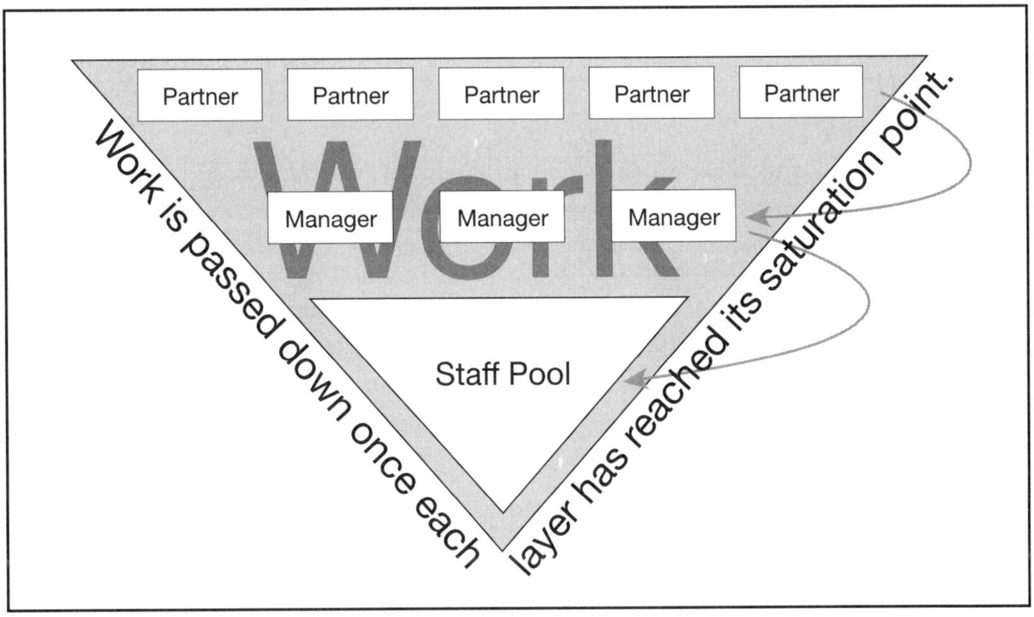

The Problems

In an upside-down pyramid environment, firms seem to have an attitude that subordinates (1) are employed to do the work that their superiors don't want to do and/or (2) are considered to be administrators providing assistance when needed. Utilizing this process, owners and managers are overworked, and staff is underworked and poorly trained. There are three major problems created by this process:

1. Owners doing nonowner work
2. Undertrained staff
3. Owner conflict

These three problems are discussed in more detail below.

Problem 1. Owners Doing Nonowner Work

This work-flow process can easily harm the profitability and long-term viability of the firm. For example, instead of pushing work down to the lowest possible level, nearly the exact opposite happens. Work is performed by the most experienced person possible. Although one could surmise that this approach would garner higher fees (because the work is performed by people with higher billing rates), most of the time, that assumption is wrong. For much of the work we do as CPA firms, our total fees are either fixed-in-fact or in-presumption. Obviously, fees are fixed-in-fact when a specific project price was specified. The fees are fixed-in-presumption when we do recurring work, like preparing a tax return each year, and the client assumes that this year's fees will be similar to those charged in previous years (unless the scope of the work changed). So, if you consider that much of our work is fixed in price, then using more experienced people than necessary to do the work only creates larger writedowns. If you take the position that your more experienced people do the work faster so that writedowns are not a factor, then I would respond with "I'll bet there is higher level work your experienced people are avoiding that should be done by them instead." If owners or managers tie themselves up doing work that is below their capability, they are not only doing work someone else could do at a lower rate, but they are also diminishing the amount of time they can devote to work that only they can do.

Problem 2. Undertrained Staff

Because these firms follow a "work first, manage second" strategy, at every level of the firm, employees are poorly trained. The response as to why is simple. It commonly is, "If I were to give this work to someone below me, I would have to spend so much time supervising them on the project that it is just quicker to do it myself." My response ... "The roles of both owner and manager are based on the philosophy that you are supposed to get the work done through others."

> **O—ᴨ Key Point**
>
> As a manager, your title is descriptive of your job—to manage. Otherwise, your title would be "doer."

So the next time you hear yourself utter the words, "It will take too much time to train my people to do this," stop and remind yourself, "Hey, it may take longer, but my job is to train them so that they can do this work." By the way, another classic reaction from this reversed work-flow pyramid is that employees rarely get feedback on their work. Instead of the owner or manager sending back a list of errors for the originator to fix, the senior people reviewing the project make corrections and get the work out the door. Once again, if this group shirks its responsibilities, it creates employees below them that lack the necessary competencies.

Problem 3. Owner Conflict

Finally, this upside-down process stimulates owner conflicts. There is little financial leverage under this model, which creates economic frustration. Conflicts arise because of the disparity of roles and duties between owners. A number of owners are embracing their responsibilities while others are functioning in the safe and unchallenging space of being glorified managers (unchallenging only because that is what they were doing before becoming an owner, so they are really hiding in their previous jobs).

The Solution or Reversing the Pyramid

Reversing the work flow is a very straightforward concept: Owners must start focusing on owner-level work, which includes creating and implementing strategy; developing systems that benefit the entire firm rather than an individual; managing clients; actively nurturing new business; and performing only the highest level advisory or expert work. Managers must do more manager work, which is made up of overseeing the work queue, supervising and training staff, providing guidance when necessary, reviewing work, and talking with clients. Finally, the staff needs to become the workhorse. Consider this process. When work comes in, everything that can be delegated to staff is delegated. Next, everything the staff can do with additional supervision and training is passed down and monitored as well. Once staff has no more bandwidth, managers can begin to perform the detailed work. This approach *reverses the pyramid* so that owners are freed up to spend more time building client loyalty, managers are freed up to spend more time developing their people and taking on responsibilities to manage mid-level clients, and staff receives the constant focus and training to help them evolve at a much faster pace. This reshuffling of work typically increases revenues and profits because:

- The owners spend more time assisting their top clients, which uncovers more opportunities to serve them.
- The owners perform more advisory and specialty premium billing work generating higher fees.
- The managers are generating opportunities as well as premium billing work because they have been assigned client management responsibility for the firm's mid-to-lower level clients.
- The staff are more productive because their work queue is better managed and their skills are improved because of the increased scrutiny and oversight by mangers.
- More work is written up because more work is being done by the right level of people.

Reversing the pyramid is an important SOP foundation for the firm to build upon. There are four steps you can take to reverse the pyramid. They are:

Step 1.   Assign interim roles.
Step 2.   Transition and fire clients.
Step 3.   Staff firm for nontax season.
Step 4.   Avoid discounting fees.

These steps are discussed in the following sections.

Step 1. Assign interim roles.

As you manage the firm's employees while working on reversing the pyramid, keep in mind that everyone in your organization is probably pretty busy already. Excess capacity has to be created from somewhere and one likely place is at the staff level. A high priority is to correct the situation in which staff are at their maximum utilization given their *current level of knowledge and training*. However, as I have stated before, you are probably underestimating staff. If there is a shortage of managers to manage the work, then you have to be willing to develop or hire additional ones. This obviously is a priority, too, and will take time. As an interim step, which assumes the firm has committed the necessary resources for training or hiring, some owners in the near term of six to nine months can be assigned the temporary role of manager. And some managers can temporarily take on the role of senior staff. At least with these modifications, except for those filling temporary roles, everyone else can start functioning in their appropriate capacities.

Step 2. Transition and fire clients.

Besides the capacity you might quickly gain from better utilization of staff, the most fertile other area is through *firing a bunch of clients*! A critical first step in this process is to break the firm's clients into two categories; top clients and everyone else. For those 20 percent of your clients (top clients) that make up 80 percent of the firm's revenue (just using a general rule of thumb), owners need to change their focus and start scheduling a significant portion of their time to be out in the field in front of these clients to make sure the firm is adequately serving them. This means that, generally speaking, in order to free up time to do this, all the client responsibilities for clients that fall below this 20 percent need to be considered for transition to junior owners, directors, or managers. This includes functions like staying in contact with these people and managing and collecting the billings. For managers to have time to take on this additional responsibility, they need to push down the work they are currently managing to their senior staff. And finally, to give staff some room to take on additional responsibility, some clients need to be let go.

To be frank, I don't actually believe in firing clients, even though I have emphatically stated otherwise. For me, unless there is an ethical issue or the client is just too mean to work with, I don't fire them—they fire me. For example, if someone has been with me for a long time and their rate structure is low, when the gap gets to be too big, I just raise the rates back to what they should be. If someone is always making me drop other work because they want last-minute service, I jack up their rates and charge them a premium for their service. If they are difficult to work with, then I might tell them that either I am going to

triple their fees or they need to fall in line with certain expected behaviors. The point is …
most of the targeted clients will fire themselves. But I am always surprised by the number
of people who are also willing to pay the higher fees. Consequently, the first reason to put
clients through this process is to get their rate structure in line with the service level you are
providing so that the work is profitable.

Firms don't actually have *nearly as big a staffing shortage as they have an unprofitable work
overage*. Too many firms have justified taking on marginal work with the idea that it will
keep their people busy during down times. My philosophy is simple.

O— **Key Point**
Unprofitable work is unprofitable work, regardless of the season.

My personal experience is that most firms could easily:

- Reduce their total gross income by 20 percent by firing clients.
- Let a few marginal employees go because, as a result of workload reduction, you don't need as many people.
- Make more money because the work you have in-house is more profitable.
- Incur far fewer hassles because your marginal employees and unprofitable clients are not there constantly lighting fires that everyone else is forced to put out.

Thus, one of the best ways to solve your staffing shortage and any underperformance in
profitability is firing your marginal clients!

Step 3. Staff firm for nontax season.

To me, the real issue almost always comes down to management (or the lack thereof). If
you truly have twice the work during tax season as you have the rest of the year, then staff
your firm at the level of staff you need for the whole year and use resources such as part-time
help, working with other CPA firms, outsourcing, and firing marginal clients to get you
through the peak season. To hire workers all year long so you can make money on them
during tax season and then donate all of those profits away during the rest of the year is poor
strategy (and a waste of your life).

Step 4. Avoid discounting fees.

There are only a few good reasons to offer discounted fees, such as:

- You are trying to break into a new marketplace or service, and you are providing an incentive to build clients or references (which means the discounts are offered for a specific period of time and don't become the normal pricing).
- The length of the project provides an increased utilization rate that makes up for the discount.

Otherwise, most discounted projects are just hidden firm losses. This committed workload creates a spiral that has a long-term negative effect on the firm. Because there is so
much work to do, even though some of it is bad work, everyone spends all of their time
doing it. Clients that actually need help and are even willing to pay a premium for that assistance are ignored because no one can give them the attention they need on a regular basis.
Because these clients are ignored, the firm often either loses them or forgoes lucrative additional work. This can put the firm in the position of needing to find more marginal work

to keep people busy. The key to reversing the cycle is to free up the owners and managers and put them in front of their clients; have owners do high-level premium advisory work; push work down throughout the organization; and force the discounted, marginal work out the door and down the street to one of your competitors.

Accountability

Accountability is another part of the SOP foundation that is required if you want your firm to evolve to a higher level. Accountability is a simple concept under which people are given the appropriate authority and responsibility to accomplish their work and are answerable for their actions or inactions. However, few companies implement this effectively. Accountability attempts to minimize the subjectivity of evaluating employee performance. Using objective measures as much as possible, employees receive clarity regarding the following:
- Exactly what is expected of them
- The system that has been put in place to measure and report their performance
- Performance measures that are based on unbiased and fair information

Accountability is central to not only motivating the workforce, but also to giving employees a sense of satisfaction about their accomplishments. In my opinion, a quality system of accountability has seven elements. Employees should:

Element 1.	Receive wages and benefits in line with those of the employee's peers.
Element 2.	Have a challenging job.
Element 3.	Know what is expected.
Element 4.	Be held accountable, as much as possible, to nonsubjective measurements
Element 5.	Learn on the job.
Element 6.	Receive adequate training.
Element 7.	Be rewarded for overachievement.

Each of these elements is discussed in the sections that follow.

Element 1. Align wages and benefits.

It is easy to identify what your employees' wages and benefits should be as compared to their peers. Look at surveys (like the MAP Survey), contact friendly firms, or join CPA firm associations to find out what comparable firms in similar geographic or demographic locations are paying their people for various positions. What's hard is to find a way to integrate your compensation system with the objectives of your firm.

The Problem

If your firm wants to pay your employees the lowest possible wages, then it should come as no surprise that you are likely to attract marginal performers. However, there are compensating factors that offset wages. These factors include a better work environment, telecommuting, flexible hours, a positive work climate, job training, day-care, and/or the many other alternatives that can counteract wage depression.

Nevertheless, paying the highest possible salaries is not necessarily a good answer either. If you commit to higher salaries, there is less opportunity to pay for superior performance.

> ### 🔑 Key Point
>
> Firms should look at wages as a function of performance and return on investment more than position.

Here is the general problem with salaries paid for positions: It is a common belief and practice that people deserve a raise once they have worked in a position for a specific period of time. Obviously, people improve their earnings much more rapidly through promotions, but longevity slowly but surely also raises salary levels. This old paradigm is one that needs to be challenged for the sake of our long-term, not our short-term, viability. Over and over, I visit firms with several employees who are paid 20 percent to 100 percent more than their market value, or more important, much more than their efforts warrant. How does this happen? Simply and systematically; through occasional merit increases and regular inflation compensation adjustments, employees' salaries can easily get out of sync with their contribution.

The Solution

It is my belief that everyone, from the receptionist through the chief executive officer and managing partner (CEO/MP), should be paid based on performance. Rather than defaulting to paying employees for showing up and putting in their time on the job, we should try to identify exactly what we want—and pay for an end result. This way, when people accomplish more, they get paid more. If employees can't live up to the total demands of their work, the workload should be reshuffled and their pay should decrease according to the relative reduction in output. Moreover, employees who can't perform to a minimum work standard can't keep their jobs.

Objections

Two objections are commonly voiced when I verbalize my approach.

Objection 1.

The objection first is, "It takes an act of Congress to fire someone; you trivialize a significant process." It is true that the process of firing people has become a human resources nightmare for most companies. Why? Rightfully so, it is hard to fire someone if he or she doesn't have objective expectations to meet. If employees are judged on meeting a set of output targets (what they produce), and they fail to meet those targets, then management has just cause to discharge them (assuming those employees have been adequately trained or have presented themselves as having appropriate skill sets). Firing someone should be difficult if management:

- Fails to clearly communicate the output targets to employees,
- Allows the targets to change with the wind, or
- Conveniently conjures targets at a moment's notice (usually around evaluation time).

Employees shouldn't be fired just because their managers won't take the time to manage by clarifying exactly what is expected from their subordinates.

Objection 2.

The second common objection I receive is, "The approach not only sounds too hard to implement, but doesn't appear to be worth the trouble." I understand this position, and quite frankly, at first glance, I would agree. However, think of the system we have in place today. We award merit and inflation increases to employees who can be counted on to show up for work, are good at performing their jobs, have positive attitudes, and are loyal to the firm. This system works well if you assume that there is an unlimited number of promotion opportunities available within the organization (because higher level positions have different monetary ranges). Given that there are fewer jobs at the top than at the bottom, and that our professionals are working longer, there is very limited upward mobility in most firms. So, for our average good workers who will be seldom promoted, we embrace a pay system that constantly provides minimal salary increases until we price them out of the market for the positions they hold. Then, during an occasional rush of fiscal prudence, we fire them for their loyalty in an attempt to better manage the company budget. The worst part of this story is … the only real mistake these employees ever made was being loyal to the firm and being subject to bad wage practices for too many years.

Now, I want to discuss the tendency to judge employees on "linger-put" versus output; linger-put being how long employees hang around or linger.

↯ Sample Scenario

Through skill development, Susan learns to work smarter and accomplish her current eight hours of job duties in five hours. As a reward, she receives a pat on the back, three more hours of work, and a tribute such as, "It must feel good to know that you are one of the 20 percent of us that does 80 percent of the work." Now, on the other hand, Tony (another employee) has been around the block often enough to recognize time management training as just another way his superiors can squeeze more work out of him. He knows the answer. It's simple. If he just looks busy and uses the organizational techniques taught during the training, he can convert his eight hours of effort into ten.

In various management sessions I conduct around the country, most owners assert that Tony will be fired for his insubordination. I challenge that assertion; for the most part, managers are not armed with the one critical ingredient needed to identify Tony's substandard behavior: They do not know how long it should take him to accomplish the work he has before him. Project planning and objective output that would give them this insight is rare. So, since the management is unable to identify Tony's passive-aggressive behavior, he will likely get treated in one of two ways—if not both. First, he will be paid overtime or get comp time for the extra work hours. Second, some of his work will be shifted, probably to Susan, since she has extra time. This kind of system makes you wonder why anyone bothers to deliver any effort at all. The example also shows why it is imperative that we begin emphasizing employee output rather than linger-put.

Along these same lines, it is also critical that we align our employees' motivations and our expectations to support the objectives of the firm. Consider this scenario, which assumes that personal billings are our only interest.

> ↯ **Sample Scenario**
>
> David is a manager and is paid $75,000 a year. He worked 2,400 hours last year and billed 1,600 hours; his billing rate was $125, and his realization was 80 percent, earning a total net billings to the firm's clients of $160,000. Now Diane, on the other hand, is a manager who was paid $70,000, worked 2,080 hours, billed 1,100 hours at a billing rate of $150, and had a realization of 94 percent, earning her total net billings to the clients of $155,100.

Who is the better employee? Most owners would choose David because he billed more hours, billed more dollars, and worked late all the time. However, Diane's profit ratio was 2.2 times what she earns (net billings against salary) and Dave's was 2.1. Dave's work grossed a margin for the firm of $85,000, while Diane's grossed $85,100, with an annual investment of $5,000 less.

The point of this example is not to debate a few dollars, but to ask, "How do you align your employees' wage goals with the firm's profit motives?" A simple way might be to set a *minimum net billings to salary* ratio and pay employees a percentage of everything they earn over that ratio. This way, the focus isn't on billable hours (which really do not mean anything), hours worked (which we shouldn't really care about), or billing rates (which should be a function of expected utilization, not total hours). By making it clear to your people what the fair objective measures are, they are armed to do what is best for themselves and the firm. Note that, of course, many factors get in the way of this—ranging from getting someone who will take on the low margin work, to the motivation to overbill a client, or to billing uncollectible fees.

Element 2. Offer a challenging job.

Offering a challenging job is much harder than it sounds. A challenging job is one that occasionally, not regularly, requires the individual to get outside his or her usual comfort zone in order to perform the work. An example might be to compare a manager who is expected to stay in the office and perform queued up work all day to a manager who is expected to apportion time between queued up work, mentoring and training staff, and managing a select group of client relationships. The latter should be a more challenging job because it incorporates broader expectations, whereas the former is more similar to a staff job (assembly line production). A challenging job incorporates several features, such as:

- A positive learning environment
- A philosophy that supports risk-taking so people are comfortable about trying new tasks without fear of reprisal
- Management's comprehension of the employee's skill level
- Projects that occasionally, though not always, really stretch the employee's abilities
- Most of the time, meaningful work to do

Element 3. Communicate clear expectations.

How do you inform employees of their exact job responsibilities? In most small companies, and in some large ones, managers only give each employee a vague insight into what is important. The beauty of this system is that when it is time for an evaluation, depending on the manager's subjective feelings at that moment, the employee can be rated anywhere from inadequate to superhuman.

When I ask management why a system this imprecise continues to be used, the common reply in confidence is, "This system gives us maximum flexibility. We don't want to be pinned down to a specific job expectation. What's important can change hourly around here! And we don't want our employees hiding behind some established job description. I don't want to hear anyone say, 'That's not my job.'"

This management response is exactly why many employees feel insecure about their performance. If an employee doesn't know exactly what is expected, then, regardless of the quality or quantity of the work done, he or she cannot feel satisfied. However, if a job is well defined with clearly explained expectations, an employee is empowered with two important tools:

- *Tool 1. Self-evaluation.* Employees are more apt to go home feeling good about what they have accomplished when they can compare what they have done with what was expected.
- *Tool 2. Defense.* At evaluation time, the employee does not become a casualty just because his or her management is having a bad day. Instead, the manager is forced to judge performance based on facts, not emotions.

How do most companies outline job expectations? Formally, this is most often done through job or position descriptions (i.e., outline expectations in billing performance, client contact, firm support, and mentoring and training) and compensation plans (pay is tied to expected performance). Position descriptions should be a two-way negotiation. The manager has specific job functions to perform, and the employee offers certain skills and talents. The position description is a short-term contract outlining what is expected. Not everything asked of an employee has to be listed in the job description, but the primary day-to-day, month-to-month consumers of time should be clearly identified. The compensation system then defines the priorities for each of the objectives identified. For example, if the role of *mentoring and training* is not backed up by economic gain or sanction, then it will fall off the employee's "to-do list."

Element 4. Give objective performance measurements.

As I have mentioned many times thus far, a critical step to being accountable is to utilize performance measurements, as much as possible, that are not subjective. The hard part is coming up with objective measures that will drive the desired performance.

Objective measures come in two basic forms, namely, lag and lead measures. An example of a lag measure might be *new client project dollars billed.* It is called a lag measure because it is the final result of staying in contact with your clients, identifying opportunity, selling the firm as the service provider, and keeping track of the hours worked on that project and the amount billed. This indicator lags behind the performance it measures. A lead measure is just the reverse. It indicates a direction even though it is too early to establish results. An example of a lead measure would be "the number of clients you visited last quarter." This lead measure creates a metric that is a logical prelude to generating the desired lag measure (i.e., new client project dollars billed). In this case, if a firm is looking to increase work from current clients, it is fair to assume that the greater the number of times their CPAs are in front of their clients, the more new work will be developed. When you are initiating change, you develop lead indicators to measure compliance with the necessary steps in the process. When the desired behavior becomes routine, you can switch to just monitoring lag metrics to measure the effectiveness of the efforts being made.

The Problem

When you talk about pay-for-performance, most employees get excited. To them, there will finally be a system in place that shows everyone how well they carry their weight. As well, it will highlight the shirkers. Rarely does anyone think they are part of the marginal performers' group. However, in practice, the closer to actual implementation, the more nervous everyone gets because, in reality, no one is sure. On one hand, we all can identify those whom we perceive do less than we do, which makes us feel safe. On the other hand, there is a general lack of trust between management and employees that definitely comes into play when new systems are under consideration.

It is key to understand that any time performance measurement systems depart from objectivity, employees immediately begin to rely on relationships for survival. This creates a bad situation because employees working in relationship-centered, rather than performance-centered organizations:

- Are constantly insecure about their jobs.
- Overcommunicate; gossip is rampant and the grapevine is overactive.
- Suffer morale problems attributable to excessive employee positioning and posturing; people step on each other in their efforts to stay in the good graces of a manager or owner.
- Are often inefficient because they spend too much energy playing politics rather than working.

The Solution

There are several solutions for a firm to consider. They are:

1. Provide regular feedback.
2. Base performance on outputs.
3. Understand how to hold employees accountable.

Each of these solutions is discussed in the following sections.

Solution 1. Provide regular feedback. To avoid these negative effects, owners need to provide employees with information such as job requirements, expectations, and performance feedback—regular feedback being essential. For example, reconsider the preceding sample scenario with David and Diane. If we expect each of them to minimally perform at a 2.25

ratio (of billings to salary), then both David and Diane should receive weekly reports not only showing how they are performing, but how their peers are performing as well. This kind of awareness will not raise the performance of your superstars (they live and breathe the business every day anyway), but it will sure raise the bar for those showing up at the bottom of the list. Although many people don't mind the obscurity of disappearing in the middle of the pack, no one likes the spotlight of being at the bottom. This kind of recognition lays the foundation for a performance-oriented organization.

Solution 2. Focus on outputs. Whenever possible, job performance should be based on outputs rather than inputs. For example, having 8 chargeable hours is an input, but billing and collecting $1,200 for that day's work is an output.

Solution 3. Maintain employee accountability. Accountability is also facilitated by management's understanding of the difference between setting goals and holding employees accountable. All too often, management misinterprets the old Army slogan, "Be all that you can be." Instead, it is necessary to distinguish between motivating employees to stretch their capabilities to reach personal goals versus maintaining accountability for the work that needs to be performed. Consider these questions before continuing:

- *Question 1.* "How high should you set your employees' performance goals?" The possible answers are "(1) easily within their grasp or (2) just out of reach."
- *Question 2.* "Where do you establish minimum acceptable performance standards?" The possible answers are "(1) at a level of accomplishment just above showing up for work everyday and doing a reasonable job or (2) "unique to each individual's capabilities?"

Consider the following story.

⇄ Sample Scenario (Part 1 of 3)

Bob is the senior tax accountant for the firm and is considered one of the best employees in the department. Last year, he worked an average of 50 hours a week and did high-quality work. Now, a new year is starting. The organization embraces a pay-for-performance philosophy. Therefore, it's time to determine what to expect from Bob over the next twelve months. Because Bob is such a good employee, and because the plan is to promote him to manager soon, the management wants him to stretch his abilities. The firm believes that goals should be set at the furthest reach of an individual's grasp to achieve the highest level of performance. So, Bob is given some lofty goals, tied in with some nice bonus incentives.

Bob steps up to the challenge, and it quickly becomes apparent that he is taking the objectives in stride. He puts in more than 60 hours a week during tax season, and still manages to put in more than 50 the rest of the year. His work has never been better. However, at year-end, he falls a little short of the targeted objectives.

If you were the firm's management, what would you do? In group discussions, most owners answer that they would reward Bob with only the performance bonuses he actually achieved. Why? The answer is, "Because he did not meet the identified objectives." But maybe it would be wiser to avoid digging a hole that one cannot get out of by thinking through this situation differently. First, remember that the goals set for Bob were lofty in the first place. Second, the intent was to give Bob a work target that would stretch his capabilities. Third, Bob is one of the firm's best employees. In a nutshell, an employee who has put in a record year, is being told, "You are getting only the bonuses that you have actually achieved." Any firm that actually follows this modus operandi will successfully run off every good employee it has.

Nevertheless, in this situation, most companies do one of two things; both bad. The most common response is to restructure the goals (or move the bar) so that Bob's actual level of accomplishment allows him to attain the new objectives. Thus, he "earns" the performance incentives. The second option is that Bob is denied the pay tied to performance, but is compensated with a bogus reward that is created to make up for the shortfall. Given this, let's continue with our story.

> ### ⮀ Sample Scenario (Part 2 of 3)
>
> It's objective-setting time again and because the firm was so generous last year, this time the management really wants Bob to earn his keep. Bob is told as much, and exceptionally high goals are set for him for the upcoming year. Bob is considered potential owner material and the management wants him to learn the ins-and-outs of how the firm works. Bob makes a valiant effort, too. His average workweek exceeds 60 hours. His billings are higher than they ever have been, and his clients rave about him. But still, at year-end, Bob falls short of several outlined targets.

If you were the firm's management, again, what would you do? The answer is that you are likely to make good on all of Bob's compensation, even though technically he has not earned it for the second year in a row. Why make these exceptions? The answer is easy … because Bob is too valuable to lose. He is the best worker in the tax department. So, the saga continues.

> ### ⮀ Sample Scenario (Part 3 of 3)
>
> In year three, Bob is burned out. He realizes that he must spend more time with his family if he wants to avoid a divorce. Bob still performs quality work, but he only puts in about 45 hours a week. His work is still excellent, his clients still love him, but his output was significantly smaller. By year-end, Bob is not even close to any of his annual targets.

Once again, what would you do if you were an owner? In almost every instance of this scenario, management around the country responds that Bob should receive "no performance bonuses." The reasoning behind the response varies, but included the following:
- Bob missed his targets by too great a delta.
- The drop in Bob's performance evoked an unwillingness to break the rules for the third year in a row.

- Bob did not try hard enough or had developed a bad attitude towards work, compared to his enthusiasm in previous years.
- Bob performed significantly less work than had been normal for him, even though his work was still high in quality

Management's rationale, in short, is that the system in place clearly calls for Bob to be denied performance pay. And because of his marginal output during the year in question, there was no reason to create some special compensation reward.

Now, let us step back and analyze exactly what Bob has been taught about accountability. The answer is, *"Nothing!!"* This system, which exists throughout the country, makes it clear that what Bob does is not as important as his boss's attitude towards him. He has been taught that accountability is much less about meeting expectations than about maintaining a relationship with someone who can adjust the bar. Any time you use the "Bosses' Attitude" as the underpinning of "Employee Accountability," you come up with "The Good Ole Boy System," which means that, "it's not what you do that's important, but who you know." Accountability has to be firmly entrenched in ideas and ideals such as the following:

- Each employee knows exactly what he or she is accountable to perform.
- Whenever practical, the results of each employee's work should be objectively measured, monitored, and reported.
- Employees should be able to easily assess whether they are meeting or exceeding expectations.
- Performance measure bars should remain constant and not shift with the wind.
- It is up to the employee, not the manager, to ensure that the proper levels of output are achieved.
- Although personal growth goals can be customized to each individual's capabilities, performance measures should be based on the assumptions that would be made if a "generic" or average employee was filling the specific position.
- Achieving less than the organization's minimum level of performance means the employee does not get to keep his or her job; for that reason, these bars should be set exceptionally low.
- Incentive systems need to be in place to reward everyone achieving output in excess of the minimum expectations bar.

In Bob's situation, only the first three of the key factors listed above were present. In addition, *performance measures were established to push the capabilities of a particular individual,* rather than reward achievement that exceeds the norm (which Bob did all the time). Bob's personal growth goals could have easily been the same as those identified above. However, the system was doomed to failure in the moment that lofty personal goals were tied to incentives. In other words, if incentive goals are based on an individual's capabilities, the result is multiple bars for different people doing the same job. This is not fair because you are, in a sense, handicapping your best employees so that your average ones can keep pace.

Element 5. Support learning on the job.

It is interesting to me how quickly people lose sight of what allowed them to gain the skills they now possess, namely, through the process of "failing on the job." Typically, each of us was given projects just a little bigger than our capability, and we failed our way through them, learning important job and life lessons, including what never to do again. Now that we know how to manage these complex projects, many of us are reluctant to provide to others the same safety net that benefited us. Often, we take the conservative posture that "the risk is too great to let our staff learn on our clients." However, we would not be where we are today if someone had not taken that risk with us.

I want to share with you the responses I get from almost every firm I have ever worked with:

- The owners say, "I can't pass that work to the managers because they are not ready or capable. I would delegate if they were ready."
- The managers say, "I would pass on more work to staff but they are not able or willing. I would do so if they were."
- So, the conclusion at every level in the firm is, "I am capable, and everyone below me is not. When they are ready, I will respond appropriately."

> **O━ Key Point**
>
> Your best investment for building value in your firm is to spend the time and money required to develop your current employees and future leaders.

This requires significant change in philosophy. For those with the responsibility to manage people, the thinking needs to change to, "My job is not to do the work myself, but to grow my people so that they are ready and prepared. They need an opportunity to learn with a safety net underneath them. If they are not ready, it is because I have failed in my job as their leader."

Please do not assume that I am advocating an environment in which marginal workers have a safe haven. Actually, quite the opposite is true. If someone fails often, making the same mistakes over and over after they have been trained not to do so, then they are not "failing on the job," they are either not trying or just incompetent. Regardless of the reason, the answer is the same—"Let them go." But more often than you expect, when you give someone enough rope and support, they will make mistakes along the way, but their performance will also surprise you in a positive way.

Delegating Versus Dumping

Most people confuse delegation with "dumping," a situation described in the Situational Leadership™ materials and course training by Dr. Paul Hersey's Center for Leadership Studies. In his book, The Situational Leader,[3] Dr. Hersey explains that you manage people by providing the level and amount of direction and motivation according to their readiness and ability to do the work. Delegation becomes an alternative when the employee is ready, capable, and self-motivated, and the manager has a high degree of confidence in that employee for a specific task or project, which will translate to a low level of both direction and support.

Too often, CPAs believe their subordinates are incapable of doing the work currently queued up as long as they think they have bandwidth to do it themselves. These CPAs realize that they have misjudged the capabilities of their "direct reports" only when they:

---

[3] The *Situational Leader* by Dr. Paul Hersey, published by the Center for Leadership Studies, Escondido, CA, 1997.

- Are literally out of time and have reached the project deadlines.
- Still have too much work on their plates to complete without assistance.
- The client is beginning to squeak.

At this point, work that just a few hours ago was deemed undoable is readily dumped on the desk of an employee with the note, "Get this back to me by tomorrow morning."

> **O⟍ Key Point**
>
> Dumping the work is not ever an acceptable management alternative.

The idea that you would not pass on the work one day because you, the supervisor, would have to hold their hands all the way through the process, and then the very next day, put that same subordinate in a "sink-or-swim" position is about as far from management as can be imagined.

Obligations When Delegating

As the delegator, you *cannot* give up your obligation of *oversight*. And just as important, the delegatee *cannot* be released from his or her obligation to *keep the delegator informed*.

Either your employees are ready and you are holding them back, which shows your failure to manage, or they still are not ready for the work you are giving them, which also shows your failure to manage. Either way, the finger points to the same person.

Element 6. Provide adequate training.

Today, because of the demographics I described earlier, we have to work hard to find qualified workers. This means that we cannot be cavalier about the people we have, especially if they want to do a good job. We have to provide an environment that allows them to be successful.

Our role as leaders and managers is to help our people evolve professionally as fast as they are willing, ready, and capable. We have to keep in mind that we are working in a different staffing supply/demand curve today than yesterday … and we have to adjust our approach to leverage today's reality. It doesn't matter what we did or what we had to do. What matters is whether you can correctly assess the pool of people available to you, nurture that group, and find a way to create synergy between their talent and the well-being of your firm.

I am reminded of a story that happened at a week-long leadership workshop I was co-facilitating. During a discussion about training and mentoring, in a moment of frustration, one of the participants commented:

> We used to do a lot more training than we do today. As a matter of fact, we hardly do much training outside of on-the-job stuff any more. We really got frustrated, investing our money on people and still seeing some of them leave. We felt like we were throwing our money away training the community; some employees even wound up with our competitors." My cofacilitator responded, "What's better, spending the money training your people to make them more effective and having a few of them leave, or not training any of them and having them all stay?

Obviously, it costs a great deal of money to develop your employees. So you have to be conscientious about determining what the training investment will be and what can be expected from it. But when you consider that employees are the single largest asset and expense in service businesses, poorly leveraging this investment is totally unacceptable.

Element 7. Reward overachievement.

Receiving reward for overachievement acknowledges the successful culmination of the other steps. If employees know exactly what is expected of them, have been learning on the job, have taken their training seriously, and are producing at a high level, rewarding them is a vital affirmation step. Or another way to put it is … if you ever want to see their superhuman effort repeated, you had better recognize their performance.

> **O─ Key Point**
>
> Receiving reward for overachievement is the capstone of the accountability process.

As we discussed earlier, there are many ways to motivate and reward your people. Compensation is rarely the top motivator, but it is often one of the employees' top "score-keeping" mechanisms, which is why pay-for-performance is such a fundamental component of SOP foundation. Pay-for-performance creates a way for each employee to assess his or her own accomplishments, as well as provide a way to compare themselves to their peers. It is a reward mechanism and an overachievement communication device (as well as an underachievement communication device). However, this is just one—albeit a good one—of the many solutions you can leverage. Although it is clearly up to you to select whatever techniques are most desirable to motivate and reward your people for their superstar production, the key is to make sure you choose something and implement it as soon as possible!

A Final Word on Accountability

Accountability is not passive. Accountability requires a change in the philosophy of most organizational cultures. It demands that employees, not management, be and feel more empowered regarding their performance. It is up to the employees to keep their jobs, influence how much they earn, determine how much work product they produce, and so on. It is up to management to become the resource to help those who want to help themselves. If an employee wants to perform just at the minimum bar, that's fine. Don't kid yourself—every firm I have worked with could use more "minimum bar" producers. Minimum bar producers are *not* marginal employees. They are employees who are producing good work at a pay commensurate with their level of production. Generally speaking, minimum performers should earn a base wage (less than the average for that position that you pay now). From this level of performance and higher, the more people accomplish, the more they earn. But the key is, incentives are earned each year the employees produce, rather than being earned once, such that their salaries are adjusted for all time.

Roles And Responsibilities Of Managers

This section will cover many topics related to the roles and responsibilities of managers. It will define types of managers, utilizing part-time managers versus full-time managers, and the structure of reporting models.

Types of Managers

The first thing I would like to challenge is that the title of *manager* is too broad. It is better to break this down into two common categories in CPA firms; the *technical manager* and the *supervising manager*. A similar distinction can apply to owners as well; the technical owner and the client relationship owner.

Technical Managers

Let's start by introducing the technical positions. Typically, in firms, the technical managers or owners are known to be technically competent, produce quality work, and crank out product all day. They are the kind of people you can hand a project to and never have to worry about it again because you know it was done correctly. These people typically have the title of *manager* purely because their experience and billing rates warrant such a status level, not because they actually manage anyone.

In many environments, you will find some of the people that fill this role are good in client communications, but terrible at interacting with the internal staff. These people tend to hold themselves to a high standard for the technical quality of their work. They are the minority to which owners will actually delegate work. Technical managers tend to believe in the superstar model, which is compatible with their attitude toward those around them, and their expectation that other employees should take the initiative, as they have, and figure everything out on their own. They believe that stars will emerge the same way cream rises to the top, without assistance. The stars can then be leveraged, and everyone else can be ignored.

Several points need to be made about the technical manager position:
- These people are very valuable, either in full- or part-time roles.
- These people do not manage—they crank out work. Some also have mid-level client relationship responsibility.
- Technical managers should be rewarded for their superior output of work.
- Technical managers who are prone to condescending behavior must be stopped. The compensation system must include penalties that can be imposed on those whose poor treatment of others creates chaos.

The ideal is to create an environment in which everyone's skills can be best utilized. Technical managers who are inclined to predominantly crank out work can be put in positions that allow them to do so. Nevertheless, they cannot be allowed to start fires throughout the firm as a result of their lack of emotional control and respect for the work of others.

Supervising Managers

Now let's talk about supervising managers. It should be no surprise that a supervising manager actually supervises staff. Unlike with technical managers, these people should default to getting work done through others rather than themselves. Supervising managers should be held accountable for their own personal production, but with lower targets than those of their technical manager counterparts. Their real focus, however, is the production of the staff below them. This means that the job of supervising managers includes scheduling the work, training and mentoring their people, as well as queuing up work for the technical managers when necessary. To summarize, supervising managers are responsible for:

- Managing people.
- Scheduling the work and making sure everyone that reports to them is busy.
- Identifying areas in which people need extra attention and providing the necessary training or mentoring so that the staff can continue to develop.
- Recognizing that, although they can do the work faster themselves, that is not their job. It is their job to find a way to plan the work, break it down as necessary, review the work, and provide feedback and training to their subordinates about the work they have done.
- Keeping their subordinates busy first, and then taking on the overflow work.

A supervising manager should be rewarded more for the achievement of those who report to them than for their own personal production, assuming the supervising managers meet certain minimums.

A Final Word About Technical Managers and Supervising Managers

Every firm needs both technical and supervising managers. But it is important to create a clear distinction between the roles of each. Note that good supervising managers are more important to a CPA firm's future success because they are developing the managers and owners of tomorrow. Technical managers are more important to maintaining today's project quality and timeliness.

You may be surprised to find some people you have tagged as technical managers want to be supervising managers because of the added status of managing staff. If this happens … great! But you need to make it clear what you expect and monitor them closely to ensure they are providing the necessary training and mentoring support structures to those who report to them.

Part-Time Versus Full-Time Managers

Because of the staffing shortage that the profession has faced in recent years, firms everywhere began to leverage their production capacity by utilizing a highly talented, part-time labor pool. Although I believe that every firm should be imaginative in creating an environment that will attract part-timers, they should not fill the role of supervising managers.

The Problem

Unfortunately, many firms have told me that their best supervising manager candidates ("best" being the person with the attitude and aptitude to manage people) are part-timers. However, here is what always happens.

Sample Scenario

A part-time manager works three days a week (let's say, for this discussion, Monday through Wednesday). Projects come in, are scheduled, and are delivered to staff, so as to work around the part-timer's schedule. Clients call in on Thursday, Friday, or Saturday (when the part-time manager is unavailable) and change their deadlines, or the staff gets stuck on a certain phase of a project, or a project encounters some last-minute problems as it becomes due. Then, the work falls to an owner or another manager to handle who (1) has to be brought up to speed, and (2) has to drop everything they have planned to resolve the crisis, and get the work done and out the door on time.

Some people would argue that this should not be a big problem because a part-timer working Monday through Wednesday is at the firm more than they are gone (since they are on three days a week and off two days). However, the real hurdles are problems of timing and capacity. The timing problem is easy to see. Fires that break out on Thursday and Friday have to be handled by someone else, which creates duplication and frustration for everyone. Second, by definition, part-timers have a potential capacity problem. For example, if something serious comes up late on Friday afternoon, a full-time worker would be expected to come in and handle it on Saturday. But, if something occurred late Tuesday evening, the part-timer would only have Wednesday available to work that week. His or her time may have already been scheduled, so that even if the immediate situation is resolved, pushing off the work planned for Wednesday until Monday might not be acceptable to another client. The point is that there are too many times when either timing or capacity availability from your part-time workers are incompatible with the needs of the clients.

The Solution

For this reason, experienced part-time workers should almost always be put in technical manager roles. Because the scheduling of the work queue for technical managers is overseen by either a supervising manager or owner, when problems occur as a result of timing or capacity, someone else can easily pick up the ball and run with it. Also, part-timers are best leveraged in either small or large projects, both of which usually have more flexibility in both timing and capacity. They should also be used, because of their experience, as overflow workers. An example of overflow work might be when a supervising manager has some specific work that needs to be done today, like reviewing a complex tax return before it goes out, when the owners are all out of the office.

Part-time workers, as much as possible, should be left out of all administrative functions. Their jobs should be to crank out work, not help provide guidance through committee involvement. Firms need to make the best use of the limited hours these talented part-time accountants have to offer and sitting in on management meetings isn't an optimal use of time. Obviously, my discussion would not apply to someone that is part time for a short period, and will join or rejoin full-time status soon.

Exceptions

Are there exceptions? Yes, there are always exceptions, but they should be rare. For example, two part-timers could share the same supervisory manager's job (one working Monday through Wednesday and the other working Thursday through Friday with overflow responsibilities on Saturday). Another example might be someone who can work four days a week with some capacity to handle some overflow work either after normal hours during those four days or occasionally picking up a half day on the fifth day.

Staff Reporting Models

Depending on the size of a firm, staff will be predominantly assigned according to either a traditional hierarchy (reporting to a manager, who reports to an owner) or to a pool. Either can work; both have strengths and weaknesses. Both, in my opinion, though they function differently, need to be structured under direct reporting relationships. The following sections show how these two can be seen conceptually. They will cover types of staff reporting models, reporting responsibility, and project responsibility, and they will conclude with summarizing points.

Types of Staff Reporting Models

As mentioned, there are two types of reporting models for staff—the direct report model and the staff pool model. Both are discussed below. Also discussed is a hybrid model that is common in firms.

Direct Report Model

Under the traditional direct reporting model, it is up to the manager to keep his or her direct reports busy. In effect, this implies that there is enough work that needs to be done for the manager to keep the assigned staff fully utilized. For example, consider a firm's audit department with three staff members who report to a manager, who reports to an owner. If you choose this organizational approach, existing projects should provide the audit department with more than enough work to keep all five people busy. On the rare occasions that there is down time, the manager must work with other departments to find work to fully utilize his or her staff.

Staff Pool Model

Conversely, under the pool model, shown in figure 3-2, work can come from anyone because no one consistently has enough work to fully utilize all the time of a specific number of staff. Therefore, you have multiple work instigators (which might include every owner and manager), who then make requests of the scheduling supervisory manager, who then allocates that work to members of the pool. The pool model is often chosen to solve the political problem of superstar allocation. If a firm is small, it might have a couple of superstars (who might be staff or managers) that each owner could keep busy all the time. But in order to avoid playing favorites (giving one owner access to the firm's top talent all the time while forcing the other owners to utilize weaker team members), firms will construct a pool to share their top performers.

Figure 3-2

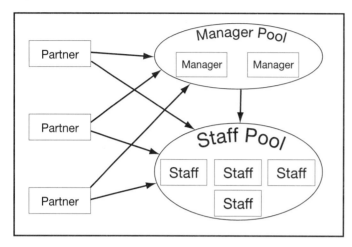

Pools don't have to be made up of staff only. Some firms have staff pools and management pools. Both can work assuming the right structure and SOPs.

Hybrid Staff Report Model

Unfortunately, too many firms adhere to neither the direct report or the staff pool model. Instead, these firms have produced hybrids that are foundationally dysfunctional and are always breaking down. Under this system, no one actually reports to anyone and each person can report to everyone above them, depending on the project. The way it works is simple, and it applies to all managers and owners. Suppose a manager or owner has a project to do. Depending on the complexity of that project, he or she will enlist the help of a manager or staff member or both.

One result is that no one specifically or exclusively manages anyone else. Thus, staff or manager evaluations, training, mentoring, coaching, and career development are considered to be more of a group project, even though a particular manager might be assigned to the task, especially in order to meet human resources' requirements concerning evaluations.

This kind of organizational chart is often found in firms that use the superstar model because the assumption is that the cream (the top performers at each level) will rise to the top on their own and will demand the care and feeding they need. The rest are just workers and will be leveraged as well as possible.

Reporting Responsibility

From an operator perspective, whenever possible, everyone should report directly to someone in order to ensure, most simply, that someone takes responsibility for overseeing the professional development of every individual. Accountability and employee performance is most consistently and effectively implemented, monitored, and administered under this structure and each employee knows exactly who is responsible for his or her training, assignments, and evaluations, and who will defend him or her if that becomes necessary. Any time you have a situation in which a number of people are charged with these responsibilities, the usual result is that none is done well (because everyone hopes someone else is taking responsibility). In the pool model, without direct reporting, while the best talent is constantly overworked, the average employees are marginally utilized. Moreover, the average talent in the pool will likely suffer from malnourishment in both career training and career development. I am not saying that the average worker won't have access to training, but rather that his or her training will be more generic rather than tied to the individual's personal goals and career path. For training to have maximum impact, it needs to be part of a well-thought-out career development program, not just random continuing professional education (CPE) courses.

Nevertheless, in firm after firm, management balks at the idea that everyone needs to report to specific people. Managers argue that the firm's staff accountants need to be accessible to everyone. They are apprehensive that the concept of direct reports would create nothing but bureaucracy and empire-building (as they quickly claim it has done in the past), and enable the hoarding of talent so that certain owners and managers always have the resources they need at their beck and call. My response is, "All of these things can and will occur if you assume that the firm will not properly manage the situation. But without proper management, nothing has much chance to work."

Project Responsibility

Please don't confuse reporting responsibility with matrix project responsibility. Reporting responsibility is what we have been talking about, or the question, "To whom do you report?" Matrix project responsibility reflects the reality that, given the number of different projects throughout the year, a staff member might report to or work as a team member with almost every owner or manager in the firm.

The Problem

Employees in CPA firms are constantly screaming because priorities are continually being reshuffled by a number of people, which leaves employees not knowing how to order the priority of the projects for which they are responsible.

> ### ↹ Sample Scenario
>
> Let's assume Beth is a supervising manager who schedules work for all of the staff members each week and the work allocated to each person is expected to consume their available time. Now, let's add Sandra, an owner, to the mix. She walks in on Tuesday and makes this request to one of the staff members: "I need some help on this right now. Could you put everything down and prepare this schedule before 2:00 p.m. today?" Then, at noon on the same day, Bert, the CEO/MP and controlling owner of the firm, comes over to that same staff member and says, "We need to take a long lunch and talk about a project that I think we are going to land and which is a perfect fit for your background."

Obviously, any intelligent staff member working in a pool that did not have direct reporting responsibility would abandon's Beth's weekly plan to take care of Sandra. And most staff members wouldn't dream of telling the CEO/MP that they are too busy to hear about a potential career-boosting assignment, especially when the 2:00 p.m. deadline is from an owner with less clout than Bert. Still, it really does not matter how the staff person would have made this call. The point is that it should not be left up to a staff member, in the first place, to decide who to disappoint in this web of requests. In other words, it is not fair, or justifiable, to put your subordinates in the position of having to resolve conflicts between owners and/or managers about job priority.

What I regularly hear from managers and owners alike is, "Whenever one of the senior owners makes a request, my projects automatically get set aside, even if they are higher priority work to the firm." The problem is that even if the CEO/MP is making these work requests, the person who decides how to reshuffle the work should be someone who has knowledge of the entire project queue and deadlines. Under the system described by the story above, this firm will typically move from handling one client crisis to the next because the work plan is continually being usurped by projects of convenience. Potential results include even more client chaos if the firm misses the deadlines of higher priority projects that are queued up and in process.

The Solution

If you want to utilize a pool and take care of your clients with the least number of internal crises, you have to develop an SOP that outlines how work is scheduled, what constitutes something that can override the schedule, and what process is to be followed when those overrides are necessary. I am aware that overrides to the schedule will be common. But those overrides will be far less costly to the firm if they are managed within a process that identifies what fires *are about to be started* by the priority reshuffling being proposed.

I believe that any time a particular workload and skills justify full-time support, direct reports make the most sense from the standpoint of accountability. If you have a situation in which the demand for talent is inconsistent, a pool makes more sense. Nevertheless, even with a pool, once again in my opinion, someone needs to have the direct responsibility for managing that pool. So, in light of the dysfunctional hybrid shown in the graphic, I propose a different hybrid, granting, obviously, that the specifics of a given situation always dictate what structure has the best chance of success (see figure 3-3). In this case, the CEO/MP is the direct supervisor of both the owners and the supervisory manager. The supervisory manager is the direct supervisor of the staff pool. The supervisory manager also has access to the technical manager for assistance with more complex projects. The technical manager reports directly to one of the owners. The point is that, at times, it would be appropriate to have both direct reports and a pool, depending on the workload of the owners, departments, or managers. In reality, all three owners have access to both managers and the four staff members, even though, in the graphic, the CEO/MP is responsible for the owners and the supervisory manager's training and career development, and the resolution of priority conflicts. As for the technical manager, the owner that supervises him or her would be responsible for those managerial roles.

Figure 3-3

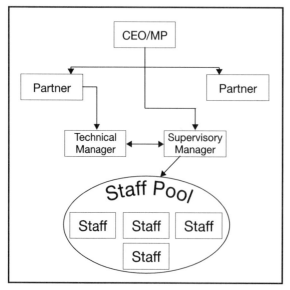

This may seem foolishly theoretical rather than practical, but any effort to clarify how reporting, authority, and responsibility works within your firm will return rewards very quickly. You will find that once supervisors at every level know who they are responsible for, and that their success in managing those people has a significant impact on their compensation, the result will be a heightened interest in performing the tasks of the career development (e.g., providing coaching, training, and feedback on work performed) of their direct reports. Just as important, you will find that your weak people are flushed out much faster. The reason is simple: A weak team member who has little impact on another's personal performance or success is merely considered a nuisance to be avoided. If that same weak team member directly and regularly affects another's performance and success, he or she is immediately shown either (1) how to evolve or (2) how to find the exit. This level of focus on your people, regardless of the outcomes (employees who either improve or are fired) benefits the firm.

A Final Word About Staff Reporting Models

Consider the following summarizing points when conceptualizing how your staff can be held accountable, fully utilized, and developed:

- In a pool, a supervising manager should be in charge of the schedule and every project has to be cleared through the schedule. The primary job of the pool manager is to manage the work queue, schedule the projects, assign the work, train and develop the staff members, and resolve the client work conflicts that normally arise. The workload comes from the other owners and managers because work initiation is not a primary responsibility of a pool supervisor. When the workload is low, the manager will be motivated to solicit work from other areas within the firm since his or her performance is heavily weighted towards the pool's overall performance against budget.
- With direct reports, the manager has to be held accountable for the full utilization of staff. Direct reports are a reward for the manager who can initiate and control enough work to keep his or her people busy rather than to schedule everything through the pool. Since the manager is responsible for the full utilization of assigned staff, when the workload is light, that manager is responsible for soliciting work from other areas in the firm. Underutilization of staff reflects negatively on the success of that manager and he or she will lose direct reports that are not fully utilized.
- If an owner or manager requests work from a staff member in a pool, that staff member immediately reports the details to his or her supervisory manager so that the work can be properly managed. If the work can be done as requested, the supervisory manager should adjust the schedule to reflect the additional work. If there is a conflict, it is up to the supervisory manager to approach the owner or manager involved in order to come up with an equitable solution.
- If a supervisory manager misuses his or her scheduling power and becomes a gatekeeper who is rude and abusive, or plays favorites, or is not focused on the best interest of the firm, he or she should be removed and transitioned to the role of technical manager.

- An organization can have either direct reports or a pool, or both. Regardless, an employee who has multiple supervisors is in an untenable position. Note, however, that an employee may nevertheless report to a number of people in the course of working on various projects throughout the year.
- Direct reporting can create silos, which precipitates owners and managers hoarding personnel, fighting over who gets access to the best talent, protecting personnel because they are valuable to an owner even though they are burdens to the firm. These situations are management issues that have to be addressed quickly by the CEO/MP. The compensation system is one of the CEO/MP's best tools to promote compliance.
- You can have management pools manage staff pools, but if you do this, you need clarity about the roles and responsibilities between managers (like scheduling, training, and the balance of individual work performed with the time spent managing others) and a compensation system that discourages the predictable abuses.
- Too often, firms have a couple of managers managing a total of three or four people. One supervising manager can easily handle four to six people. Still, do not just allocate your staff equally to those people who have manager titles. Decide what makes sense and who can best fill the role of developing your people. Minimize the supervising managers to a sensible number, and transition the rest of your managers to be technical managers.

If you use direct reports, too many people may wind up reporting to one department or owner. At this point, the CEO/MP should propose to the board that the workload be rearranged so as to be more evenly distributed. The board in turn should do everything possible to support this request. Large imbalances in workload construct silos, an "us-against-them" mentality, and often trigger the early formation of a spin-off competitor to the firm.

> **⊙ᴍ Key Point**
>
> Regardless of whether you use pools or traditional direct reporting, each staff member needs to be managed by someone specific (i.e., managed, not just administratively reporting to someone).

Although every organizational option you come up with will have strengths and weaknesses, you have to make sure that regardless of the variation you choose, your people are developed, held accountable, have access to a clear conflict resolution hierarchy, have an opportunity to grow, and are not put in the position of having to fight their boss's battles.

SOP Programs That Support Employee Performance

Below are eleven suggestions for ways to formally document the process that supports employee performance. Included in the discussion are:

1. Performance review system
2. Pay-for-performance compensation system
3. Business development program

4. Leadership development program
5. Motivation and rewards program
6. Partner-in-training program
7. Career professional program
8. Owner evaluation
9. Intern program
10. Employee orientation program
11. Mentoring and coaching program

Performance Review System

A performance review (PR) system allows the staff and managers to understand what is expected of them and how they perform against that expectation. This system should include information about reviews, including how, by whom, and through what process they are conducted; the rights of the employee; the rights of the reviewing manager; and the impact of reviews on continued employment.

Pay-for-Performance Compensation System

A pay-for-performance (PFP) compensation system aligns performance with the strategic initiatives of the organization. It changes when the strategic initiatives change, is predominantly based on objective criteria, pays for billing and management performance, and maintains client relationships. There is a thorough discussion of this system in the following section of the chapter.

Business Development Program

A business development (BD) program identifies firm-wide how additional business will be generated for the firm, including various approaches for growth by attracting new business and referrals of new clients; increasing "the share of the wallet" of existing clients; defining the marketing duties expected at various levels of employees; and gathering the resources required to support these efforts.

Leadership Development Program

A leadership development (LD) program helps people understand how they behave, how to better monitor and control their own behavior, how to influence the behavior of others, how to communicate more effectively, how to manage client relationships, how to develop long-term relationships, and how to appreciate diversity. The program could also address the attitudes and values encountered between the various generations working in your organization.

Motivation and Rewards Program

A motivation and rewards (MR) program identifies unique ways to motivate and reward your employees other than through direct compensation. The program can ensure client contact and involvement in firmwide meetings. Motivations and rewards may also provide employees with health benefits, 401(k) plans, travel, firm outings, day-care, and flextime.

Partner-in-Training Program

Everyone should know and understand the minimum that is required to become a partner. The typical firm just lists a number of subjective criteria. As we have discussed in this chapter, although objective criteria should not replace all subjective measures, they should replace many of them. A partner-in-training (PIT) program should clearly identify the requirements to become a partner and specify the title and compensation changes—if any—that are part of participating in the program. Typical partner requirements include the following, at the minimum:

- A minimum size of client book
- A minimum amount of new business or clients
- The ability to maintain and grow whatever size client book is managed
- Leadership qualities and characteristics

In the PCPS Succession Survey, the participants were asked about "identified and formalized requirements for new owners," and were given an answer choice that requested them to select all that apply. The responses follow:

- We do not have formal written requirements, but rather informal ones
  that change based on the perspectives of the current owners.   70%
- We have identified crucial competencies that must be met in order to be
  considered for ownership.   33%
- We have identified minimum and documented subjective qualities and
  characteristics that must be met in order to be considered for ownership.   24%
- We have created a non-equity partner track to make sure new partners
  fit culturally with the firm before becoming equity owners.   22%
- We have identified and documented a minimum client book size that
  potential owners must meet in order to be considered for ownership.   11%
- We have identified a net revenue per partner requirement, so partner
  slots open up as the firm reaches revenue thresholds.   11%
- We have identified and documented a minimum new business
  development amount for potential owners to meet in order to be
  considered for ownership.   6%

As you can see, most firms have not truly formalized this process but the requirements are pretty basic for most of those that have. As for book size, my personal experience is that firms, depending on their size, set the minimum bar between $250,000 and $1 million. In a reverse pyramid, it is difficult for a partner to grow his or her book beyond about $400,000 because, at that level, the partner is so busy doing the daily work, he or she does not have any time left for building client relationships. However, if the pyramid works optimally, then a partner could easily handle $1 million or more. Obviously, this is more about a dollar volume in combination with client volume, than either factor. For example, a partner could potentially manage $20 million if it entailed only one client relationship. Alternatively, $600,000 might be a stretch if that total was made up of $10,000 clients. One thing is certain: The bigger the dollars, the further away the partner is from doing any detail work and the more his or her job is purely the management of projects and clients' expectations.

And the bigger the dollars or the larger the volume of clients, the more you can bet that the partner has direct reports that do most of the day-to-day management of the client base.

Career Professional (or Career Manager) Program

A career professional (CP) program clearly identifies the expectations, titles, compensation alternatives, and other benefits that are available to those who do not choose or have not been chosen for the owner track. This also includes a road map of the training, technical capability, personal characteristics, and leadership skills that employees need to maintain their positions.

Everyone should know and understand that becoming an owner is not the only viable and respected career path. Many firms create nonequity owner positions for senior-level people who do not want or do not qualify to become owners. Other firms have director positions, senior manager positions, senior consultant positions, or use a number of titles to convey respect. Earnings that exceed the norm, along with the titles of these positions, acknowledge the level of expertise that they require. In addition, career professionals are often highly technical CPAs who are great at what they do, but do not want to be distracted by firm politics and/or management.

Owner Evaluation and/or 360 Feedback Program

An owner evaluation (OE) and/or 360 feedback program allows the owners to be evaluated by their peers and their employees. This feedback is compiled to allow each owner the insight of a comparison between how they believe they perform and the views of others.

Intern Program

Firms of all sizes are discovering the benefit of working with local colleges (from community colleges to major universities) to establish programs that give the firms access to some very talented part-time help. Interns used to be hired to shuffle paper and file. Today, however, many firms use interns to do basic tax return preparation or routine audit work. Moreover, most firms make offers to those interns—not because they have to as part of the program requirements, but because those interns prove themselves to be valuable. An intern program identifies the number of interns in the firm's system at any one time, how interns are recruited, program benefits, intern duties, and the feedback process.

Employee Orientation Program

An employee orientation (EO) program identifies how new hires are educated about the firm and its practices, procedures, systems, and culture. Such a program likely includes a road map and checklists for each employee's first days or weeks on the job that specify the content and timing of each employee's introduction to the firm.

Mentoring and Coaching Program

As for mentoring and coaching, the AICPA's Women's Initiatives Executive Committee has put together mentoring program guidelines that are a great beginning if you are interested in moving in this direction. Although the guidelines build a framework for the program, the materials in this chapter absolutely apply to the foundation upon which this program should be built.

Compensation Systems

It is possible to tie all of the concepts presented so far together into a compensation program. So, let me share with you my approach, though it certainly is not the only one that can work. I believe that a person's pay should be a function of:

1. *Level of job.* This refers to the level of competence required to do the job, whether intern or managing owner.
2. *Expectations of the job.* This refers to the assorted roles and responsibilities of positions, such as the difference between supervisory and technical manager.
3. *Return on investment for that job.* This refers to the gross margin that is anticipated to be returned by an individual for the firm's investment in payroll.

The following sections outline the specific steps to creating a compensation system framework. But first we will begin with a look at the problems in typical compensation systems and what criteria are currently in use by firms.

The Problems

I surveyed a small group of about 40 CPA firms to accumulate some basic information about their compensation systems. These firms were hand selected and ranged in size from $500,000 to $50 million in gross revenue, with the median-sized firm a little under $4 million. From that survey, and based on my consulting experience, there were six typical compensation system problems:

Problem 1.	Nonalignment of compensation with the current strategic objective
Problem 2.	Rewarding past work rather than what is being done today
Problem 3.	Focusing on billable hours
Problem 4.	Ignoring growth from existing clients
Problem 5.	No incentives for client transfer
Problem 6.	Basing retirement formulas on salary

A brief discussion of each problem follows.

Problem 1. Nonalignment of Compensation With the Current Strategic Objective

In other words, instead of the firm's current strategy driving how incentives and bonuses are paid out, it is a fixed system that rarely changes. Most commonly, formulas are substantially revamped when a large block of ownership and voting changes hands (i.e., retirement or demerger). This tends to lead to compensation systems that pay for unwanted performance like logging charge hours rather than accomplishing what the firm has deemed important. Examples of compensation not aligned with the current firm strategy include:

- Continuing to do work for marginally profitable clients rather than making the effort to either convert the work and fees to a more suitable arrangement or running them off

- Letting the day-to-day minutia of the practice give you an excuse for not setting up meetings to maintain visibility with the top 20 percent of your clients
- Not giving the time agreed as important to develop new skills or services
- Doing work below your level (the reversed pyramid)

Problem 2. Rewarding Past Work Rather Than What Is Being Done Today

Too much of the compensation is paid on the book-of-business managed even though owners have effectively turned the responsibility of taking care of some of those accounts to other people. The owners are being paid an annuity for effort made 10 years ago and, therefore, they become complacent about making the required effort today.

It is common for compensation systems to be developed with some objective criteria. The problem is that it is also common for those criteria to be virtually negated when the CEOs/MPs or compensation committees use their discretionary pool to equalize the effects of the objective formula. In other words, the owner earnings are adjusted back to fall in line with previous years' allocations, regardless of current performance.

Problem 3. Focusing on Billable Hours

Owners and managers at every level seem to be overly focused on the billable hour—doing the work themselves—instead of providing the necessary training so they can push work and account management to managers and staff.

Problem 4. Ignoring Growth From Existing Clients

Little attention is paid in compensation systems to the growth of the book managed from existing clients. The growth focus for most firms seems to be on new clients, which puts the emphasis in the wrong place. Incentive pay for new clients is a good idea, but it is more in line with an expectation for the senior owners or the firm's marketing initiatives. Incentives paid to grow additional services (your "share of the wallet") with existing clients are a far more important, achievable, and sustainable growth emphasis for all owners and managers alike.

Problem 5. No Incentives for Client Transfer

Few incentives or repercussions are included in the vast majority of compensation systems for transferring clients to other owners or managers. Systems usually pay CPAs to bring in business and manage clients, but they do not pay to transfer those clients to owners and managers with the additional bandwidth to serve them. Client transfers increase in importance when you have owners who are a few years from retirement. Most of the time, the transition of those clients occurs too late, because too little pressure was placed on the retiring owner to make this transition timely. The end result is usually lost clients or senior owners who creatively extend their retirement pay by continuing to perform a function that should have been passed on to others years earlier.

Problem 6. Basing Retirement Formulas on Salary

Retirement formulas are all over the lot, ranging from those based on the market value of the firm to those based on salary, and everything in between. One of the biggest disadvantages of salary-based retirement pay (the retirement payout amount calculated as a multiple of salary) is that it is too closely tied to annual production. Few firms freeze the retirement pay under these systems three to five years out so that the retiring owner is encouraged to shift his or her focus to the transitioning of clients rather than maximizing retirement payout. Under salary-based retirement payouts, retiring CPAs tend to hold off transitioning clients because their final retirement amount is negatively affected by limiting the book of business managed.

Current Criteria

In the PCPS Succession Survey, the respondents were asked, "What criteria do you use to determine owner compensation (select all that apply)," the responses were:

- A salary or base draw   82%
- Ownership percentage   48%
- The size of the owner's client book or fees managed   34%
- New business developed   34%
- Billable or collectible hours   32%
- Profitability of book   30%
- Performing certain identified firm functions (chairing committees, certain leadership roles)   29%
- Growing the existing business with a current client   21%
- Capital accounts   20%
- Training/development of staff   19%
- Cross-selling other services into your client base   14%
- Business transferred to other owners or managers   13%
- Profitability of department   11%
- Leverage of work being done (ratio of partner to staff work)   10%
- Client satisfaction goals   9%
- Other, specified by the respondents   9%

Another question, and the answers obtained from the Succession Survey was the following:

Which of the following describes (select all that apply) your current compensation plan for retired owners. Our firm's compensation plan:

- Does not address these issues.   41%
- Will pay retired owners a salary to continue working for the firm.   24%
- Will pay retired owners a percentage of their billings or collections for client work.   23%
- Will pay retired owners for the book of clients they still manage.   4%
- Have been made available to every retired partner.   21%
- Will pay retired owners to bring in new business.   14%
- Will pay retired owners to remain active in the community; serve on boards of directors; be involved in charity events.   5%

The Solution

Key Point

Compensation should be based on firm strategy.

Every time you change your firm's strategy, you should immediately realign the compensation system to support it. Compensation systems should be built to reward the behaviors you want continued, effect the changes that you want started, and penalize the actions that you want to prevent. If you look at this from a 30,000-foot level, you want your system to motivate owners to do owner-level work; managers to do manager-level work, and staff to do staff-level work. You also want to highly compensate your exceptional employees, reward your good workers, and drive off the marginal ones.

Most compensation systems reflect a philosophy of "to-the-victor-goes-the-spoils." Therefore, although the system can be tweaked annually, it rarely changes very much. As you know from the survey results covered above, these systems might not be modified for 10 years or more. Some of this might stem from the reflexes that support either the superstar or operator model. People operating under the superstar model tend to feed the superstars and starve everyone else. This is great if you are one of the "chosen," but not so great if you are part of the herd. On the other hand, operators tend to try and feed everyone, and because of that, they can stifle the superstars. If an organization has been run by operators for too long, these firms often find themselves gradually losing their entrepreneurial spirit. As stated earlier, either system will work. The superstar model is great as long as the superstars are active and driven, but it is a difficult model to transition, especially with any consistency, to new leadership. The operator model, while far better suited for succession in my view, requires implementation by visionary superstars who have to voluntarily give up the power and authority they have earned in order to set up a system for the benefit of those that follow.

The problem is … there is a naturally occurring conflict between the superstar and operator models and it goes like this:

> Most businesses are founded and become successful built on the superstar model. However, for them to profitably thrive either past a certain growth threshold or through generations, they usually have to shift to an operator model. So, without the superstar, the business probably would have never made it off the ground … but without an operator taking over, the limits of the organization are tied directly to the personal limitations of the founding superstar.

We see this all the time in corporate America. When a start-up company does well, once the business grows to the point that demand for products/services is recurring and predictable, it doesn't take long for that organization to move their founding superstar to a board-level position so the company can put talented operators in place to methodically grow and manage the organization profitably.

So, if you are a superstar firm (which most CPA firms are modeled after), some of the concepts introduced in the following sections will contradict how your system has worked. Moreover, implementing these changes is apt to be uncomfortable for the firm's superstars, who will be asked to give up more than they might want.

Build A Pay-for-Performance System

There are four basic steps in building an effective pay-for-performance system. They are:

Step 1. Identify personal billable production for each staff member.

Step 2. Adjust personal billable production to match expected revenue target.

Step 3. Establish performance targets for (a) staff, (b) managers, and (c) owners.

Step 4. Conduct performance evaluations.

Guidance on each step is given below.

Step 1. Identify personal billing production.

Your first step is to create a spreadsheet listing every billing employee, and his or her budgeted charge hours, billing rate, personal expected realization (not a generic realization), and salary. It is important to look at the performance history of your employees as you populate this spreadsheet rather than record your expectations because the purpose is to identify actual anomalies. I created the billing worksheet below (table 3-1) to use as an example as we work through the steps.

Table 3-1: *Billing Rate Analysis*

Billing Rate Analysis				
Accountants	Budgeted Charge Hours	Billing Rate	Salary	Suggested Multiplier
Avg Paid CEO/MP	975	225	270,000	0.85
Avg High Paid Partner	1,000	210	240,000	1.25
Avg Low Paid Partner	1,300	185	150,000	1.65
Avg High Paid Manager	1,300	150	82,000	2.25
Avg Low Paid Manager	1,500	120	60,000	2.50
Avg High Paid Staff	1,500	105	52,000	2.75
Avg Low Paid Staff	1,700	90	40,000	3.00

This data provided in the chart above gives insight into the establishment of billing rates that are commensurate with salaries, realization, and utilization.

Then, you need to plug in a multiplier that you think is fair; but don't worry too much about accuracy at first. You will be making multiple passes at this, so just start with something. Here is a general set of guidelines that I often use in my first round of analysis:

CEO/MP	.85
Senior owners	1.25
Junior owners	1.65
Supervising managers	2.25
Technical managers	2.75
Senior staff	2.75
Staff	3.0
Bookkeepers	3.5

Notice the differences between the multipliers of the supervisory manager and the technical manager and the senior staff. The supervisory manager's personal production objectives are lower, reflecting that he or she is required to schedule work, develop staff, and be accountable for the group's production. The assumption being made on behalf of the technical manager and staff senior is that these positions do not manage much and are more focused on personal production. The more jobs require people to spend time producing through others, the more personal production requirements must be lightened to allow these staff enough time to manage their direct reports.

Also, just so you know, the CEO/MP is assumed to spend a great deal of time managing the firm. If the CEO/MP carries out administrative duties similar to those of the other senior owners, the multiplier should probably be closer to 1.25. If, however, the CEO/MP spends most of his or her time managing the firm (which is certainly appropriate as soon as the firm achieves revenues of about $3 million and higher), then the multiplier should start declining. Once a firm gets to about $6 million in size, the CEO/MP should not be spending more than 250 to 400 hours of chargeable time working with clients; if they are, they are neglecting the firm.

Create an internal billing rate or multiplier.

Rather than use the formula adopted by many CPA firms (which is based on an external rate [i.e., 4 x (salary/2,080 hours)]), I have developed one around an internal rate. The reason is simple. With the expansion of services CPA firms offer, expected utilization can vary dramatically. Consider these examples:

- A budget for a tax person might be 85-percent utilization with a 90-percent realization (1768 hours chargeable at 90 percent of fees).
- A budget for someone predominately performing advisory work could be 60-percent utilization at 98-percent realization.
- A budget for someone performing business valuations may be planned for 70-percent utilization at 95 percent of fees

So, when you calculate billing rates, in order to give each employee a chance to be of value to the firm, their rates have to be balanced with utilization expected, given the type of service performed. Very few nontraditional services can come close to the full utilization percentages we have become accustomed to from our traditional services. So, under the traditional formula, people with the same salary are assigned approximately the same billing rate. But unfortunately, this approach, applied to staff supporting nontraditional or niche services, likely sets them up for failure. This means that billing rates have to be disengaged from status in order to give these more unique services a chance to contribute value to the firm. For example, it is reasonable for a manager performing niche specialty work to have a much higher billing rate than an owner carrying out traditional work due to the differences in expected utilization.

To compute what I call the *multiplier*, the internal rate is simple. For each position, given its level and expectations, and the payroll dollars invested in it, there is a required return. This multiplier sets a generic revenue expectation or gross margin for various positions in the firm. So, looking at the chart above, if a firm pays a manager $82,000 and that the position has a 2.25 multiplier, it means that this manager should generate, on his or her own personal production, a collectible $184,500 dollars (a gross margin of over $100,000 assuming 100-percent realization). Here are some thoughts to consider about multipliers:

- Depending on the position you hold, the multiplier changes. For example, the multiplier for the CEO/MP is the lowest, while the multiplier for staff is the highest.
- For the most part, owners, based on this survey, especially senior owners, basically pay for themselves and earn just a little extra that drops back into the firm kitty. Younger owners and everyone else in the firm are expected to make a higher contribution to overhead as a percentage of what they are paid.
- The multipliers calculated above were based on the survey results. The multipliers ranged from .85 for the CEO/MP to 2.75 for highly paid staff. Note that these numbers have not been adjusted to represent best practices, but are averages for the firms in the survey. Therefore, it is solely up to you to choose what level of return you think is fair for your people.
- Recent findings, based on data not collected in the original survey, are that general accounting staff might average about a 3.0 return with paraprofessionals (like bookkeepers) averaging around 3.5.

All of these results and the spreadsheet are for information only and meant to be a starting place to begin your analysis. This information should not be utilized as an authoritative guide and any changes you make to your compensation system should be purely based on your judgment of what is appropriate for your firm, not the calculations that result from using these formulas. Nevertheless, this tool should help you develop some basic comparisons between your people, in terms of how they perform, against the investment you make in them.

Identify disconnects.

I created the spreadsheet below to first help firms understand the disconnects between their billing rates, budgeted hours, and the return on investment matched against the salaries they were paying. So, let's walk through the examples and see how these averages provide us with some interesting insight (see table 3-2).

Table 3-2: *Billing Rate Analysis*

Billing Rate Analysis				
Accountants	Realizations	Budgeted Revenues	Suggested Revenues	Billing Shortage (Overage)
Avg Paid CEO/MP	90.00%	197,438	229,500	32,063
Avg High Paid Partner	90.00%	189,000	300,000	111,000
Avg Low Paid Partner	90.00%	216,450	247,500	31,050
Avg High Paid Manager	90.00%	175,500	184,500	9,000
Avg Low Paid Manager	90.00%	162,000	150,000	(12,000)
Avg High Paid Staff	90.00%	141,750	143,000	1,250
Avg Low Paid Staff	90.00%	137,700	120,000	(17,700)

Assuming a generic 90-percent realization for each of the preceding positions, here are two examples of how these numbers work out.

Highly Paid Owner Example:

Let's take the highly paid owner. If he or she bills a thousand hours at a rate of $210 with a 90-percent realization on that time, budgeted revenues total $189,000. Now, compare that amount to his or her expected return on salary based on the multiplier. In this example, you would multiply 1.25 times salary to arrive at a total of $300,000. The variance created is $111,000. Although this spreadsheet is only intended to help you think through the connection of these variables, such an extreme variance points out a conflict. In this case, the owner in question is underperforming in terms of personal production, to the tune of $111,000. However, there could be many valid explanations. For instance, this owner may have spent a great deal of time during this period marketing and bringing in new business or implementing a huge administrative project. So, if this were the case, the multiplier pertaining to personal production could be too high. Alternatively, something more basic, such as the billing rate, expected charge hours, realization, or utilization are in conflict with each other. If you assume, for the sake of discussion, that the multiplier and salary are acceptable, then maybe a solution would be a combination of new expectations. By upping the budgeted charge hours to 1,150, the billing rate to $270, with earnings at an average realization of 96 percent, the shortfall is only $1,920.

Low Paid Manager Example:

Consider the low paid manager. With a $60,000 salary, expected charge hours of 1,500, a billing rate of $120, a multiplier of 2.5, and a realization rate of 90 percent, this person is $12,000 more profitable than the expected return demands. In my opinion, this person should be earning incentive pay because of this overperformance.

As you can see, this worksheet is meant to help you identify anomalies in your pay system. The multipliers that you decide are appropriate for your employees are totally up to you. Nevertheless, if you consider similar multipliers for similar positions, and then compare the results against expectations and wages, you will be surprised by who turns out to be out of sync. You can fix the variance by changing any one or any multiple of the variables, and by adjusting any or all of the following:

- The multiplier, in the light that someone has specific or unique duties different from those of others in the same job category
- The billing rate, which is usually way off for some people
- The expected charge hours
- The salary
- The realization rate

Interestingly enough, the worst violations of this formula usually concern part-time employees. Firms often uncover significant imbalances between what they pay their talented experienced part-time staff and the return in revenues produced by those employees. Most of the time, the billing rates for these people are way too low. Sometimes, it is because their realization has fallen to a ridiculous level. Regardless, any variance of more than a couple thousand dollars should be reconciled; a solution should be identified and implemented.

Finally, some of the suggestions that the spread provides for each position above are outlined in table 3-3.

Table 3-3: *Billing Rate Analysis*

Billing Rate Analysis				
Accountants	Calculated Targeted Hours*	Current Expected Multiplier[†]	Automated Suggested Billing Rates[‡]	Rate Variance Current to Suggested[§]
Avg Paid CEO/MP	1,133	0.73	262	37
Avg High Paid Partner	1,587	0.79	333	123
Avg Low Paid Partner	1,486	1.44	212	27
Avg High Paid Manager	1,367	2.14	158	8
Avg Low Paid Manager	1,389	2.70	111	(9)
Avg High Paid Staff	1,513	2.73	106	1
Avg Low Paid Staff	1,481	3.44	78	(12)

*Calculated Targeted Hours is the number of hours that would meet the suggested multiplier without changing rates or hours.
[†]Current Expected Multiplier is the multiplier that is currently calculated considering current hours, billing rate, and realization.
[‡]Automated Suggested Billing Rates is the billing rate that would allow the current hours and realization to achieve the suggested multiplier.
[§]Rate Variance is the increase (decrease) between the Suggested Billing Rate and the Current Billing Rate.

To repeat myself, the positions in this example are generic; you will want to build your spreadsheet to include each billing employee and their historical performance data, and start working through this process.

Step 2. Adjust to reflect the reality of the firm.

Once the spreadsheet has been filled out with actual data and the conflicts identified, your next pass is to add a column showing adjusted revenue targets, and plug in suggested revenues per person. In the first round, you defaulted to the calculation of the multiplier times salary to give you a revenue target (to identify the anomalies). Now, it is time to consider what this person does and make adjustments to (1) revenue targets and (2) charge hours, realization, and billing rates.

Adjust revenue targets.

Some standard adjustments might include:

- Lower the revenue target for an individual because he or she works on a lot of marginally profitable jobs, in which case, his or her lower revenues are not the fault of the employee, but attributable to the nature of the work sold. At the same time, this worksheet would quickly point out that changes in pricing need to occur at the owner level. Still, in the near term, the employee should not be penalized because a class of work is continually being sold at a discount.

- Raise the revenue target because the technical manager works on the most lucrative projects, which are normally written up, in order to effect an adjustment to the revenue target.
- Lower the revenue target because an individual provides a significant amount of firm support, which eats away at his or her chargeable utilization.
- Alter someone's job description and duties. For example, you might decide to reclassify a supervisory manager to the position of technical manager, which would require an upward adjustment to expected revenues.

During this pass, you will be converting this spreadsheet from a theoretical analysis to one based on your situation, your employees, and your expectations. The new column ("Adjusted Revenue Targets") should approximate the firm's total revenue budget. If it does not, and it often will not, it is time to reflect on the difference between reality and perception. For many firms, when the charge hours are plugged in with expected realization rates, the calculated revenue totaled by this exercise is significantly higher than the current budget. This result is attributable to the firms' historical focus on the inputs (like hours charged) instead of outputs (like revenue billed and collected). The reason is that, although employees record their charge hours, all of these hours are rarely billed. Finally, a surprising phenomenon is that many firms fail to face that their realization is significantly lower than assumed. Recently, going through this exercise with a firm of about $3 million in revenues, it became clear that about $400,000 in profit was dropping off the table because of poorly sold jobs. The analysis of this exercise further revealed that the biggest obstacle to greater profitability was not in pushing the employees to do better work, but rather to stop the owners from giving it away.

Adjust charge hours, realization, and billing rate.

Once perceived fair revenue targets have been established for each individual, you want to adjust the charge hours, the realization, or the billing rate so that their total is closely matched to the expected revenue target. Remember that this is not a theoretical exercise. If you cannot increase the charge hours, or the realization, or the billing rate of a given individual, maybe the analysis is telling you that you are overpaying that individual. Granting that charge hours is often the hardest number to change, realization rates can definitely be improved with a little focus. As for billing rates, this number is far easier to change than most people think. Based on my experience, this number is the one that is farthest off the mark in most CPA firms. Over and over, I have convinced firms to raise the rates of some of their people (especially the owners), not by $5 or $10 an hour, but by 25 to 35 percent. The fear is always that all the clients will leave. The reality experienced is that of the few clients that leave, the vast majority are those that the firm was losing money serving in the first place. Always keep in mind that each time you let another marginal client go, you have freed up time for better serving your best clients (and usually at far better rates).

Step 3(a). Establish performance targets for staff.

Most firms have a pretty short list of priorities for a compensation system that will motivate staff. A common short list would probably include motivating staff to:

- Produce good quality billable and collectable time
- Develop technically to be able to handle more complex work.
- Look for additional opportunities to serve the clients they are working with.
- Develop interpersonally to manage client relationships.
- Refer friends and family to the firm.
- Desire to become leaders within the firm.

The first bullet on this list is usually the highest priority for firms. So, if you have established your targeted revenues for each individual, setting staff compensation is pretty straightforward from here. If any staff member overperforms their personal production targets, then he or she should make more money. I have seen firms pay anywhere from 10 to 40 percent of the excess revenues in performance bonuses for this one criterion. But any percentage will work depending on the firm's goals as long as the incentive is significant enough for someone to want to make an extra effort to earn it. For example, if you have a $40,000 per year employee and his or her annual incentive to provide a Herculean effort is $500, then you have made it clear that operating in "average" mode is the best strategy because the reward is not worth the necessary effort. However, if that effort can fairly easily convert to between $3,000 and $6,000, you have painted a different picture.

For larger firms, the difficulty of this first step is the hours of analysis that is required to try to figure out why certain people under- or overperform. Is it the result of the type of services being provided, work that is being either discounted or written up, or the organizational ability and skill level of the staff? Compensation systems are riddled with exceptions because so many variables influence performance. Many times, underperformance results from a combination of these issues. Obviously, you should not punish your employees for underperformance for which they are not responsible. For instance, consider the following:

⟳ Sample Scenario

Sally makes $75,000 and is a technical manager. For this example, assume that the firm sets her multiplier at 2.75. Therefore, her personal billings for next year are expected to be $206,250. However, Sally is the technical guru for the nonprofit niche. But much of the nonprofit work has been discounted by 15 percent or more below the standard rates. This occurs because the owner in charge of this niche (Ann) has worked with many of these clients for 25 years and does not want to upset them by dramatically raising their rates to what they should be. Ann fights to keep the rates down with the justification that much of the work is done during their low season, so it is good work because the firm is keeping their people busy.

Well, you have already heard my rant about taking on work to keep people busy and that this practice often traps firms into working harder for less. I would recommend multiple fixes. First, we need to run off some of the nonprofit work by raising rates to what they should be. Second, we cannot hold Sally, at least this year, to her 2.75 multiple because the work she does is written down before she even starts. Management has to exercise judgment about how to proceed and decide what exceptions should be made.

I would suggest, based on the information we have, reducing Sally's performance target by 15 percent (because of the discounted work) to $175,000 for the coming year. Then, I would recommend confronting Ann about the fact that her pricing practices have basically cost the firm over $30,000 in terms of just one employee: Adjusting Sally's normal goal of $206,250 downward to $175,000 in order to accommodate the in-house work generated lost profits of $31,250. In addition, part of Ann's compensation should be tied to her progress in closing the gap enough to restore standard pricing for this service area. By next year, for example, there will be an agreed-to standard for Ann's nonprofit work, possibly achieved by raising the average discount by 7 percent each year. Moreover, Ann's compensation will be reduced by 50 cents on the dollar for every dollar discounted below that agreed-to standard, i.e., any work throughout the year that was not priced at the new minimum standards. The point is that the firm is making it clear that the other owners are not willing to assume the burden of paying for Ann's pricing practices. In addition, although the firm is making an exception for Sally this year, they must tell her that the price gap on the work she is doing must be reduced over the next couple of years and that her expected target revenues will be adjusted accordingly.

The more employees in a firm, the more exceptions to the compensation system will be necessary in the first few years. That is OK as long as there are plans to progressively resolve or remove those exceptions. Typically, the analysis that paves the way for the implementation of a compensation plan focuses attention on client practices as much as on employee performance. Anomalies in client practices should be addressed by adjusting the employees' performance expectations to ensure fairness, and by then making the necessary corrections within the firm.

For the smaller firms, the good news is that these systems are pretty easy to devise because they can be tailored to one or two individuals.

> ### ⟳ Sample Scenario
>
> Assume a sole proprietor with no employees who took home $150,000 last year. This year, an assistant was hired. Obviously, the owner is concerned that his or her income will be reduced by the amount being paid to the assistant. A possible simple performance plan is for the owner to take home the same amount as last year, and then share 10 percent of the extra profits with the assistant. If the assumption being made here is that the owner would not have been able to overproduce last year's success without the additional help, then the objective is to motivate the assistant to help free up the owner's time (making it possible to provide more client services), rather than to isolate and delegate specific activities.

In the end, regardless of the size of the firm, the first step in any compensation system is to determine the performance that is anticipated for the salary being paid. In the example of the sole proprietor above, the expectation was increased firm billings.

The following discussions will cover timing of rewards, communicating the program, timing of incentives, creating policies, and creating innovative incentives.

Timing of Rewards

In order to set up your compensation system so that your top performers are being paid incentives by the beginning of the fourth quarter, you must start paying rewards before the expected budgeted amounts are actually achieved. In other words, if a staff member's annual revenue goal is $115,000; you might want to start paying incentive pay around 93 to 95 percent of that number. Think of it as greasing a wheel. As individuals approach their annual numbers (which should be based on average expectations, not personal capabilities), they start earning incentives, which motivates them even more to make a charge in the final weeks or month of the year. Consider the following.

💲 Sample Scenario

The firm has an owner (Sheryl), a manager (Lee), and a CPA staff member (Lila). Sheryl wants Lee to meet a personal performance goal of $100,000 in billings over her salary. Lee is paid $75,000 a year. So, staying with the idea that the incentive plan should start paying for performance below the annual target, Sheryl sets the base incentive bar for Lee at $165,000. However, because Lee can easily hoard work and Lila would then sit idle, Sheryl's plan also requires that Lila must meet a minimum billing number (say, $108,000, since her annual budget is $115,000) if Lee is to qualify to be paid under this compensation system.

In short, Lee must be motivated to produce, Lee must be motivated to manage Lila's work, and Lila must be motivated to bill. Therefore, one possibility is to pay Lila 10 percent of the collectible personal billings over $108,000 up to her annual budget of $115,000. Then, that incentive can be accelerated to 20 percent for the collectible billings above $115,000. Lee's compensation might work the same way, except Lila has to meet her minimum bar of $108,000 for Lee to qualify for her plan. Additionally, Lee will be paid 5 percent of everything Lila bills above $108,000. So, at a minimum, for every dollar over the annual budgeted billing amounts for her employees, Sheryl will get to take home an extra 75 cents on the dollar because of excess performance.

Now, I am not suggesting that this scenario is suited to all situations—what motivates people will vary from firm to firm. The key is to devise a system that is tied to objective criteria. For example, one firm I work with sets annual revenue targets for the firm. If the targets are met, everyone in the firm and their families goes on vacation together for a week to some exotic location. Nevertheless, this system, which works fantastically for a firm with 15 employees, will not work for a lot of firms because it can also allow some team members to hide and get a free ride on the backs of the workers while enjoying the same reward. Peer pressure helps, but if management is not willing to support that peer pressure by getting rid of slackers, a system like this will fail quickly.

🔑 Key Point

The key is to put together a system that fits the personalities of your employees and hence is meaningful to them.

Communicating the Program

In my experience, discussing the compensation system with the staff helps them grasp that their total collectible billings are a major determining factor in how much they can make. Giving them some input into their billing rate and write-ups or write-downs becomes an important part of the process. I interviewed a firm recently that allows employees to set their own salaries. Notwithstanding the control mechanisms that are also in place, the philosophy is, "What you ask for in salary sets your hurdles and targets, and as long as you can meet those targets, more power to you." Many times, staff discussions about the connection between personal earnings and billings creates a new perspective. If employees want more money, they realize that they have to come up with a way to increase their overall billings (and they understand that hours worked is not their only lever). It also needs to be clear that a major criterion for success continues to be client retention and loyalty, which means that billing fees that are unacceptable to clients can backfire. Once the staff understands that multiple metrics have to be balanced, they are empowered to look at their value differently. But, once you empower them, do not be surprised if they start challenging the status quo. This might come in the form of pressure on the owners to stop assigning discounted work to do, raise billing rates, stop writing off time staff believes was good work, or give staff input regarding their client billing. Many owners will instantly react, believing that staff demands of this kind violate the owners' authority, but on reflection, it should occur to owners that the staff is only asking for better management of the firm and its profitability. That is not so bad.

On the other hand, some staff want more money, even though they are already overpaid, (i.e., all their variables are already maxed out). In these situations, the real value of the compensation system is to make clear to the owners that they are treating the other employees unfairly by continuing to provide the overpaid staff with raises. It is a victory for any compensation system if its implementation convinces owners to hold firm about people who are not generating a fair return or pulling their weight.

Timing of Incentives

Incentives paid have been discussed only as if earned annually, which, in my view, is the reality. However, firms do not have to wait until the end of the year to pay incentives. Many firms will advance performance pay quarterly or semiannually. This can be best accomplished through personal budgets that take into account the seasonality of individuals' work. For example, if half of an individual's total billable time accrues during the tax season, his or her performance targets should be in alignment. Otherwise, you will end up paying some bonuses after peak season only to find the employee falling short of his or her annual targets by year-end. This puts you in the awkward position of having paid incentives when none was actually earned—and you can bet this will never be reconciled.

Creating Policies

Consider the following two policies regarding pay for performance:

1. Compensation systems can be changed at any time. They are not annual contracts. They can be altered without advance notice. All compensation earned under a previous plan will be honored, and as of the date of the new plan, all compensation will be paid in accordance with it.

2. Pay for performance is based on achieving annual targets. Any person who is not an employee by the end of the pay-for-performance term is not eligible to be paid incentive pay.

These two policies are critical because you need the ability to change the compensation system whenever required to motivate or demotivate certain behaviors. Returning to an earlier scenario, assume that Sally's annual target was reduced because of the discounted nonprofit work she was assigned, but midway through the year, a large very lucrative nonprofit job was sold, and Sally is the lead. You would want to be able to adjust her target to reflect the changed environment. Or, conversely, if someone is taking advantage of the compensation system in a negative way that was not anticipated, you need the right to be able to plug the hole immediately. As for the annual requirement to earn incentives, some firms, as a policy, do not pay any incentives for midyear departures because their systems are based on the premise that the employee shares in any excess return on investment for his or her position. Midyear departures mean that there will not be any excess return to share, given rehiring costs and the productivity losses incurred until the replacement staff gets up to speed. Other firms might create a more flexible policy by only paying incentives for performance that exceeds the annual targets, not the period-to-date targets. Firms that decide to pay for midyear departures based on period-to-date performance need to understand that an irregular workload flow might generate additional payroll costs that could only be earned resulting from timing rather than because of profit gains that will be enjoyed.

Creating Innovative Incentives

Besides personal production, are there other incentives to pay staff? Yes. Referring back to the preceding list, it is easy to pay staff for new clients or the growth in business from existing clients. An example would be a family member or friend who becomes a client of the firm. These new clients, generated from long-time personal relationships, are about the only new business you should expect from staff. The largest business development area that staff can influence, which they should be compensated for doing, is identifying additional work with the clients they currently serve. This is the growth gold mine that few firms tap with their younger employees. A common inducement is to pay 10 percent of the first year's billings for the additional project. Some firms pay this for two years. Personally, I would recommend payment only during the first year because payment over multiple years means committing future dollars. Such commitments are entitlements that immediately reduce the size of your future compensation pool and limit your flexibility in devising the following year's program. The final, most common, approach is to tie financial rewards to subjective requirements such as how the direct supervisor believes the individual is developing technically or in a leadership capacity. But as I have said so many times, when deciding what emphasis to place on incentives, first consider the firm's strategy, then identify the behaviors you want to reward or penalize, then put together whatever system makes sense for you, your employees, and your firm for the coming six months to a year.

Step 3(b). Establish performance targets for managers.

In my view, the compensation of technical managers should be evaluated just as it is done for staff. They, too, must mostly be enticed to produce. Just like staff, technical managers should be rewarded for identifying additional opportunities for servicing existing clients. Incentives should also encourage them to bring in new business, although the likelihood of this occurring is minimal. However, working existing client relationships is a completely different story because technical managers have plenty of opportunities to identify additional services to offer.

The scenario with Sheryl, Lee, and Lila above should give you good insight into my approach to supervisory managers. Supervisory managers, in my opinion, need to be motivated to produce through others. Unlike the technical manager, who will be predominately rewarded for his or her own production (billings, business growth, client management), supervisory managers should be rewarded for the accomplishments of their staff. This will motivate the supervisory managers to spend time making their people more productive by developing, mentoring, and coaching them. If you set up a system that allows a supervisory manager to make money through his or her own personal efforts rather than through the people managed, do not be surprised if they ignore their staff and crank out the work themselves. My advice is to pay supervisory managers for their personal accomplishments, but pay them more for the total production over target for all the staff they manage.

A number of firms have created situations similar to that described for Lee above. In these firms, the supervisory managers had to meet certain minimum performance numbers. Moreover, staffs, cumulatively, had to meet certain minimum performance numbers for their managers to be eligible for the incentives. The trick is to play with the numbers and alter the variables to ensure that the supervisor is always better off when he or she met his or her minimum performance requirement and the staff exceed theirs. You want to convince the supervisory managers that the best way to overachieve is to invest in their staff. Since performing through others is foreign to most CPAs, it may take a strong incentive (or disincentive) to convince these managers to change their habits. However, once they do, the pyramid will reverse very quickly, and the staff will either start developing or be asked to leave at a much faster pace. Obviously, just like the technical managers, supervisory managers should also be given incentives to manage client relationships, look for growth opportunities among their clients, and attract new clients.

In summary, at the technical manager level, the biggest incentive areas tend to be personal production and client management (growth, loyalty, satisfaction). For supervisory managers, the biggest incentive areas tend to be staff production, client management, and personal production.

Step 3(c). Establish performance targets for owners.

Obviously, this is the most complex part of the compensation plan, mostly because it is so political. Owners do not like to be accountable. At the owner level, many firms expect owner performance that is similar to that of technical managers, as previously described.

However, owner responsibilities should more closely emulate the supervisory manager (i.e., with an emphasis on how well work is done through others and the development of those below you) with the added caveats of a focus on business managed, new business sold, and clients transitioned.

The roles and responsibilities of owners within firms are often very vague, which is a second hurdle. The primary obstacle in analyzing owner compensation is balancing expectations between performance pay and owner benefits. With staff, because owner benefits are not applicable, you can focus most of the system on a philosophy of "What have you done for me lately?" With owners, the question is, "What have you done for the firm since your induction as an owner?" The theory is that owners are partially being paid for the cumulative benefit and value provided to the firm. Otherwise, the concern is that owners will burn out early under the heavy pressure to constantly perform as superstars. The discussions that follow will cover benefit creep, ownership and retirement, and ownership and compensation.

Benefit Creep

Many firms, especially larger ones, tie owner salaries to their shares or units (ownership). The problem with this is "benefit creep." Here is what happens. Each owner is allocated a percentage of the budgeted profits as annual earnings based on his or her share of ownership. As excess profits above budget are realized, additional shares are generated. These shares are then distributed back to the owner group; some firms do this on a pro rata basis while others distribute them equally among all shareholders. Add a couple of retiring senior owners to this scenario, with their shares and clients being allocated to the remaining owners, and benefit creep is in full swing. The following is an example.

> ### 🔁 Sample Scenario
>
> Bill, Sam, and Jerry were all owners, each owning 33.33 percent of the firm. Jerry retired and Gale was brought in as an owner to replace him. Gale was given an ownership interest of 20 percent, with the remainder of Jerry's shares going to Bill and Sam (giving them both 40 percent each). Later, Howard was added as a 10-percent owner, which reduced Gale's ownership to 18 percent, while Bill and Sam dropped to 36 percent each. Then, Sam retired, and the shares were distributed by ownership percentage again, with the result that Howard owned 15.62 percent, Gale 28.13 percent, and Bill 56.25 percent. So, as several owners were added or retired, Bill, who started with 33.33-percent ownership of the firm, ended up with 56.25-percent ownership.

By itself, Bill owning 56.25 percent of the firm is not a problem. In my opinion, the problem is that all of this happened through the natural evolution of a flawed share-redistribution SOP foundation. Moreover, what if Bill has been the weakest link in the chain during the last seven or eight years? What if all the other owners had to constantly carry more than their share of the burden to make up for Bill? What did he do that warranted such a powerful controlling ownership position in the firm now? What if owner compensation was budgeted profits allocated based on shares? Assume that when Bill joined the firm, his allocated profits amounted to $175,000, but now because of benefit creep, it starts at

$500,000. How is the firm balancing benefit creep with accountability, value to the firm, and performance in this case?

We have been talking about shares, but the same creep is likely occurring with book of business managed. Bill might have managed a $350,000 book in the beginning (which is the smallest book of the three owners), but, by now, he might be managing a $1.5 million book. This is fine if Bill actually generated most of this business; however, it is an entirely different matter if the lion's share of this business was transitioned to him from retiring owners. Benefit creep was developed to protect owners, but it is also a strategy that can easily undermine a firm over time.

Just so you know that I am still on earth, I can hear you say, "This is irrelevant because if Bill hasn't been performing, he would have been fired a long time ago." My response is … "Very few firms ever fire owners, and when they do, it is apt to be the result of a violation of ethics, values, or a major personality conflict rather than accountability." The reason is simple. Although everyone knows who the weak owners are, the other owners will not turn on them for fear that once the weak owners are removed, they might be next. Nevertheless, benefit creep can be kept in check in those few firms in which there is decision-making authority that can and will:

- Fire or at least demote owners over accountability.
- Hold back some portion of the owner allocation and pay it based on established and predominantly objective performance criteria. Note, however, that this will be ineffective unless the firm holds back enough compensation to create a significant incentive (or penalty).
- Reallocate shares based on a significantly altered owner's value to the firm.
- Give the management team the authority to shift out-of-balance managed books of business.

Otherwise, you can easily end up with owners who are so overpaid that even dinging them by 20 percent will not matter. Or, just as bad, you wind up with exceptionally large books of business being underserved by these same owners, which puts those clients and the firm, at risk of significant loss. In the end, terrible as it may sound, adjustments are necessary if an owner's value to the firm, including his or her ability to manage the client book, is far greater or less than his or her ownership and/or compensation percentage. Thus, although I am not suggesting that there are easy solutions to this problem, I am suggesting that irrevocably tying together ownership and compensation is not in the firm's best interest.

This is not to say that seniority and past contribution lack residual value. They absolutely do—just as much as is currently attributed to them under many systems. For instance, maybe the firm should pay some portion of its compensation purely on ownership and shares (maybe 25 to 40 percent), and tie the rest to performance. I am also not opposed to agreements that give certain owners a minimum salary regardless of their activities in recognition of their seniority or lifelong value to the firm (unless those owners are not performing at a level where they can continue as owners). At least with this understanding, going forward, fair performance assessment has a chance to occur because the subjective perks are known and have already been built in.

Often, owner compensation systems are created, and performance objectives are identified, after significant efforts have been made to develop and monitor objective criteria. Nevertheless, by the time the compensation committee massages the results, anyone could guess within $10,000 what each owner was going to make based on previous year's allocations. Firms that allow such a sham effort to implement pay-for-performance in the owner group, in my opinion, are wasting the time and money of both the management and the firm.

Ownership and Retirement

I believe that ownership and retirement should have more in common than ownership and compensation. Compensation is about what you do to make the firm more successful. Ownership is about your share of the market value of the asset called the firm. Many firms tie retirement payout to some multiple of salary, but consider this logically. If you buy a stock on the stock market, your ownership is based on the value of the organization, not what you personally do to support its operations. If you own part of a CPA firm and it doubles in value over the ten years you work there, it seems to me that you are entitled to your share of the gain. So, if the business is worth $1.5 million and you own 15 percent of it, whether you made $75,000 or $300,000 last year seems irrelevant.

Why has this approach been abandoned by so many firms, even though it makes so much sense? Quite frankly, I think some firms hope this strategy can counter benefit creep. Rather than everyone being assigned shares that constantly grow as people retire, everyone is assigned an ownership interest that does not change. So the "salary-tied-to-retirement" alternative has been created to recognize ownership and contribution without actual ownership. Two major problems have spawned from this derivation:

1. Equalizing ownership makes it increasingly difficult to create the necessary decision-making authority to operate the firm. This "we-are-all-the-same" approach puts owners with strong business acumen and vision in weak positions and owners with weak business acumen and vision in strong positions because everyone has the same voting rights. And because, in the end, voting rights rule the day, the results have been disastrous for many firms.

2. Because salary often drives retirement payout, in the waning years of an owner's career, the retiring owner is motivated to continue business as usual to maximize his or her retirement payout rather than being motivated to:

    a. Transition clients to younger owners and managers.

    b. Introduce others to that owner's business network.

    c. Get more involved in visible community activities and boards to bolster firm image and public relations.

    d. Mentor and coach others to expedite their development in the technical or niche expertise being lost.

Ownership and Compensation

Sometimes ownership and compensation get disconnected for the wrong reasons, which generates a web of inconsistencies. For instance, a number of firms do not consider firm management a top priority job (i.e., developing budgets, establishing performance goals for each person, holding people accountable), but rather consider client work the only real priority. The result is that not enough planning gets done in advance and too many decisions are tactical. Here's a story to consider.

> ### ⮂ Sample Scenario
>
> A small firm has gross revenues of about $800,000. One of the two managers of the firm, Dave, expressed an interest about a year and a half ago in becoming an owner. Because the sole proprietor, Becky, has been so slow in responding to Dave's request, Dave finally tells Becky that he is going to start his own practice. Becky, realizing that Dave has strong relationships with $200,000 worth of her business, offers Dave a 25-percent equity interest to stay. Becky rationalizes that she did not give away the farm with this offer because she knows she can still set the salaries, control the bonuses, and dominate the voting with her 75-percent share. So, Dave takes his 25 percent of the business and goes back to work.

There are a number of problems with this situation. First, Becky should have been proactive regarding Dave by deciding how she wanted to handle this. If Dave was owner material, she should have come up with some alternatives that were better thought out rather than waiting for this impasse to unfold. For example, she might have gotten back to him immediately with a set of reasonable criteria that he needed to meet in order to become an owner. Or, Becky might have created a principal position so that Dave could share in the profits for a couple of years, which would allow her to assess how he worked out as an owner before complicating the arrangement with equity. If, on the other hand, Dave is not owner material, Becky should have immediately started shoring up her relationships with the clients Dave regularly contacted.

Second, no one should ever be put in a situation in which he or she can hold the firm hostage to meet demands. Nevertheless, it will occasionally happen regardless of what you do, and firms need to be willing to stand up and fight. Dave should have had to sign a noncompete or employment agreement when he first started having regular contact with the firm's clients. Such an agreement would have made it more difficult for him to take clients or, if he did take them, at least he would have had to pay for them. Either way, having an agreement in place changes Dave's position dramatically. For example, if Becky wanted Dave to become an owner, she would have been in a position to charge him for the privilege. Since he would have had to pay her for any clients he took if he started his own business, paying her for a share of the ownership would sound reasonable. She might have offered Dave that same 25-percent equity interest at the cost of $200,000 (to be paid over a number of years through whatever arrangement suited the situation, whether that be partly cash, partly the deferment of salary increases, partly the deferment of bonuses, or partly payment through growth in profits). But the bigger word of warning is that if Dave is not owner material, it would have been a mistake to make him an owner, regardless of how much he might financially hurt Becky in the short run; marginal owners hurt the future value and success of the firm far more than any price you have to pay for letting go of unsuitable candidates.

In larger firms, because they tend to be more operator (corporate) run, no owner candidate that tries to blackmail or force the owner group into making him or her an owner will succeed. The individual who takes such an action has proven that he or she is not owner material because it is impossible to build a firm with owners that constantly hold each other hostage. But to be fair, because larger firms typically have created policies and procedures around issues like owner requirements, the process is more formal and proactive. In smaller firms, however, owners often procrastinate to the point that they practically require employees to use threats to be taken seriously. This state of affairs highlights the problem of not taking the job of management seriously as much as it illustrates anything else.

Third, giving Dave 25 percent of the firm is probably only the first of many bad moves. Logically, Becky will not want to put much value on that ownership interest since she gave it away, so she will start coming up with other variables to stalemate the impact of Dave's ownership interest on his compensation and retirement.

Although compensation, ownership, and retirement go hand in hand, they have become a tangled web in many firms. As discussed above, ownership can become the major determining factor in annual pay, which then drives the retirement payout calculation. Often, compensation is so interconnected with ownership and retirement that it cannot be used to support strategic achievement.

I have yet to observe a system that I considered exceptional by itself. I have been introduced to systems that seem to work well because (1) a number of SOP foundation processes and procedures are in place to support them or (2) the owners have a relationship and commitment to *each other and the firm* that overcomes the weaknesses of the system. Such support structures do not erase the weaknesses of imperfect systems, but they minimize the predictable damages. On the other hand, I have encountered systems that are the underlying source of chaos and conflict in firms. The issues in these troubled firms are so personal to each owner group that, rather than try to describe them, I have only identified some of the problems that are apt to appear. However, you may want to consider the following in developing the next incarnation of your financial remuneration web:

- As you know, tying ownership to retirement is acceptable because there is always a direct correlation between ownership and the sale of a business (whether selling the entire business to an outside organization, or only part of it to the other owners). This is especially applicable to the small firm. If it is appropriate, consider using the fair value of the firm as part of your formula for determining the retirement benefit amount (and maintain that formula within a regularly reviewed and updated SOP). Connecting ownership and compensation is an entirely different matter. Ownership can correctly be a factor in compensation, but if ownership drives compensation, the connection disables a critical management tool for motivating and punishing behaviors and performance.

- Keep in mind that in larger firms, retiring owners are too common to permit the continuous complexity of having to determine the firm's current value. Just like their corporate counterparts, larger firms create more shorthand methods of determining retirement benefits. For example, a top 10-sized firm pays owners their capital and a multiple of the owner's salary over five years as the retirement payout. A Big Four firm just pays the capital account. In this situation, the retiring owners only get their 401(k)s and capital accounts (which can be quite large), based on the theory that the owners were paid enough each year in salary and bonuses that they should have enough money on which to retire.

- Owner compensation should pay for business growth with existing clients as well as new clients. Too many systems only focus on new clients. Selling additional services to existing clients is a much better long-term strategy for building the business because so many more people can have a positive impact.

- All owners should be responsible for cross-selling added, needed services to the clients they manage. However, not all owners are equally suited for new client development.

- Owners should be compensated when they transfer clients to other owners or managers (assuming the relationship, not just the work, is transferred). In my opinion, transferring a client should be thought of as selling additional business. The owner who gives up current client relationships should be rewarded for being willing to:
  — Give it up to someone who has more time or skills to better service the client.
  — Reduce his or her book of business managed.
  — Put the firm and the client before him- or herself.

- If a firm is subject to the negative outcomes of benefit creep, either in the share of ownership or the client base managed, they need to be put in check by a strong SOP foundation, similar to that discussed above.

- Owners, just like managers, should be held responsible for the production of any of their direct reports who are either over or under budget. If the production is under budget, the negative incentive is subtracted from other earned incentive amounts.

- Billings managed should be part of the owner compensation formula. But equally important is the identification of key accounts (the top 20-percent clients and referral sources) and the institution of incentives and penalties regarding the adequacy and frequency of contacts being made to manage those accounts. In your compensation system, you want to avoid paying large sums of money every year for owners who just sit on their clients. For example, consider the owners who habitually pass off work to others and have not had direct contact with their accounts in years. Generally, the more an owner's income is based on work performed years ago rather than current work, the more complacent the owners are and the greater their unwillingness to take on actions and activities for the benefit of the firm.

- Owners should be severely financially punished whenever they lose a client as a result of lack of service. There is no excuse for this. If an owner cannot adequately service all of his or her clients, those that cannot be serviced need to be transitioned. If transitioned accounts are lost as a result of a mistake made by a junior staffer learning to managing accounts, at least the firm gained some value either in life lessons or insight into this junior's ability to manage accounts. Both of these outcomes are better than an owner who hoards clients and does nothing to take care of them, thereby guaranteeing that these clients will seek out a competitor firm that will show interest in them.

- Individual performance plans are a must for owners. What is expected; how it will be measured, monitored, and reported; what goals are set? However, no performance plan is better than a performance plan with no teeth (i.e., reward or penalty for action or inaction that is sufficient to hold owners accountable). An ineffective performance plan makes a mockery of pay-for-performance in full view of your employees.

- The bulk of the reward of the CEO/MP or, potentially, this owner's team should be based on the overall success or achievement of the firm. The CEO/MP's incentive should not be about client work, but rather whether the firm met its goals as identified and agreed to between the CEO/MP and the board.

- The owner group should also have an incentive to meet their profit targets, but in combination with all of the other targets previously identified in this chapter.

- In the last three to five years before retirement, owners should be operating on a transition plan laid out by the CEO/MP that identifies which clients to transfer, to whom, and by when. The largest clients need to be transitioned first because it takes several years for the replacement owner to develop strong enough personal relationships to be able to maintain those accounts. For the larger accounts, you want the retiring owner to be active for a minimum of a couple of years to support this transition. A major part of the retiring owner's compensation plan during this period should entail adhering to and following the transition plan. If the retiring owner decides not to follow the transition plan, then the annual fees for any clients lost for the first 18 months after his or her retirement should be deducted from the retirement payout amount.

- Although it might make sense for retired owners to be invited to select board meetings as advisers, it does not make sense for them to have a say in firm direction, nor does it make sense for them to continue to manage some client relationships. Although retired owners should be allowed to continue working on accounts they have managed in the past, the management of those relationships should be carried out by an existing owner. No client accounts should be managed by someone who is not an active part of the firm's leadership.

- It makes sense to pay retired owners to bring in new business and for the firm to support them in their charity and community efforts as long as they positively represent the firm.

- Offering selected retiring owners consulting agreements to continue working with the firm after retirement taps into an excellent source of talent. However, retired owners should preferably be paid as a percentage of the billings and collections (25 to 40 percent). Hourly billing can work with the proper controls. Salary deals rarely make sense, however, and are often just disguised extensions of the retirement payout.

- The obligation of the retired owner is to either speak positively about the firm, act positively to support the firm, or do nothing at all. Should a retired owner disparage the firm during the term of his or her payout, either in whole or in part, the payout should be in jeopardy.

Step 4. Conduct performance evaluations.

If a well-thought-out compensation system is created, performance evaluations are done every day and week by the employees as they compare their performance to their objectives as well as to the accomplishments of their peers (hence, the importance of routine firmwide shared performance reporting). Then, the only thing left is the subjective part of the evaluation in which the supervisors rate their direct reports on measures such as the following, to name just a few:

- Being a team player
- Self-development
- Self-motivating
- Attitude
- Control and delegation
- Decisiveness
- Resource utilization
- Time management
- Leadership
- Project management
- Client relations
- Developing others (mentoring and coaching)
- Stress tolerance

The AICPA's *Management of an Accounting Practice Handbook* has a lengthy section entitled "Personnel," so there is no reason for this book to reinvent the wheel. Therein, the subsection entitled "Performance Evaluation Systems," has a number of examples, to assist CPA firms in putting together the subjective section of their appraisal forms and processes. But the key is that with a pay-for-performance system (which routinely measures, monitors, and reports), people can determine on their own where they stand at any time. Returning to a thought covered early in this chapter, recall that a critical motivation for people is their feeling that they have done a good job or have made a difference to the company they serve. What better way to cultivate this feeling than to give employees the power to self-assess their progress.

A Final Word About Pay-for-Performance Systems

If all you want to know about pay-for-performance is how to make this concept work for you right now because when you decide it's time to go, you plan on turning out the lights and walking away, then just take any concept that rings true to you and plug it in to your formula. Alternatively, if you are looking for something that will endure through changes in leadership, then consider developing a much more formal system for performance objective identification, monitoring, feedback, and evaluation. Obviously, the latter will take significantly more time, money, and energy to put in place, but you are doing it so that it will become a routine process (part of your SOP foundation) that current and future firm members adopt as a normal part of good business management.

Also, you need to keep in mind that there is no single compensation system that will work for every firm. And even a system that works perfectly for you today may become an albatross a couple years from now because it is out of step with the new behaviors that you will need to motivate. Strategy identifies required behaviors and actions, accountability drives the compliance that produces these behaviors and actions, and compensation is the infrastructure "stick" that supports accountability. So, do not be surprised if your employees do whatever is reinforced by your current compensation system.

> **O—¬ Key Point**
>
> If you are asking people to perform one way, but paying them to perform another, you must, to put it simply, "Change your approach so that you are consistently putting your money where your mouth is!"

Conclusion

We want to elicit the best of the people we have because they all come from the same labor pool, which is not nearly as wide or deep as we would like for it to be. Except for new graduates (who have virtually no track record), everyone you consider hiring is probably someone who was let go or walked away from another organization as a result of some level of dissatisfaction on one side or the other. This is not as ominous as it sounds because one firm's bad employee might be another firm's outstanding performer as a result of differences in culture, job duties, or training. Recognize that the labor pool is probably not as deep as the personnel pool you already have, but the people you already have must be supported by the right SOP foundation. So, make the effort to get the best out of your good people and do not be shy about trading in your marginal ones.

Chapter 4

Growth and Transition: Increasing the Value of the Firm

The objectives of this chapter are to:
- Present fundamental growth philosophies.
- Confirm the premise that firm growth is referral driven.
- Discuss the importance of synergy between new and existing services.
- Define the fortress and empire approaches to marketing.
- Outline steps for creating an effective business development plan, including classifying clients and utilizing passive and active marketing.
- Give an overview of transitioning business to the right staff.

For any business to be successful, it must, most simply, offer a product or service that the market wants to buy, and then must sell that product, and deliver it at a profit. When you ask most CPA firms about their business development strategy, the most common response is, "We do good, timely work and are responsive to our clients." Our profession is built around the model of "if we do good work, they (clients) will continue to come." The problem is, that was then, and this is now. Good quality work is not enough. The environment is more competitive. Our clients need and are asking for additional assistance from their trusted advisers about how to become more successful. These pressures, plus the many others discussed in this book thus far, create an environment that requires a more formalized marketing approach to compete than has ever been needed before. For these reasons and more, I have developed this entire chapter to walk you through how you might approach creating a marketing standard operating procedure (SOP) foundation for your firm.

Although there are many sophisticated marketing strategies that your firm can embrace (and that are not covered in this chapter), the steps outlined below are the basics of professional services marketing. Leveraging various add-on strategies can be very beneficial, but putting them in place before your "perpetual marketing engine" is running at full speed is like building the walls of the house before you have a permanent foundation on which to set them.

This chapter takes the same approach by laying out how some basic marketing SOP foundations should drive the future growth of your firm. We will focus first on reasons why marketing is important to an SOP foundation. Discussions on growth, business development, and then transitioning business to the right people follow. We will conclude with an outline of steps that you can work through to create an effective business development plan.

Why Marketing Is Important to an SOP Foundation

There are three reasons that explain my rationale for why marketing is worthy of this kind of attention.

Reason 1. Marketing is an ongoing SOP process.

First, marketing is an essential operating process for any business, in any industry, in any country, at any time. Marketing is not something you do when business opportunities dry up … it is a foundation process that needs to occur all the time. If your firm is not identifying and providing additional services to your existing clients, or new services to new clients, over time, it will start shrinking due to normal, "not-your-fault-and-nothing-you-can-do-about-it" client attrition (death, selling the business, retirement, or moving away). Because our relationships with our clients are so personal and intimate, with little effort on our part in the past, we have easily leveraged our naturally occurring referral network. This has been our marketing salvation. However, in our profession's current marketplace—in which one firm's new client is likely some other firm's lost client—marketing is starting to assume the same prominent role that it occupies in businesses everywhere. And the more competitive our marketplace becomes, the more dominant will be the role of marketing in a firm's future success.

Reason 2. Marketing is the least understood SOP strategy.

Second, marketing is probably the least understood of all the SOP strategies most commonly implemented by firms. I want to dispel the air of magic that surrounds marketing. Selling new business is not the result of being a "silver tongued devil," but rather the process of helping your clients understand how you can help them. When you provide professional services, your referral network (clients and other referral sources) will drive your growth.

If you are "out of sight" of that network, you are most likely "out of mind," too, which minimizes your growth. So, I describe simple systems and strategies to make sure that your firm builds its critical marketing foundation on some rock-solid ideas.

Reason 3. Marketing can generate owner conflict.

Third, most important, and as a result of the first two issues, marketing creates some large chasms between owners, and these have to be bridged. Too many business development owners use their marketing prowess to hold their technical owners hostage. And interestingly enough, because of that prowess, firms too often misdirect resources away from structuring and formalizing the marketing function. This in turn encourages even more reliance on the marketing owners to bring in business, thereby making them even more indispensable, more valuable, and more highly compensated. Unfortunately, no matter how good your marketing owners are, if the firm growth exceeds a certain level, these owners will not be able to generate enough volume without systems to support them. So, please, save yourself a great deal of growing pain and owner disputes in reaching an outcome that always ends up the same.

> **O⟐ Key Point**
>
> To sustain your firm over time, you have to convert marketing from an individual function (i.e., the superstar model) to a firm-wide function (i.e., the operator model).

Doing this is also a great leveler. It puts the technical and the business development owners back on more equal footing, thereby closing the gap between them. Closing this gap is essential if you want the necessary buy-in to support the on-going development of SOP foundation throughout the firm. And SOP foundation implemented throughout the firm is a critical success factor supporting seamless leadership transitions and firm succession.

Size of Firm Commentary

The business development information and approaches covered in this chapter are as applicable to sole proprietors as they are to the top-10 largest firms. Of the material covered throughout this book, the issues discussed here are the most universal and the approaches described are the most uniformly applied. The greatest differences emerge as a result of the magnitude of the processes, support, systems, training, and reporting required for the larger firms. Obviously, the fewer the number of people required to buy in to this approach and modify their current behavior, the easier the implementation will be.

Although many of the principles outlined in the transition section at the end of the chapter apply to all sizes of firms, they are best applied to the day-to-day operations of firms ranging from about $750,000 to $20 million in revenue. For the sole proprietors and firms under $750,000, the transition issues are very relevant if the firm is being sold (because the owner can typically significantly affect the overall price paid by the buyer based on how the transition is handled), but less relevant the rest of the time. For firms with revenues of around $15 million and more, the transition issues are far less important. Achieving compliance with the transition objectives is very straightforward in these firms, given their corporate style of governance and engrained approach of managing the firm's clients (rather than an individual's clients).

Growth

One of the single biggest factors in determining the value of a firm is its total revenues. Obviously, many other factors come into play and affect the final price, ranging from the type of clients served, the skills of the employees, the likelihood of client retention, transition arrangement, the quality of the fees, realization, and utilization. However, well-managed and sustained growth is the easiest way to improve the market value of your firm.

In the preceding chapters, both the "one-firm model" as well as "reversing the pyramid" were discussed. Your approach to addressing each of these areas will have a significant impact on how you tackle the growth objective. Regardless of those differences, there are some fundamental ideas that I believe apply across the board. These ideas are:

Idea 1. Client relationships take time.
Idea 2. Mergers and acquisitions are costly.
Idea 3. Superstar models are limiting.
Idea 4. Firmwide marketing SOP foundations succeed.

Each of these ideas is discussed below.

Idea 1. Client relationships take time.

Owners have the primary responsibility of managing all of the firm's *top* client relationships. Owner time must be free to adequately address this responsibility, which means that many mid-level client relationships will have to be pushed downward to the professionals in the next lower tier of your firm (typically, the managers) in order to free up owner time to adequately address this critical responsibility. From the 30,000-foot level, client management includes:

- Continuously updating your understanding of each client's current and future priorities.
- Identifying additional services that would be beneficial to those clients.
- Managing the work performed for those clients.
- Billing and collecting fees.
- Maintaining client satisfaction with and loyalty to the firm.

In most firms, unfortunately, owners get too caught up in "doing client work" rather than "working the client." The most successful firms embrace the general rule that "as much as possible, the owners' job is to be at their clients' offices managing those relationships." This usually equates to owners' splitting time between maintaining client contact for business development purposes, performing high-level for-fee advisory services, and managing and coordinating the various projects performed throughout the year.

Many firms have also invoked a team approach to managing their top clients. There are a number of reasons. First, this duplication of effort improves client service and increases loyalty to the firm by providing the client with more than one contact person who is knowledgeable about the client's situation and projects. Second, this practice facilitates transition by providing clients with more than one ongoing relationship with someone in the firm. As owners retire, clients feel less abandoned because their relationship with the retiring owner is not the only one that has been nurtured.

Key Point

Managing the firms' client relationships is not a job that can wait until the work queue is empty (which is how most firms proceed), but rather *is* the job, whereas working the queue is a very low priority.

Idea 2. Mergers and acquisitions are costly.

The second strategic issue is one, I believe, of misplaced comfort. Most firms, when faced with the objective of growth, default to merger or acquisition. From my perspective, this is one of the most costly alternatives a firm can choose. Why?

1. Because you roughly pay about 75 cents to a dollar for every dollar in revenue you acquire.
2. You end up buying a lot of clients you do not really want or who do not fit your client profile.
3. You inherit all of the bad billing practices, from fees to realization, of the other firm and its employees.
4. You take on a culture that, more often than not, is vastly different than yours.
5. You are apt to end up with a key owner or manager who will be problematical to work with in the future. (Typically, this situation generates a struggle that disrupts the firm for years and yet is usually resolved only by running off these inherited owners or managers).
6. You have to spend the money to retrain the people in the acquired company to work with your technology, systems, processes, and methodology.

And I could go on for paragraphs. It seems pretty straightforward that buying or merging a practice probably costs firms at least 1.5 times (and often twice) whatever they pay for it by the time the new organization matches the operation of the old one (before the purchase or merger) in efficiency and effectiveness. And by the way, this positive assessment assumes that the combined practices actually reach that synergistic point … too many times, that goal is never achieved. My experience suggests that the actual price of acquisitions and mergers can exceed the numbers given above because of the number of firms that have to:

- Spin a small group out of the combined firm as a result of unresolvable culture conflict.
- Over time, fire a substantial percentage of the purchased clients as a result of incompatible fees or services.
- Fire or arrange early retirement or a special deal for an owner who is incompatible with the attitudes and objectives of the new organization.

- Fire or arrange early retirement or a special deal with some of the talent that was given a high value on paper during the negotiations for the merger or acquisition, but who, in reality, prove to be too disruptive or uncooperative to keep.

It might seem like I am bashing mergers or acquisitions, but I want to make it clear that I am not. There are many instances in which a merger or acquisition is the best strategy for growth. However, it should rarely be the *default-business-development-strategy* that it has come to be. I believe merger and acquisition has become prominent in our profession because of the almost mystical view of marketing. Since most CPAs matured by thriving in a technical environment, the sales, marketing, and business development side of the profession is foreign or unnatural to them. However, rather than try to understand and leverage marketing, firms try to take a shortcut by buying another firm's "magic" in this area.

Nevertheless, many firms would say, "We acquire other firms to gain access to their staff as much as to their clients." But my observation, as a privileged outsider sitting in on many of the owner discussions regarding acquisitions and mergers, is that such deals are almost always driven by the desire for firm growth. If acquiring staff is the central concern, there are other far less expensive and chaotic SOP foundation processes to consider (for instance, intern programs and recruiting programs).

Idea 3. Superstar models are limiting.

Put this into perspective. Firms, on the strength of one or two business developers, can grow from revenue of about $200,000 to several million dollars. However, firms that take this approach confront a natural limit because the growth engine rests on a couple of superstars. The problem is that, as firms grow, the impact of the superstars shrinks. For example, in a firm with about $1 million in revenue, one or two people can have a huge impact on growth by bringing in several hundred thousand dollars in new business, a much more significant increase than the same amount of new business would be in a larger firm. As firms see their annual growth percentage continue to shrink, they often decide that the solution is to bring in other superstars. For example, the business developers in two firms engage in a well-intended but unrealistic dialogue in which they agree that they could substantially grow the business if they just had enough support staff to do the work. The flaw in their logic is that lack of staff is less of an obstacle to growth than the circularity of the following line of reasoning:

1. Given the burden of client responsibilities, firms hit natural limits on how much business they can actually develop.
2. Although firms are willing to focus more time on business development, their compensation systems do not allow them to do so unless they give up their powerbase, i.e., the daily management of clients.
3. No sooner do firms begin to think that their compensation issues can be addressed, than they are forced to recognize that most of their new business comes from referrals from their existing clients. Consequently, business development is less effective without the regular client contact that is sustained by managing client work.
4. In the light of item 3, the business developers renew their focus on working their client base and referral sources to develop more business.

5. The process of item 4 takes time, forcing the business developers to quickly hit the natural limits of how much business they can actually develop.

In working with firms of all sizes around the country, it has become clear to me that relying on a few individuals for firm growth becomes a failing strategy as the firm grows larger. And relying on a combination of firms to solve the growth problem often creates a significant number of internal problems, higher costs, and lower profits and distributions for the owners, which are not the objectives that drove the idea of growth in the first place.

Idea 4. Firmwide marketing SOP foundations succeed.

The solution that is left, which is to create a firmwide marketing engine with all owners and managers having some responsibility for growth, is least often chosen. What truly baffles me is that a firm with $3 million in revenue will not blink an eye about buying a $1-million firm (which will likely cost them at least $1.5 million or more for the reasons I discussed above), yet that same firm probably has a marketing budget of less than $75,000 per year.

So, here is the question in a nutshell: Why is it that the same $3-million dollar firm identified above will not even consider the commitment of $1 million to a marketing budget, spread out over several years, which would allow them to organically grow (i.e., grow it themselves) $1 million in revenue? Moreover, this kind of commitment would not entail the added obstacles and costs of merging cultures, taking on bad clients, and weeding out problematic owners. Best of all, the firm would be developing a capability that it can replicate over and over.

Business Development

Unsurprisingly, the rest of this chapter is devoted to understanding how firms have gone about creating their firmwide marketing engines. Business development, just like everything else discussed in this book, starts with a plan. But, before starting the plan, there are some marketing concepts that need to be clarified. The following sections cover referral marketing, niche marketing, new services selection, and fortress versus empire marketing strategies

Referral Marketing

My business development methodology for marketing CPA firm services begins with my foundation premise that service businesses, *especially professional service businesses, are predominantly referral driven*. This means that although firms can use a variety of media to advertise and expose their practice (like TV, newspaper, radio advertising), very little will come of this investment without the support of referrals. This statement seems controversial and at odds with the approach of firms across the country. A look at the marketing effort and investment of most CPA firms suggests that most ignore the importance of referrals in the implementation of their plans. Consider the potential effect that my view would have on developing an effective approach to business development and marketing: If CPA services are referral driven, firms should *not* spend any time or money on any development efforts that are not primarily tailored to *push the referral button*. Once a firm has a strong foundation in referral-driven marketing, then and-only-then should efforts be put into place to support nonreferral, prospect, and new client marketing. In most firms, the reverse is true ... firms spend the largest amount of their marketing budget on nonreferral, prospect, and new client marketing, which leaves little to tap into their greatest growth asset, namely, referral marketing.

Referral marketing is simply marketing to those individuals and businesses that already know and respect your firm. These sources are current clients; friends and family of the firm, as well as supportive professional resources (such as attorneys, insurance agents, stockbrokers, and bankers that currently work with the firm). Why is the referral so important to firm growth? Simply, no one wants to experiment or rely on luck when it comes to obtaining assistance on important financial matters. An analogy can be made to the medical profession. If you need a heart doctor, the most common first tactic would be for you to ask those you trust for a referral to someone they trust. Looking for assistance in the Yellow Pages may be efficient, but is fraught with risk. Unanswered questions are:

- What experience does this person have?
- How capable is he or she?
- How many times has he or she successfully resolved problems like mine?
- How can I tell whether he or she is competent?

Suppose someone emphatically tells you about how satisfied he or she was with a particular professional. As a result of that assurance, you will be far more comfortable and far more likely to contact that professional in order to get access to his or her expertise.

My approach to marketing focuses on developing two basic types of referrals. The most obvious approach is to attract new clients to your firm through referrals from clients, friends, or other professionals. Second, educate your clients about the diversity of services you offer. This will encourage existing clients to make referrals from, for instance, other departments in their organizations, or other kinds of engagements that they may be seeking.

> ### 🔑 Key Point
>
> Based on my personal experience consulting with CPA firms over the past 25 years, a conservative estimate is that referrals account for more than 90 percent of the annual growth of most firms.

These statistics are the basis of my advice to focus almost all of a firm's marketing resources on referral marketing. If increased share of the wallet (growth of services for existing clients) and referred new business is the most likely source of a firm's revenue growth, then these areas should be the focus of the business development plan.

Niche Marketing

As you might guess, there are also times when referral marketing is the wrong strategy for a CPA firm. Consider this simplistic case study as the beginning of our discussion of alternative strategies:

⇄ Sample Scenario

Winters and Associates, a successful CPA firm, decided to expand its offering to include the nontraditional service of technology support. As a logical place to start, this service was marketed to their existing client base. Immediately, there were several leads. Within six months, the technology projects fully utilized what normally would have been off-season idle time by the technology-savvy management and staff. Yet, additional requests were still coming in. Rather than miss these lucrative opportunities, management hired a full-time information technology (IT) expert for the sole purpose of satisfying the growing client demand for this service.

Six months later, after adding and shifting personnel to operate this new growing IT department, the pent-up demand from the existing client base had been satisfied. The technology support requests continued, but slowed down. Over the next 12 months, the nonbillable time of the technology staff was growing and becoming problematical.

Management recognized that the firm's financial resources were being drained and that the owners' willingness to support this service was dwindling. Some IT people were shifted back to more traditional departments. But in order to salvage the IT service, management also put together a comprehensive marketing campaign to expand the firm's IT visibility. The result was an even more restricted cash flow because, although the expanded marketing effort generated significant interest, the new business was slow to materialize. The firm quickly discovered that it takes more time and is much harder to sell IT services to new clients than to sign up existing clients for the same services. The owners were not willing to support the losses being incurred by the technology department, at least not for the time it would take for demand to catch up with supply. They decided to go back to their bread-and-butter services and leave technology support to other CPA firms. This decision prompted one of the owners to leave to start a technology-focused CPA firm; he took several of the firm's key employees and a good number of the clients with him. It took Winters and Associates years to recover from this technology adventure, specifically, from the losses incurred by launch of the technology niche service and the personnel losses triggered by the formation of the spin-off firm.

This story should sound familiar and any number of niche areas could be substituted, including wealth management, valuation, litigation, or elder care. Even if your firm has not experienced this, you most likely know firms that have. Historically, CPA firms have had difficulty implementing various nontraditional services, mostly as a result of three factors:

1. Lack of synergy between new niche offerings and existing services
2. Lack of differentiation between the objective of developing new clients and that of growing the "share of the wallet," i.e., providing more services to existing clients (In other words, what is the source of the growth?)
3. Inconsistently focused firm marketing, with little distinction between owner and manager marketing responsibilities and the implementation of an administratively delivered campaign of referral development

New Services Selection

For the past 25 years, CPA firms have continued to expand their scope of services. In the beginning, expanded services were usually a migration of existing services, or even the result of a redefinition of the scope of a service rather than truly new services. For example, many CPA firms offered informal tax, estate, or wealth management planning as part of their tax return preparation process. Many of those firms either gave away these additional services or charged minimally for them. Therefore, as time went on, it became increasingly more important for firms to formalize these augmentations of their primary service so clients would understand the following:

- The unique services being delivered were not a normal part of the tax return process.
- Their CPA firm had special expertise to share, which allowed the firm to differentiate themselves from other CPA firms.
- If they were interested in receiving any of these augmented services, their fees would rise.

Firms experienced little resistance to expanding their services because, in the beginning, these new services, by the nature of their migration, were very synergistic with each other. For example, tax return preparation can naturally lead to tax planning, which can naturally lead to discussions about estate planning.

As firms evolved and the redefinition or formalization of their traditional services was complete, firms continued to mine this successful strategy by adding new services. Conversations among owners shifted to "What niche service or specialty area should we develop next?" In some cases, firms added new services that were synergistic to their existing services. For example, a firm with a number of clients who are wealthy individuals could easily add wealth management services. Or, a firm with a specialty niche, like construction, might add an estimating or bonding support service. A synergistic service is a new service that is a natural extension of services that fills the additional needs of existing clients.

New Service Selection and Island Services

For many years, CPA firms all over the country added new services at a phenomenal pace, encountering little resistance, and mostly enjoying success. Even notwithstanding economic ups and downs, firms find that a service expansion strategy has limits. One of those limitations arises when offering a nonsynergistic service. Why? Because with each nonsynergistic service, long-term profitability requires the development of a new marketplace (i.e., a new client base). Most CPA firms did not understand and anticipate this. Instead, firms assumed that all new services have an equal chance of generating demand, and drew no distinction between existing clients (those currently being served) and prospects (potential clients). Firms lose a great deal of money in the process of learning to make this distinction; the preceding example of Winters and Associates' expansion into IT is common. Technology services are synergistic if most of a firm's clients are businesses and a variety of operational support services are already being offered by the firm. However, technology is not synergistic if most of your clients are individuals or businesses that are too small to be able to afford this level of expertise. I describe any service that is not synergistic with the needs of your existing clients as an *island service*, meaning that it stands alone. For an island service to make sense for a firm, it:

- Must be part of their long-term service strategy (it may be an island service now, but given the clients the firm is trying to attract, the current island service is just the beginning of a set of synergistic services).
- Should be a differentiator service. (In other words, you might not plan to make much money on the service itself, but you use the provision of this service to open new doors and attract clients away from competing firms because it is seen as valuable).
- Needs to be profitable.

For a long time, many firms believed that picking a service out of a hat gave as much chance of success as any other method of deciding which services to provide. However, over the past five or six years, firm after firm has found that adding nonsynergistic new services can be very expensive, both in terms of the costs of maintaining the expertise to deliver these services, and the costs of later discontinuing them. The costs are financial losses, the departure of owners that developed island specialty niches, and the lost focus of the firm. So, before a firm launches a new service, it needs to answer some key synergistic questions, including:

- Why are we launching this service? (Are our clients demanding it, or do we have an owner interested in providing it)?
- What will likely happen if the service succeeds or fails? (For example, if the service succeeds, will it likely be spun off because it is so disconnected from the other efforts of the firm? If so, are you just funding a start-up business for one of your owners to steal?)
- Does this service logically fit with the other services you offer?
- Logically, will this service be useful to your current clients? (If not, do you have a strategic purpose to attract a new set of clients?)
- What are your expectations for this service? (When will it break even? How long are you willing to support it? How do you define success so that you will know when it has been achieved?)
- Who is going to champion this service? (Does that champion have any clout with the existing owner group? If not, have you anticipated that the service will probably be doomed when it hits the first bump in the road?)

A Final Word About New Services Selection

To summarize the common failings encountered in this area, it is important to understand that:

- All services are not alike; they do not all have an equal chance of success.
- A service that is synergistic for one firm does not mean it will be synergistic for every firm.
- Island services that are not strategically initiated will wind up costing the firm a great deal of money if you eventually decide to shut them down.

Once you have decided what services to offer and promote, the next question is, "Who is going to buy them?"

Fortress Approach Versus Empire Approach Growth Strategies

Most firms think marketing is synonymous with new client development. However, marketing is about *all* business development. Before you offer any service, you need to understand who the service is targeted to serve, and why it is important for you to serve that market.

To help firms work through this, Michaelle Cameron, Ph.D., a professor of marketing for Saint Edward University in Austin, and I developed marketing concepts called the *Fortress* and *Empire* approaches. Here are some very basic definitions we have attributed to these terms:

> Throughout history, fortresses were built in order to protect communities from outside forces. Barriers were created, like walls and moats to fend off would-be attackers. The vast majority of the daily needs of the community were supplied from within the walls of the fortress.
>
> *Empires* were built by conquering new territories and expanding well beyond original boundaries. The community's needs were supplied through a combination of the resources available within the empire's own fortress and in the new wealth found in the annexed/conquered provinces.

Given these definitions, the following sections address how we use these terms to drive the marketing strategy of professional services development.

The Fortress Approach

To us, the *fortress approach* embraces a focus on client retention, an objective of service extension ("growth in share of the wallet"), and a strategy of new clients through referrals. The goal is to inform the community (existing clients, friends, and supportive service professionals) about the diversity of services offered by the firm.

> **O—¬ Key Point**
>
> Remember, the vast majority of your clients think your firm offers no more than the services they currently buy from you.

Therefore, by developing overall client awareness about all of your services, you generate several predictable outcomes for the following reasons.

1. Because you have made your clients and friends more aware of the number of services you offer, they are far more likely to ask you for assistance. Without this contact, those same clients might seek assistance from others because they are not aware that your firm can help them.

2. A potentially even greater impact may be that those same people are in a far better position to refer work to you now that they know you do more than just their kind of work.

3. You enhance client loyalty to your firm when clients feel their trusted professionals can help them in additional ways (even if they don't need those services right now). Logically, even more loyalty accrues to the firm when you actually provide those additional services.

4. By building a wall of services around your clients (and making them aware of those services), you are less likely to find one of your competitors infiltrating your client base by providing the services that your firm offers and could be providing.

A real plus of the fortress approach is that it typically returns the greatest benefits in the shortest amount of time (whether that benefit is profits, utilization of services, or attendance at an event). It is far easier to get the attention of and engage with people who already know you, trust you, and have confidence in your ability to provide services. So, assuming you are making contact with clients and/or referral sources with unsatisfied needs, you can use inexpensive media to quickly tap into established relationships to attract attention and sales.

The Empire Approach

A second marketing alternative, the *empire approach* is usually taken to acquire new clients or develop a new niche specialty. It requires a long-term horizon and is time and resource intensive. You use the empire approach when you expect the demand from your current client base will not fully utilize the service supply. The success of this service depends on adding new clients, i.e., new territory must be conquered. Consider the technology service in our earlier sample scenario. As often happens, the firm in our example found quick success by going after their untapped client demand with their newly offered service. This is an important initial strategy when launching an empire service because you can underwrite part of the cost of launching a new service by skimming the cream of demand from your current clients while you develop your longer term market. However, as many firms do, our example case overlooked the second part of that approach, the "*while you develop the longer-term market*" part. Since the technology service was not synergistic with their other services, the firm did not have an existing client base that could sustain the necessary supply-to-demand ratio. By the time Winters and Associates realized that a mix of new and existing clients would be required for the technology service to be successful, the firm had lost almost a year of critical empire-building, marketing time. It is important to note here, for clarification that the marketing campaign approach and messaging is vastly different depending on which strategy (fortress or empire) you choose.

Fortress Approach Versus Empire Approach and Marketing New Services

Randomly picking new services to offer in order to make a few extra bucks is most likely to prove extremely costly to the long-term positioning and success of the firm. Here are the steps, in order, that your firm should take:

1. Strategically determine what services your firm wants to launch.
2. Understand whether a given service is synergistic or an island service.
3. Consider both the fortress and empire approaches to determine the best marketing strategy.

If your current client community can continually purchase most of the supply available for this service, a fortress approach will be best. If the service cannot be supported long term by the existing client base, then you need to reevaluate why it is important to offer this service in the first place. Once you are satisfied that launching your new island service is the right course for your firm, then you will need to look to the empire approach for guidance as to how to proceed.

Fortress Approach Versus Empire Approach and Their Markets

The following are three examples that demonstrate the two marketing approaches and the audiences to which they cater.

Example 1. Fortress Approach:

The current clients and your referral sources (professional relationships [attorneys, insurance agents], friends, family) with whom you already have relationships. These people know you, and respect and trust your firm. They are likely to at least glance at any message and information you send them.

Example 1. Empire Approach:

Prospects and nonclients have no relationship with you and will most likely immediately trash, delete, and ignore anything you send them until your organization becomes a known quantity.

Under the fortress approach, it takes only *months* for your marketing to begin to have an impact on current clients and referral sources. Under the empire approach, it takes *years* to have the same impact on prospects and nonreferred clients because there is no existing relationship to leverage.

Example 2. Fortress Approach:

Current clients and referral sources not only have no problem buying services from you or referring services to you; many of them want to. If you tell them you can help them in a specific area, they are easily convinced that you are capable of delivering new services to them because they trust you. And they will continue to trust you until you give them reasons to feel otherwise. The only issue is to match their needs (or the needs of the referred party) to your skills. Therefore, much of your marketing efforts with this group should be focused on helping them understand the various ways you can provide assistance.

Example 2. Empire Approach:

Prospects and nonclients do not know you, do not trust you, and do not have any reason to believe that you can help them. In order to get them interested in talking to you, you have to convince them that your special expertise, knowledge, and skill is uncommon. Given the critical difference between the empire and the fortress approaches, it should come as no surprise that empire marketing efforts are all about establishing niche expertise. Once prospects (nonclients that are not referred to you) start believing that you have unique expertise, you are about halfway there. Next, those same prospects have to have a need that is not or cannot be served by someone they already trust. Logically, when you market to prospects, many times, your efforts first benefit everyone but you because your messages will prompt the prospects to contact their current service providers for the assistance you are trying to sell.

Under the fortress approach, new business and service opportunities are generated much more quickly and at far less cost than current clients and referral sources. If, for example, you send these clients a mailing, you can depend on them to read it the first time they get it. Because you are educating this group about the range of assistance that your firm can provide, they (or people they know) will call you as opportunities arise. Under the empire approach, you have to travel down a much longer road to reach prospects and nonclients. First, you have to convince them that you have special expertise that would benefit them. This is especially difficult; since they do not have a relationship with you, it is hard to get their attention long enough to get them to listen to you. The bad news is that, even if you manage to get their attention, you still have to be lucky enough for the prospect to decide to seek assistance from you, rather than from some other professional with whom they already have a relationship.

Example 3. Empire Approach:

In marketing to prospects and nonclients, it is best to target niche industries or service areas, because, first, you are trying to convince them of your expertise. The reason is simple. You are trying to convey the message that you know, understand, and can help the prospect better run their organizations or manage their problems. It is easier to accomplish this if you can mention the specific concerns, obstacles, and opportunities that face them. So, if you target manufacturing prospects, you are more apt to get their attention by speaking their language about the pitfalls of MRP (materials requirement planning), the value of doing some simple capacity planning and the avoidable costs of rework and idle time. If the messages you send are general in nature, these prospects, with whom you have no previous relationship, have no reason to believe that you understand their world. What is true for an industry is true for a service. For example, it is far easier to catch the eye of a litigation attorney who might need assistance in an upcoming case if you talk about how you have provided litigation consulting services that have delivered value to the final outcome of a trial, how your experience testifying on the stand has benefited those you serve, or tips and tricks that experts need to be aware of when being deposed.

Under the empire approach, although niche industry and service marketing helps you convince prospects of your expertise much more quickly, it still takes a lot of time for you to build a brand with someone who does not already know you. (For example, consider a mailing. You will be lucky if a prospect pays enough attention to the first three or four mailings to recognize your name and logo. After six or seven pieces, your name and logo might start to seem familiar to the prospect because he or she has seen it so many times. This recognition might induce the prospect to glance at your materials to see why you are being so persistent in making contact. By the eighth or ninth contact, you will probably get a full reading of your materials—the level of attention you would have received had you sent this piece to a client or referral source for the first time. Consider a niche marketing approach, in which you stay the course long enough to create awareness of your organization. Your marketing efforts are fundamental to getting the prospect's attention. Nevertheless, even in this instance, most of the time, a recommendation by someone in your fortress is still the final trigger that prompts the prospect to contact you.

The Empire Approach and Prospective Clients

Given the preceding discussion, it would be easy to conclude that the empire approach is best avoided. However, even though the empire approach is definitely more time-consuming, costly, and slow to bring results, there are many times when it is absolutely the best alternative. Here are a couple of examples in which empire is the optimum approach:

- Offering technology services even though most of your clients are individuals
- Launching a litigation support service to litigation attorneys even though you do not specialize in serving the legal community
- Offering the utility industry support services even though your client base is predominantly small businesses
- Offering wealth management and investment services even though the bulk of your clients have total assets of less than a couple hundred thousand dollars

Another common example of today's market opportunities is the service area that has been legislatively created and has a short window of opportunity to leverage. Consider services required by the Government Accountability Office (GAO) and the Sarbanes-Oxley Act. Because of this legislation, organizations of all sizes either must or have voluntarily opted to create a more distinguishable line between attest and nonattest services. As you know, for these clients, this means you either have to give up the attest or the nonattest work that you have historically provided because you are no longer permitted to do both. Although this seems like bad news, the good news for a marketing-oriented firm is that the new rules apply to every other CPA firm. Given the likelihood that all of the other local and regional CPA firms have a combined client base that is larger than yours, practitioners have had an opportunity to acquire far more new work than the amount of work they had to give up. Therefore, there was a unique and rare opportunity to pick up lucrative projects from organizations that were also being happily served by your competition. Several examples that come to mind are:

- Reviewing internal controls and making recommendations for improvements
- Projecting revenues, expenditures, and fund balances
- Assisting with various technology strategy and implementation projects
- Investigating fraud matters

In these cases, you should use the empire approach to target prospects in industries you currently serve for those services that can no longer be performed by their auditors. Examples of industries affected by this legislation are government agencies, schools, Securities and Exchange Commission (SEC) companies, certain nonprofits, and many more. Considering both discussions above, either because of the service-synergy disconnect or the forced change resulting from the legislation and its rules, the empire approach is the best way to leverage these kinds of situations.

The Empire Approach and Existing Clients

It is right about here in my discussions with firms that the question arises, "If niche marketing is the most effective for prospects and nonclients, then why not use the same approach on your current clients and referral sources?" The answer is, "You might!" If, for example, your firm has a specialty in construction, then you might create a campaign with messages targeted specifically to them, and since the messages are focused on specialty and expertise, the same campaign could also be used to market to prospects. This type of approach will help your current clients think of new ways for you to serve them, remind them of why your firm can uniquely serve them, and also keep you in their minds, for referral to their contractor friends and associates. Although this campaign will likely attract some interest from prospects a year or two from now, the real benefits you are more likely to reap in the short term are growth in "share of the wallet" for services with current clients and new client referrals.

Consider this interesting twist: You also want to do some marketing of the general services you offer to your niche or industry clients. Why? If you *only* market niche specific messages to your contractor clients, then you may unintentionally limit the universe of referrals that will be provided by those clients. In other words, contractors have many friends, associates, and family who are not contractors. So, if these other parties ask these contractors for referrals, the contractors may refer them to a firm other than yours, in the belief that you specialize exclusively in their industry.

Here is one final idea. Because professional service marketing is as much about generating referrals as it is about selling new services to existing clients, every single client and referral source needs to be included in your contact list. Do not be surprised if that simple 1040 client sends you a great business client because the two have been friends since high-school. Because your marketing made your client aware of the many services you offer, he or she can still generate excellent referrals for your firm, even though he or she would never need those services.

Remember that, when you sell to your empire market, you are selling competence and experience. Why? Because the potential clients do not know you, you must give them a reason (your unique ability) to call you instead of someone they already know. When you sell to the fortress market, you need to focus your messages on how you can help. Why? So the clients or referral sources, who already trust and respect you, can quickly determine how your skills and experience can be applied to their situations or those of their friends.

Fortress Approach Versus Empire Approach and Marketing Tools

Now, rather than apply this logic (fortress or empire) just to services, let us put this in a larger perspective using common marketing tools. Take a newsletter for example. It is normal for CPA firms' newsletters to dedicate 70 percent or more of their available space to technical matters. This type of newsletter conveys that you are an expert and a competent service provider. Here is the question: "Is the newsletter, in the situation described above, being used to support empire or fortress marketing?" If you answered, "Empire," you are correct. Demonstrating expertise and competence is important if you want to interest people who are unfamiliar with your work. Now, let us change the newsletter to focus the same amount of content on "success stories (stories about services performed at various clients)," narratives about new employees and their skills, and ways you can help your clients. This newsletter is now ready to support a fortress marketing approach. Over and over, the problem with most firms' marketing is not the tool or medium they are using, but how they are using it. Too often, empire marketing messages consume fortress marketing campaigns and vice versa. Coming back to our first newsletter example, if a newsletter is focused on convincing your audience of your expert and technical ability, and you send it to your current clients, you are wasting time, money, and paper. A common comment from the audience is, "I don't read the technical stuff in the newsletter because that is what I pay them to do. If it applies to me, they will call me." So, the newsletter is not a bad idea; how you deploy it can be good or bad. Messages that will motivate the fortress marketplace are completely different from those necessary to motivate the empire marketplace. If you use both strategies in your firm (which is common), it is easy to get sloppy about how you communicate to each group. Look at each marketing piece you are utilizing and consider each of the following:

1. Determine whether it is targeted at prospects or clients or referral sources.
2. If it is targeted at prospects, it should focus on expertise and competence:
   a. Use a more niche industry or service-oriented approach to make your messages resonate.
   b. Plan on a one- to two-year conversion rate, and make sure you have included many contacts into your plan over that time.
   c. The empire approach is commonly marketing to some people who do not know you, nor do you know them. Consequently, you have to use more generic media, such as newspapers, trade magazines, radio, purchased company lists. These media and approaches also raise the cost because you are spending money contacting people who will never have an interest in your services. (Your cost per contact is low, but your cost per qualified contact is very high.)
3. If it is targeted at clients and referral sources, it should focus on helping the audience understand how you can help:
   a. Market to all of your clients and referral sources because you are looking for both new client referrals and "share of the wallet" growth.
   b. The whole point of your campaign is to stay on the minds of those people most likely to hire or refer you.
   c. Because you know exactly who makes up this audience, your cost per qualified contact is very low.
4. You should only sell one or two services at a time. If you try to sell too much, you will end up not selling anything. (Note that if you try to sell too many ideas per contact, because of the minuscule amount of time and attention you get from your audience, you will not convey a clear message. And more often than not, you will appear to be a jack-of-all-trades and a master of none. Singular, simple, clear, concise, and repetitive messages are the fundamentals of selling.)
5. Do not spend time and money marketing to your empire audience until you have a strong foundation of marketing to your fortress (unless you lack a fortress to market).

Once the fortress marketing engine is in place, you can layer on various empire campaigns. The most common mistake is that firms rarely do any marketing, and when they do, it is all empire marketing. This is a terrible use of resources when 80 to 90 percent of your growth every year will come from either client service growth or client referral.

By incorporating and utilizing the approach best suited to the services you offer and the marketing tools you use, you should:

- Improve your ability to plan because each strategy has nuances and market reactions you can anticipate.
- Be better able to respond to your marketplace with appropriate services.
- Be able to more consistently send messages that will motivate your clients and prospects to action.
- Significantly improve your odds for success when launching new services.
- Enhance client satisfaction and loyalty.
- Be able to accomplish all of the above more efficiently and at less cost than evolving without the use of this methodology.

> **⊙┱ Key Point**
>
> Once your fortress is protected, it is the right time for some well-planned, strategically initiated empire building.

We hope this discussion about fortress and empire has made it more clear how to best leverage your marketing resources. We hope this discussion also helps you take a fresh look at the services you offer and the synergy between them. Finally, we hope we drove home the point that you need to build a marketing engine to support your fortress before you spend much time and energy trying to expand your empire.

Passive Marketing Versus Active Marketing

Now that we have established who we are marketing to, and how to approach our marketing messaging, let us consider the three strategies of marketing. They are:

- Passive marketing to our clients and referral sources
- Passive marketing to targeted, segmented, or niche prospects
- Active marketing in addition to our passive marketing to all top clients through personal contact

The preceding three strategies create the foundation of a marketing approach that I call "the drip system." The purpose of this approach is to keep your firm in the minds of your clients and referral sources. To do this, you have to devise ways to stay in touch with your targeted audiences about once a month to once every six weeks. Do not expect a flood of responses from the use of this system. Expect the same result you would if water was dripping out of a faucet. In the beginning, the drip from the water has very little cumulative effect. But, after hours, days, months, and years, the accumulation of water becomes substantial and begins having a substantial impact. The same is true with this marketing approach. A constant drip of contact from your firm to your targeted audiences will build a greater awareness of the services you offer, a higher chance of referral from that same audience (in mind versus out of sight), and increase the likelihood that your audience will contact you to help assist them.

Now, let us discuss the distinction between the terms passive and active marketing as used in this document.

Passive Marketing

Passive marketing refers to the way we contact the targeted, segmented, or niche audience. For example, typical passive mediums include client letters, postcards, e-mails, and trade-specific advertising (i.e., an industry-specific magazine). I call this a passive strategy because owners and managers do not have to be involved in the day-to-day implementation of this approach. This strategy is really an administrative function once the various messages, media, and time frames are decided upon. It is the foundation for creating a firmwide marketing engine.

Active Marketing

On the other hand, active marketing efforts revolve around face-to-face contact and logically center on one-on-one interaction. This approach is considered active because all of those who have client account management and/or referral source relationship responsibilities will be asked to actively and proactively create, maintain, and report back on how their regularly scheduled personal visits and discussions are progressing. This strategy is far-and-away the most effective technique for attracting new business (both growth in "share of the wallet" [new projects] and new referrals). This is your marketing workhorse.

If active marketing is so effective, should all of your marketing efforts be focused on this approach? No, and the following are the reasons why:

- If everyone in your organization made personal visits with all of your clients, you would likely go broke due to nonbillable time.
- You want to be in mind throughout the year with your clients and referral sources, not just occasionally. Creating a marketing engine that runs all of the time pays dividends, especially when augmented by personal visits.
- Not all of your clients are worthy (i.e., return-on-investment worthy) of a personal visit. It does not make sense to tie up a $200 per hour person to spend a couple of free hours talking to a $300 per year client opportunity.
- If your CPAs were inclined to spend all of their time selling, they would have chosen a different career. You will get significant pushback if you do not create a defined contact plan with specific client assignments, and a monitoring system to support the follow-through process.

Active Versus Passive Contact Lists

If we are not going to talk with everyone, then who gets included in the active contact list? As with most businesses, there is a generalized 80/20 rule. Although these percentages may vary for your firm, the philosophy behind it will most likely apply. This rule states that about 20 percent of your clients generate about 80 percent of your total fees. For you, 15 percent of your clients may generate 70 percent of your fees, but the point is still the same. If you made personal visits to the 70 to 80 percent of your clients that generate 15 to 20 percent of your fees, your charge hours and profitability would tank, and the amount of business gained overall would be minimal. Therefore, my active marketing approach focuses on the few clients that make up the most business rather than the reverse. It is also important to note this information in the contact list. Finally, include your top referral sources in this contact mix as well.

Although I want to make it clear that an effective firmwide business development engine has to leverage both marketing mechanisms (both passive and active), the underlying principle that permeates all aspects of the plan is the objective for clients to keep your firm in mind. If you devote all of your resources to making personal contact, then you will not be able to cycle through all of your clients fast enough to accomplish this. Your objective is to educate your marketplace as to what you have to offer them all of the time.

Think of an automobile dealership. Such a business does not spend all of its advertising dollars to make a big splash in one or two months of newspaper ads. (By the way, the ads are part of the business's empire approach, but because a dealership is a retail business, the rules are different than for professional services.) Auto dealerships typically market throughout the year because they want to be in mind when someone in their marketplace wants to buy. For example, if you are very happy with your car, the likelihood of your looking at various automobile promotional ads is minimal. However, if your car was totaled one night while parked on the street, your interest in a replacement vehicle would skyrocket by the next morning. The point is that you want frequent exposure to your targeted audience because you never know when interest will peak regarding what you have to offer.

Finally, spending time selling services to clients and referral sources is stressful and will be avoided at all costs by many of our professionals. The only way to change this dynamic is to shift the event from one of selling, to one of living up to our mantra of "being our clients' most trusted adviser." The important nuance is that the client conversation is not about what the firm has to offer, but rather, what the client's organization needs to meet its future objectives. Professionals are attracted rather than repelled from participating in these conversations as soon as they become convinced that the objective is to better assist and serve their clients. Obviously, you can only dedicate this level of resource (your people's time) to those clients and referral sources with the greatest potential.

Assume you want to remain profitable, develop more business, maintain a strategy of being kept in mind, and you want your people to be comfortable and engaged. This means that you will reserve the active component of your marketing strategy on being regularly in front of the 15 to 20 percent of your clients that make up 70 to 80 percent of your revenues as well as your top referral sources. I define *regularly* as once a quarter (with the normal tax season conversations counting as the contact for that quarter). The passive marketing strategy is used to augment the active personal marketing efforts as well as support your in-mind objective with the remaining 70 to 80 percent of your clients.

Business Development Plan

It is time to move from a philosophical to a task focus. The first step is to build a business development foundation. That foundation has four steps.

Step 1. Create an up-to-date database.

Step 2. Classify clients.

Step 3. Develop an active marketing strategy.

Step 4. Develop a passive marketing strategy.

Each step is discussed below.

Step 1. Create an up-to-date database.

You need an easy way to regularly access all of your clients and referral sources' names and addresses. An important part of this process is to also identify those clients who should not be contacted and omit them from the list. Clients that should be omitted might include those with multiple entities. Although you might definitely want this client on your contact list, you probably will not want to send that person three or four pieces of the same marketing materials. Another example is to omit a young child of a client. You may prepare that child's simple tax return, but you likely would not want to send marketing materials to him or her. What remains should be a clean marketing list of clients and referral sources that can be mailed as a normal part of implementing the drip system marketing plan.

Cleaning up the database is usually a difficult and time-consuming process; do not be surprised if it takes several months of focused effort by someone in your firm. The owners and managers will complain because they will have to go through numerous lists multiple times.

> **⊶ Key Point**
>
> You want to get the database right so that the mailing and e-mailing task of making regular contact can be done by administration, without owner and manager approval each time.

An important nuance to build into this process is the understanding that owners and managers will want to omit various clients and referral sources from certain mailings and messages. After the master list is cleaned up (by ensuring the proper names, addresses, salutations, and e-mail, and by omitting duplication), management should fine-tune the list by addressing exceptions. This step is another explanation for why owners and managers will have to make multiple passes at the lists. An example of an exemption is an owner wanting to omit several of his or her banker or broker referral sources when the firm is marketing wealth management services. As you can see, with numerous services and client personalities, list management can be a complicated process; each marketing subject might literally call for the creation of a unique list. Logically, before this process can be finalized, the database has to be bounced against each of the marketing messages planned for the next 12 to 18 months. If you do not take this approach and get all the approvals in advance, the owners are apt to procrastinate on signing off prior to each planned contact to the point that the foundation for your drip system will crumble under the weight of inconsistency.

Step 2. Classify clients.

Once the master list is clean, go through it and classify clients. Firms commonly segment clients into classifications in order to target them. For simplicity, I have used some common classifications (*A, B, C,* and *D*) and the generic definitions that follow, as a starting point. Passive marketing applies to all categories of clients and referral sources.

Active marketing is targeted for all *A* clients and referral sources. If there is personal marketing bandwidth left over, start down the prioritized *B* client and referral list. Generally speaking, firms include all *A* and what I call *High B* clients and referral sources in the active marketing program, i.e., those *B* clients with the most potential.

Client definitions are the following:

A   An *A* client is often defined as one of 15 to 20 percent of the clients that make up 70 to 80 percent of the firm's revenues. If you sorted your clients by revenues for last year, you would quickly identify those clients that generated substantial fees for your firm. An *A* client is one that you are probably adequately serving, one that will continually have new projects for you to do, and one that generates sizable revenues for your firm.

B   A *B* client is one that you are right now most likely underserving, but who has an opportunity to generate sizable revenues for your firm. For example, you might have a business client for whom you only do tax returns. However, based on what you know of the business (i.e., they are $5 million in size or have a 100 employees), you could easily provide thousands more dollars in needed services.

C   A *C* client is a client that does not have much additional service opportunity other than what you already do, and the revenues generated are small. However, they are good clients, do not have complex situations, pay you on time, pay average or better fees, and are pleasant to work with. The best description of this group of clients is they are your typical individual tax-return-only clients. Do not confuse the *C* rating with school and assume they need to become *B* clients to make the grade. A firm can have all *C* clients and do very well.

D   A *D* client could seemingly fall into *any* of the classifications above. However, these clients present at least one of a number of possible problems. They most likely are unprofitable to the firm as a result of poor rates, realization, and utilization. They are hard to work with because they are abrasive, late payers, or never timely (so they always create scheduling problems); always want special accommodations; require services that are difficult to provide (e.g., the client who is the one governmental audit you perform, which is very inefficient work for you); or only pay your last bill as an incentive for you to start their next project. None of these issues alone automatically classifies someone as a *D* client. For example, you might have someone who always pays late, but is an acceptable client because you charge premium fees for his or her work. Or, someone may constantly negotiate fees, but nevertheless involves you in big projects that are profitable. Generally speaking, most firms know quickly who falls into their definition of the *D* category. At the end of the day, you do not want any *D* clients. This means that your objective is to either find a way to convert them into *C* clients or better, or introduce them to your fiercest competitor. In the latter instance, these clients will waste your competitor's resources instead of yours.

Once again, a CPA firm having only *C* clients is not a bad thing. In this situation, the firm's client base could be described as a cluster of small clients who pay timely and are fun to work with, but who have little potential to provide additional business. In this case, passive marketing may be all you need to do. But in order to grow the organization and replace the losses of natural attrition, your passive marketing approach needs to be in full gear all the time. On the other hand, some firms have moved to a more boutique style of firm in which they are very hands on with all of their clients, have a big share of each client's professional services wallet, and have a staff that is made up predominately of managers and owners. It may be that all such clients fit into an *A* or *B* classification. Therefore, by providing a great deal of frequent personal contact and support to each of a very few clients, active marketing alone should generate the necessary new business and referrals.

The fundamental three questions that you need to be able to answer are with facts, not conjecture:

1. Do your clients know what your firm can do to help them?
2. For your active marketing clients, do you know what is keeping your clients awake at night (i.e., the concerns and opportunities they are trying to address at this time)? By the way, an important part of this process is for you to uncover issues regardless of whether or not you are able to resolve them. For issues that you cannot address, give your clients referrals to professionals who can give assistance. It always surprises me how many firms expect professionals to refer business to them, but who do not reciprocate. Providing a referral for a needed service not only helps the client, it makes the client want to talk to you about all of their issues because they want the benefit of your network. Moreover, giving referrals stimulates future referrals back to you.
3. Do your clients know what your firm's total service capability is so that they are armed and ready to refer you to friends, associates, and family?

For *A* and *high B* clients, the answers to questions 1 and 2 above should be identified through regularly scheduled contact. Question 3 should get an affirmative answer from your client and referral sources as a result of your firm's passive marketing campaign.

Now, I want to take a moment to make a special point regarding question 2. You are in danger of losing *A* or *high B* clients if the owner or manager in charge of these accounts cannot at least articulate each client's priorities. Although you probably will not incur these losses overnight, you can bet that any unserviced priority needs will be supplied by someone. And with each passing day, as CPA firms continue to broaden their scope of services, a competitor of yours will likely be called in to help. If the partner or manager in charge of these accounts can at least articulate what your *A* and *B* clients' priorities are for the next 12 to 18 months, you have a much better chance of sustaining your relationships with these clients; without this knowledge, you are likely to be blindsided. If client priorities are identified, you will be able to either deliver the needed service yourself, or, if your firm does not provide the service, you will at least be able to refer the client to a friendly firm that will not compete with you for the services you do provide.

If a client is classified as a *D*, then the person in charge of that relationship needs to develop a strategy to convert them to a *C* client. That strategy could be as simple as the following:

- We will bill them at 95 percent of the standard rates this year and see whether they want to remain a client.
- We will transition this client to one of our senior staff to manage and bill because the client's needs are better suited to the senior's experience level and billing rate.

Alternatively, the strategy could be as drastic as the following:

> The owner needs to inform this client that the account must be paid current and kept
> that way or the client needs to find another accountant.

Regarding *D* clients, a common misperception is that they are at least covering your overhead. Something you need to understand is that as long as you have these marginal clients in your work queue, they give you a sense of security about workload and cash flow, but they will keep your people from servicing and spending more time with your more valuable clients. The argument is often made that a firm would rather have a client paying a 60-percent realization of fees rather than having one person sit idle. I think a better strategy is for the firm to:

- Pass *D* clients to managers and senior staff to convert to *C* clients or get rid of them.
- Pass *C* clients to managers and senior staff to manage and bill to free up owner and senior manager time.
- Send owners or managers out to visit *A* and *B* clients more frequently.

This approach allows your people to:

- Look for better ways to serve all of the clients. This is true because owners and managers typically do not consistently spend enough time with their *A* and *B* clients, and these same people usually totally ignore their *C* and *D* clients. By passing down the *C* and *D* clients, a *D* may automatically become a *C* client because you have the right level of experience (and therefore billing rate) working on those projects. In addition, you give your less experienced people a chance to grow through on-the-job training by managing and billing clients. If they mishandle such a relationship, the loss to the firm is minimal.
- Find new service opportunities. This occurs more frequently because managers and senior staff have the experience necessary to really provide value to the less complicated *low B* and *C* clients. Because those clients are theirs to manage, they are motivated to do so. Obviously, owners and managers will find more work by staying in touch with the firm's *A* and *B* clients. The rule is well known, "The more time you spend on site with a client, the more opportunities come your way."
- Maintain and enhance their loyalty. This one is simple. The more you help your clients, the greater their loyalty to you.

Accomplishing the above is not all that difficult, but usually requires a significant change in philosophy. For most firms, it means they have to "reverse the pyramid" in order to achieve this transition, which can be a difficult battle to win in many firms.

Step 3. Develop an active marketing strategy.

Now that you have spent some time working through, classifying, cleaning up, and fine-tuning the information in your database, it is time to put together your active marketing strategy. The first step is to determine the cutoff as to the number of clients and referral sources to be regularly contacted by your people. To simplify our discussion for the sake of this chapter, let's assume everyone that you classified as either an *A* or *B* client or referral source will fall into your active campaign. From this point, it is very straightforward. The results rest on consistent implementation. The active campaign is more about "being a turtle" than "being a rabbit." Too many firms try to make up for years of lost opportunity by setting contact expectations that are unrealistic. After a month or two of everyone violating the process, the initiative dies of embarrassment. To avoid this, start slow and build! As part of active marketing, consider tying compensation to the goal of making contacts. As discussed, start with paying for lead indicators (Did the person make the contact?), and then, over time, put more emphasis on lag indicators (new projects, new clients).

For each client placed in the active campaign, consider putting an action plan in place to provide clients with regular contact and a higher level of service. Developing a client plan worksheet will help you formalize your strategy as to how you plan to best serve them as well as to record the client's priorities uncovered during each scheduled visit. An important use of a standardized report is for your owner in charge of marketing (or the marketing committee) to review each owner's and manager's plans with them once a quarter as a kind of a mini-business development session. This ensures that the firm's resources are properly allocated to those clients that need them, that all top clients are receiving timely quality service, and that the firm is not exposed to a competitive threat by underserving these important clients. All you need is a simple contact calendar so that you can map out for each owner and manager when they are expected to make their personal visits. If you want to have accountability in this area, it must be clear who is assigned to make the contacts and by when.

A firm I work with put this together a point system tracker to stimulate marketing involvement by everyone in the firm. A point value system was devised for each marketing task listed on the worksheet, based on feedback from staff regarding their perception of the effort and difficulty required to complete the task. Because this is the first year of its rollout, the total points required by each group has been set low (with the understanding that the requirement would grow). Some people are reaching their marketing goals in a matter of months. Still, when changing the culture of the firm, you want to build it around success and positive reinforcement. As I have stated so many times thus far, a good SOP foundation, whether it pertains to marketing, or compensation needs to be developed by being a turtle, not a rabbit. The key is to put together a defined program, spread the tasks of marketing to everyone proportionally in a way that makes sense for his or her job, and develop and monitor a feedback system.

Obviously, these kinds of point value system worksheets are meant to serve as samples, which should be tailored to your firm. Even better, this kind of information should be part of an automated contact management system. Some firms use the contact management component within their time and billing systems; others use software tools like Salesforce. com. Nevertheless, the forms will certainly work for small firms and as an interim approach for larger firms until a better process is put in place. Remember, to make the active campaign work, someone (or a committee) needs to review progress with each person in the active plan on a consistent basis. That same person (or committee) should also discuss what the owners and managers are finding out during their visits to ensure that the appropriate information is being gathered. If the discussions are falling short of covering the intended subject matter, consider training, coaching, or counseling as logical choices to get everyone on the right track.

Step 4. Develop a passive marketing strategy.

Since you now have identified your *A* and *B* clients, and everyone has a personal schedule of contacts to make, it is time for the owner group or marketing team and committee to put together your passive marketing campaign. The first campaign should be aimed at your clients and referral sources. This campaign should optimally identify one mechanism or medium per month that will educate your client and referral base about a service you offer. If you cannot afford one contact per month, then minimally try to make eight contacts per year. To develop this business development campaign, you need to answer these questions:

- What medium do you want to use for each contact of your target audience (letter, postcard, seminar, newsletter)?
- What is the service and message you want to send?
- When do you want this message to launch or arrive? (Either date is fine, just be clear which it is.)
- What group is being targeted with this contact?
- What is the number of pieces?
- What is the cost of each contact?

Just like the active campaign above, this is not complicated. It is more about priority than anything else. When passive campaigns stall, it is usually because the owner group will not give the proper signoffs to administration to implement the program (or they want to sign off on each piece right before it goes out rather than signing off on the entire campaign and letting it run). So, to get started, simply put together a table outlining your plan and answering the questions above.

You want this table to cover a minimum of a 12-month period. Once you have defined and priced your foundation marketing effort, if you still have money left in your budget, you should consider developing one or more niche industry or service campaigns. These campaigns should involve a minimum of three to four contacts in fairly rapid succession (over three to four months or a contact about every three weeks). Because these niche campaigns are likely targeted to prospects and nonclients, you want to utilize a unique service that will catch the attention of the narrowly segmented audience you select. For example, you might want to offer a cost segregation study to your real estate clients. This campaign might start out with a letter that introduces the service and announces a seminar you will holding, followed by a couple of postcards highlighting the seminar date, concluding with a telemarketing followup asking prospects whether they would like to attend. All four contacts should be scheduled to occur over a three-month period to achieve maximum firm recognition.

Another idea might be a four- or five-piece campaign focused on litigation support. In this instance, maybe the first contact will be a postcard on litigation support, followed by a copy of an article you have written on how to provide quality services to litigating attorneys, then another postcard, and concluding with a letter asking your attorney prospects to visit your Web site and sign up for your litigation support e-newsletter. Remember, if the marketing campaigns are being sent as part of your fortress approach, they need to focus on educating your clients and referral sources as to services you offer (how you can help). If the campaigns are being sent as part of your empire approach, they need to center around demonstrating your unique expertise (and explaining why your expertise would be beneficial to them and why you are different from everyone else).

You also want to coordinate your marketing campaigns around client purchasing habits. For example, if you were marketing to a group of government agencies about providing the consulting support that their auditors can no longer provide, you would want to send your first piece about two months before that consulting is likely to be required.

The final step in outlining your plan is to craft the proper message for each piece above. Once this has been done and approved, the passive campaign turns into an administrative process whereby the creation, printing, and mailing are done based on the timetable outlined with little to no owner involvement until a new campaign is introduced.

Transition

Now that we have our business development plan in place and both the active and passive campaigns firing on all cylinders, it is time to address the important issue of transition. We start by defining this term and discussing the two sides of its meaning. The first variation I will term *servicing transition* while the other is *firm value transition*. Although the definitions are very similar, they are applicable for different reasons at different times. Each is discussed in the following sections.

Servicing Transition

As you probably guessed, servicing transition is the transition that is most important to business development. The definition I assign to this is simply "moving the client relationship from one professional to another for client service reasons." This transition is typically done for the following two reasons:

1. *Underservicing.* The book of business managed by the professional is getting too large for that individual to adequately service all of his or her clients.
2. *Resource matching.* The resources of the firm would be better utilized and maximized by replacing the professional who currently manages the client.

Each is discussed below, followed by a discussion on the benefits of servicing transition.

Underservicing

Regarding underservicing, there are many negative consequences that emerge when this condition exists, such as:

- Lost opportunity to provide additional services and increase client loyalty to the firm
- Lost opportunity to provide additional services to create additional profits for the firm
- An increased opportunity for a competitor to be invited to the table to provide needed services

Resource Matching

Resource matching is usually done if you have someone with specific skills and expertise who better suits the services the client is currently utilizing. For example, consider an audit owner originating the first engagement who is still responsible for maintaining the account relationship even though the client's only ongoing recurring engagement is the operational consulting done by a different group within the firm.

The Benefits of Servicing Transition

For reasons such as underserving and resource matching, clients need to be transitioned. As a result of available time and/or unique expertise, the newly assigned professional is able to:
- Provide the client a higher level of service.
- Uncover additional opportunities to serve these clients.
- Improve client retention, satisfaction, and loyalty.

All of these outcomes are fundamental to improving firm growth. For example, it is hard to grow the business if you are bringing in new clients at 12 percent, but losing them at a 15-percent rate. It is also hard to grow the firm with new clients alone. Growing the "share of the wallet" you enjoy with your current clients is essential to sustaining long-term consistent growth as well. The major roadblock to properly serving the firm's top clients is the availability of time. For example, one senior owner's B client, which is too low on his or her list to ever properly service, would likely be at the top of the priority list for a more junior owner. So, as part of a viable business development plan, firms have to constantly look at their categorized client list and make sure that all A and B clients are receiving excellent care. This means that, from time to time, transitions will be necessary to maximize your business development opportunities by either better serving the underserved or by matching the clients' needs with the best service provider, who can uncover and deliver client-needed services.

Firm Value Transition

Now let us introduce the second definition of firm value transition. This topic will be covered in more detail in the next chapter, but it is simply "moving or expanding the client relationship to maintain firm loyalty and retention." It comes in two forms—transition to a young partner or transition to an account team. Each is discussed below.

Transition to a Young Owner

The most obvious is to transition a client from a retiring owner to a younger owner so that the client maintains an ongoing relationship with the firm. If a major component determining firm value is gross fees (revenue), it becomes clear why it is so important to retain clients when owners retire. And because so many owners retire without transitioning their client relationships in an adequate and timely fashion, it is the transition that tends to hurt firm value and profitability the most.

Transition to an Account Team

The second variation of firm value transition was addressed at the beginning of this chapter. It commonly shows up as expanding the client relationship through the assignment of account teams. Obviously, unless you are a very large firm, you cannot afford to double the team assigned to each client, especially not with owner-level personnel. Although account teams can be a good strategy for *A* level clients any time or in any sized firm, it can also work well for both *A* and *B* clients if the current person managing this relationship is an owner who is likely to retire in the next five years.

Conclusion

In conclusion, I hope this chapter has stimulated some thinking as to how to improve your firm's marketing capability. The development of a marketing engine is an excellent example of SOP foundation that supports the superstars, but also spreads the business development load across the whole firm. This not only makes the firm stronger and more profitable, but is essential if you want the firm's value to be based on its operational capability rather than just on an individual or two. Below is list of issues that need to be addressed as you create your firm's business development strategy. This checklist includes reminders about common pitfalls encountered, steps you should consider taking, and issues that need clarity or consideration. By making sure you have contemplated and satisfactorily addressed each issue below, you will have taken a giant step forward in constructing a critical marketing SOP foundation for your firm.

1. Make sure the services you offer make sense for and have synergy with the market you serve.
2. If you are going to support island services, use them to create differentiation between you and your competitors as a way to attract new business. And do not set unrealistic expectations for these services since they are partially meant to open doors for your firm that otherwise might have remained closed.
3. For new services, create a business plan with time frames, specific hurdles, and revenue and profit expectations. Then allow those services a chance to meet or exceed those agreed-to objectives without constantly comparing their progress to existing traditional services. If you launched a new service that was not strategically initiated, shame on you. But if it was properly initiated, give it the time it needs to pull its own weight.
4. Invest your marketing dollars first on staying in mind with your clients and referrals sources. This is where and how the bulk of your business is generated ... not from knocking on doors.
5. Consider the fortress and empire strategies to make sure you are taking the right approach and utilizing the best messages to attract your target audience.

6. Clean up your client and referral source lists (database) so that you can turn the passive marketing campaign over to one of your administrators to implement so that it will continually occur, even during tax season.

7. Consider the timing of the specific messages used in your passive campaign so that they are attempting to stimulate awareness just prior to when the clients are most likely to take action or have a heightened interest.

8. Categorize your clients so that you can ensure that your resources are being properly allocated to build loyalty and deliver exceptional service to those most important to your firm's survival and prosperity.

9. Either upgrade your *D* clients to *C* clients, or run them off. These clients are a primary cause of many firm staffing shortages, as well as the biggest obstacle to better serving *A* and *B* clients and growing their businesses.

10. The passive drip system is meant to include everyone (all clients and referral sources). The active system is meant to identify and deliver personal service to those clients needing and wanting it most (namely, the firm's top clients).

11. Do not try to make the passive campaign perfect; just set it in motion. It is called a drip system because its impact is realized over time, not based on one or two pieces. As is often said in the literary world, "Don't get it right; get it written." In the marketing world, "Don't get it right (agonizing over every word); get it in the hands of your target audience."

12. Reverse your pyramid and change your culture so that every owner, and potentially every manager, understands that it is a primary requirement of the job to stay in front of his or her assigned clients on a regularly scheduled basis. In addition, the information gained from those meetings needs to be properly recorded with the understanding that a marketing debrief will take place to devise service strategies that will allow the firm to better support those clients.

13. Transition clients to those people who have adequate time or the right skills to properly service those clients. The hoarding of clients by owners for the sake of internal power or compensation privileges will, in the end, become a critical failure factor for the firm.

14. Ensure that if client meetings are taking place, at a minimum, your people are walking away with an understanding of and can list that client's priorities for the next 12 to 18 months.

15. Consider, in the beginning, focusing some compensation around lead indicators (what people are doing) rather than lag indicators (what results were obtained). If you want to change your people's habits, you have to reward the *change steps* they are taking along the way.

16. The job of the passive campaign is to primarily generate referrals (new clients) and secondarily grow "share of the wallet." The job of the active campaign is to primarily grow "share of the wallet" and secondarily to maximize referrals. However, since the active campaign also includes visiting key referral sources, those contacts are being made primarily to motivate new client referrals.

17. Make sure that your compensation system is built to pay your people for growing the services or scope of current services (share of the wallet) to your client base. This is an area to which everyone in your firm can contribute. Too much attention, in most systems, is placed on new client generation, which is more a function of size of the client base managed (because of the likelihood of referrals) than actual marketing effort.

18. Create a marketing culture in which regularly scheduled dialogue occurs about how to best service your top clients. Remember, cross-selling is not a choice that an owner makes if you follow a one-firm concept. Cross-selling strategies are devised by owners and managers working with the firm's marketing director, or by working with a marketing committee, or because of the time set aside by the sole proprietor to devise the proper approach. Regardless, excellent client service is a function of planning, not just happenstance.

Chapter 5

Succession Strategies: Passing the Torch

The objectives of this chapter are to:

- Introduce several examples of succession with lessons to learn from each example.
- Give an overview of merger and acquisitions of CPA firms, including what buyers and sellers are seeking.
- Give guidance on creating retirement plans in CPA firms.
- Outline the fundamentals in a good succession plan.

It is time to pull all of the information that we have covered thus far together and discuss various strategies for passing the torch. The best way I know to kick off this chapter is to tell a few stories. Following these stories are discussions on the mergers and acquisitions of CPA firms, retirement planning for CPA firms, and succession planning for CPA firms.

CPA Firm Succession Stories

Below are five succession stories. Each story is followed by lessons that can be drawn from the story.

Story 1. Two Senior Partners

Consider two senior owners who own 100 percent of the firm. They are a few years from retirement. The current market is paying 85 cents on the dollar for gross revenue of the firm, paid out at 25 percent a year over four years based on client retention. The firm is billing around $2 million. There are four managers that handle the day-to-day project management and client communication responsibility for 70 percent of the billings. None of these managers has an employment agreement that requires them to pay for clients that they might take with them if they leave. The managers have signed a loose, noncompete agreement that has had sketchy success in enforcement. The two senior owners plan to sell the firm and split the take evenly down the middle. At 85 cents on the dollar, that calculation amounts to $1.7 million, but the owners are expecting at least another $200,000 loss of clients that will either leave the firm or be fired by the purchasing firm.

The two owners have had high-level talks with a larger firm that is interested in buying them, but there has been no dialogue with the four managers as to what is going on. These talks have not occurred because the managers are assuming they will buy the firm from the retiring owners at one dollar for each dollar in revenue at the time of retirement, to be paid out over 10 years at 5-percent interest. Although this agreement would net the owners at least $500,000 more in purchase price, they lack confidence that the managers can run the business profitably enough to pay them off.

The time finally comes when the owners confront the managers. It is not a pretty sight. The managers are surprised and hurt that the owners have so little faith in them. This causes them to band together and threaten to leave or to be cut in as owners in the purchasing firm. Once the purchasing firm finds out that there is dissension in the ranks, they quickly pull out of the deal because, although part of the purpose of the purchase was to expand their revenue base, another important aspect was picking up four manager-level people who did not expect owner status any time soon.

The Lessons Learned From Story 1

I have personally addressed situations like this as well as many other variations of it. Sometimes the owners go ahead and sell to the managers because they have no other choice (to stop the imminent breakup), and sometimes the business is sold at a far deeper discount than expected to compensate the purchasing firm for having to address the unresolved problems. There are two lessons to learn from this story:

First, more time and resources should have been spent developing the managers to a level at which the owners would be comfortable selling the business to them. This would mean that the management of the firm should be transitioned to the incoming managers so the owners, while they are still active, can mentor, coach, and field test the new owners. As a way to ensure stability, the owners should incorporate standard operating procedure (SOP) foundation everywhere possible (from performance measurement and monitoring to marketing to quality control to training) so that status quo operations could easily continue long after they were retired. Using this approach, the owners would not only have time to develop their buyers, and put in processes that all sides will be comfortable with, but they would also stand to gain a great deal financially because internal purchasers (like the managers in this case) will almost always pay a much higher price for the firm than any arm's-length outside buyer. In this case, the owners could have easily invested a half a million dollars in leadership and in the development of internal processes, and still come out ahead in the deal.

The second lesson is that in small to medium-sized firms, ownership percentage and realized revenue from the sale of a firm are directly proportional only when harmony exists. So, you cannot pull off a deal like this without "sweetening" the pot for the remaining players. This sweetening could come in the form of negotiating owner status for the managers in the new firm, increased pay, and selling bonuses. Regardless, these actions will reduce the owners' final retirement take on the sale of the business. In addition, if the managers are not ready to be consumed by another firm, then the owners probably cannot sweeten the deal enough to make it palatable to all parties. In this case, if the managers had decided to leave and form their own firm, they would probably take between 40 and 60 percent of the business with them. Therefore, the owners, who owned 100 percent of the firm but did not have employment agreements requiring the managers to pay for any clients they would have taken, are looking at about 40 cents on the dollar for what is left (40 cents is based on the assumption that the managers would have taken about 50 percent of the clients and the purchasing firm would have run off 10 percent of the remaining clients). So, the owners go from a theoretical purchase of $2 million over 10 years at 5-percent interest to $800,000 over four years at no interest. Clearly, there is a lot of money at stake for this situation to have been taken so lightly and handled so covertly.

Story 2. A Sole Practitioner

Sara, a sole proprietor with one administrative employee, bills about $225,000 a year and is getting to close to retirement. She has signed a practice continuation agreement with a group of four other small firms that kicks in should she die or become disabled. They have agreed to buy her practice at 90 cents on the revenue dollar, payable over three years at 33.3 percent per year, based on each year's total billings for clients transitioned. Each of the five firms, whose owners are about the same age, signs a similar agreement with the others.

Unfortunately, Sara gets pneumonia and dies due to complications. The group is shocked because she had been the healthiest of them all. Nevertheless, no one immediately took over Sara's practice. Because the agreement addressed business that had been transitioned, no one had any accountability to try to salvage Sara's business, which was simply left upon her death. Here are the circumstances:

- No one had really done any due diligence on her practice.
- No one was under any obligation to buy the practice.
- The tax season was just starting.
- Two of the four remaining firms bound by the pact were at full capacity and really could not handle any more work

Immediately after tax season, the group got together and decided how to proceed. By the time the clients were contacted, over 45 percent of the business had already found other homes. Of the remaining 55 percent, one firm identified about $75,000 dollars of work that was of interest, and a second firm found about $25,000. The remaining approximately $24,000 was of no interest to any of the firms. Finally, the administrative employee was terminated.

In this situation, a practice continuation agreement was in place, but so loosely defined that it did not provide much value. The CPA owner's spouse received $90,000 over three years instead of the expected $200,000. Because the succession of this firm was too poorly defined, no one had the obligation to properly manage it, nor was anyone accountable to maintain a certain volume of the business. The result was that a significant part of Sara's firm's value was just thrown away.

The Lessons Learned From Story 2

A couple of lessons can be learned from this situation. First, know that whatever terms and conditions are not worked out in advance *will* bite you! Work them out now!! Make sure you have addressed at least the following questions:

- Who specifically is accountable to handle this transaction (which firm)?
- What conditions trigger the agreement (e.g., retirement, death, disability)?
- Upon notice of a triggering event (e.g., retirement, death, disability), how fast is the buyer required to take over the firm?
- What is the sale price of the firm?
- How is the sale price to be calculated?
- On what date does the calculation apply?
- To what criteria does the calculation apply (all clients at some specific date, retained clients)?
- Over what period will the payments be made and at what interest?
- What is the plan to keep the existing employees?
- What is the commitment to continue to service the existing clients?
- Will the current rate structure be honored? If not, will there be a gradual price escalation or just a new "take it or leave it" price?
- If the triggering event is retirement, what are the client transition plan requirements that will meet the obligations to complete this transition?
- If disability is covered, what level of disability is required?
- If disability is covered, including short-term disability, how will that be handled differently than a sale?
- If disability is covered, is there a noncompete in place in case the disabled CPA decides to start practicing in some limited form later on?
- If short-term disability has occurred, what is the cost for this short-term assistance (percentage of billings, price per hour, minimum flat fee per day)?
- If short-term disability is covered, does a noncompete clause apply that requires the assisting firm to pay for any business that transitions to them prior to a final triggering event?
- If short-term disability is covered, what experience level of person will be assigned to temporarily handle the clients of the firm?

- If short-term disability is covered, what quality controls will be put in place to ensure that minimum standards of work are maintained during this period?
- If insurance is acquired to support this transaction and death or total disability is involved, how does that affect the payment terms?

These are just some of the most universal issues to address. If you would like more information about practice continuation agreements, please refer to "Practice Continuation Agreements: A Practice Survival Kit," written by John A. Eads, CPA, and published by the AICPA. This book explains how you can preserve the value of your practice and features a sample action plan, a sample practice continuation agreement, and sample correspondence.

Second, in small firms, especially in closely knit communities, the news of someone's death or disability travels fast. Clients, especially the larger ones, tend to have multiple CPAs that have been courting them for years. Because these clients are loyal to their CPAs, they have never seriously considered changing firms. However, once the news of Sara's tragedy reaches them, these clients will shift to other firms in a heartbeat if the buyer does not move quickly to make contact. Sole proprietorships can easily lose half or more of their value in two to three months, so response time with accountability is a critical agreement point to work out.

Story 3. A Father-and-Son Firm

This is a story of a father and son owned firm, which grows to a multiowner firm. Daniel and his son, Barry, owned a CPA firm. Daniel was a technical guru and was great at client service while Barry loved the marketing and the public relations side of the business. Daniel was perfectly happy servicing his existing clients and keeping the firm small; Barry wanted to build an empire. As dad began to slow down, Barry took over and really put the firm on the map; growing it from about $1 million, to $3 million, and then up to $8 million over the next 10 years. During this growth period, given that Barry was not a great technician, he knew he had to find and convince talented CPAs to join him, and he did this well. Barry kept marketing, the new owners started marketing, and the firm kept growing. Nevertheless, it became increasingly more difficult for Barry to continue to add additional owners by the time the firm had grown to $8 million in revenues because there was not much stock left to attract them, given Barry's desire to maintain absolute control of the firm. During this high-growth period, Barry turned over day-to-day management to others. But he never let go of the decision-making process and he continued to want to sign off on just about every decision.

This firm, from the beginning, was founded on the superstar model and virtually nothing was formalized, which allowed Barry to maintain maximum flexibility in every situation. By the end of the 10 years, this "free-wheeling" model was starting to cause problems for all the other owners, including their comfort about their future. The other owners approached Barry about instituting a variety of systems, including a retirement plan; selling more of the ownership to draw additional owners; and creating more formalized processes and procedures. Barry was not pleased by this challenge to his authority and immediately started looking for exit strategies.

The Lessons Learned From Story 3

There is one central point that comes to mind about this situation. Because this firm had decision-making authority in place, it was positioned to grow and prosper, a good thing. But as we always find out in business, what works wonderfully today may not work at all tomorrow. Because this firm's decision-making authority was based on controlling interest, the success of this entity was directly proportional to the skills and vision of that one entrepreneur. In this case, the firm had started to outgrow Barry's ability to lead it. He wanted to keep his arms around and his hands in everything, which started to limit the firm's growth, and the talent of the people it could attract. In the corporate world, this is the time when the entrepreneurial owner would be moved to the board of directors so he could continue to provide advice and counsel, and hierarchical decision-making authority would be put in place so that an operator model could be introduced to make the day-to-day management calls. Operators leverage people through systems; superstars leverage systems through people.

In this case, Barry was unwilling to step aside because he rejected the realization that his management of the business had become its biggest limitation. However, he was perceptive enough to realize that he no longer managed the clients, could no longer control the owners, and that his kingdom was about to unravel. He quickly sought out a firm to buy him out. This is one of those rare instances in which the transaction worked in the owner's favor … but not for the reasons he thought. Barry wanted to cash out, the marketplace was still paying a bounty to majority owners to sell their firms, and the other owners were willing to go along because they saw his removal as important to their future success. They could have easily split off, taken their clients, and started a new organization, which would have left Barry with far less than he got. Nevertheless, to them, swapping a dictator for a working decision-making structure seemed like a reasonable trade, so Barry got a chunk of money for his share of the business. Today, he runs a small shop and is still a very talented CPA. The sad part of the story is Barry would have been wiser to recognize his limitations and work out a deal with the other owners, rather than selling out as soon as he could. Had he done so, instead of owning the majority of an $8 million firm, today he would own a smaller portion of a much larger firm. His exit strategy today would be worth many times what he was paid years ago. Moreover, in every year since then, the other owners would have been happy to pay him much more than he has been making to continue to do public relations for the firm, the work he loves and does best.

There are moments in anyone's personal evolution when he or she has to realize that in order to get more it is necessary to give up more. The harder one tries to hold on and keep things the same, the more resistance one will encounter, the more restricted one's options become, and the more backlash force one is building. Had Barry given up trying to micromanage the details and focus his energy on the strategy and direction of the firm, he could have maintained the control he needed and given his owners enough room to build the operating foundations they felt were necessary. Also, one of Barry's driving criteria was to maximize his personal income. Once again, had he been willing to give up more of the business so that it could continue to grow, he would have owned a smaller piece of the pie, which is now a much bigger pie. For example, what's better? Owning 50 percent of an $8-million firm or 25 percent of a $25-million firm?

Story 4. Four Owners—Two Seniors and Two New

The CPA firm Cameron and Aven (C&A) has gross revenue of about $3 million. Anne Cameron is a strong business developer and Lee Aven is the firm's technical guru. Anne and Lee have admitted two other owners over the past eight years, both of them being predominantly technical.

Anne, believing that the firm's growth has reached a plateau, is rewriting the new owner requirements to focus more on new business development skills. Because Anne has the largest book of business in the firm and a controlling interest, she believes the technical owners are really a lower class of owner because, she says, "If you can't generate new business, you do not have much value to the firm." Her attitude is starting to cause conflicts between her and the other owners.

The Lessons Learned From Story 4

There are several key issues to discuss here. First, Anne is such a good business developer that her skill has actually hurt the firm because she has never committed to developing a marketing engine (SOP foundation). If business needed to be developed, she went out and did it. However, last year, with the firm at $3 million in size, Anne had a large client book to personally service and was only able to develop a little more business in excess of what was naturally lost through attrition.

Besides the need to have a firmwide marketing engine that is constantly operating, Anne needs to put emphasis on the requirement for all owners to work their client base. Instead of the compensation system focusing on new business, Anne needs to concentrate the growth of the services within the client base managed by each owner. By doing this, coupled with the integration of the newly implemented marketing engine, the majority of growth will come from expanded services from existing relationships as well as some expansion of new clients emerging through referrals.

Anne redefines the new compensation system into two equal status classifications, namely, technical owner and development owner. Each owner, regardless of classification, has the following:
- A client management responsibility for their assigned clients (loyalty and satisfaction)
- A project management requirement (total billings for their clients)
- A personal billings requirement (based on their own charge hours)
- A management responsibility (to develop their direct reports and be held accountable for them in meeting their budgeted targets)
- A firm profitability goal
- A business development goal

The technical owners, even though they have slightly higher personal billings requirements, have specific and strong client base growth goals (achieving additional revenues from existing clients managed). The business development owners have slightly lower personal billings goals and the same client base growth goals, but the added requirement to maintain visibility in specific networking organizations, charitable events, and board functions. Anne realized that everyone has to be responsible to manage and grow the clients they serve, but not everyone needs to represent the firm in "meet-and-greet" activities.

The strongest change in belief that Anne had to adopt to move her firm forward was the understanding that technical owners could not be allowed to hide behind the single service in which they specialize. Technical owners had to be responsible for selling their clients the whole array of products and services C&A offered. And if they could not do this, those owners needed to be demoted back to manager. Once Anne experienced an epiphany about all this, and explained her new position to the other owners, there was little resistance; most of the resistance had always been about developing new clients, not working existing relationships.

Anne also realized that new business was more a function of referral than of personal effort. She analyzed the firm's growth over the past five years and found that 92 percent of the growth came from providing additional services to existing clients or referred clients. This clarified that she was not working magic by bringing in new business as much as she was good at working a system. So, the best approach was to implement her system firm-wide. Finally, Anne recognized that hoarding her client book was also hurting the firm, so she delegated all of her C clients to various managers in the firm.

The rift between Anne and her more technical owners—caused by her attitude—was starting to cause cracks in the firm's armor. She had several heart-to-heart talks with a couple of her owners as well as other chief executive officer and managing partners (CEO/MPs) she respected. Anne realized that staying on the current course would probably split up the firm, which would hurt everyone, including herself. She understood that without quality technical owners managing the complex projects of the firm, client satisfaction and loyalty would fade away. She also recognized that her strength in business development had created a weakness in the way marketing was conducted throughout the firm. She figured out that she had been doing what so many owners do—she overvalued her contribution and undervalued that of others.

What is interesting about this story is that the smaller the firm, the more emphasis is placed on finding business developer owners. The larger the firm, the more emphasis is placed on finding very technical project management owners. Small firms look to people to spontaneously and entrepreneurially make a difference, while large firms have to look to firmwide adoption of process to make that difference. Both can work, but the latter is significantly more successful at supporting the succession process because of the interchangeability of people.

Story 5. Seven Owners

Winter, Winter, and Summer (WWS) is a $9 million firm that was founded by Jeb Winter. He had built a $3 million practice years ago. Ten years ago, when his firm reached $1 million in size, he decided to merge with his brother Gerald. Two years later, Don Summer merged his $1 million practice with that of the brothers. Since then, the three owners have grown the firm to include seven owners by adding two more $500,000 firms and the rest through organic growth.

Jeb is 62, Gerald is 60, Don is 59, two other owners are in their early fifties, and the final two owners are in their late forties. Each of these merged firms was built around the superstar model. In order to make it attractive for other firms to merge, Jeb and Gerald created an organization based on one vote for each owner. Nevertheless, the salaries for Jeb, Gerald, and Don are twice the average of the other four owners, with Jeb making the most and Don coming in a close second. Although Jeb is the CEO/MP, his leadership approach is very democratic. Don, on the other hand, is constantly intimidating everyone to follow his strategies. The big three (Jeb, Gerald, and Don) control about 70 percent of the firm's business with Jeb controlling about $3.6 million, Gerald managing about $550,000 (down from a million), and Don running about $2.25 million.

Both Jeb and Don have come to the conclusion that their "one person, one vote" operating model is not working well because it gives an owner with a couple hundred thousand dollars in book managed the same vote as either of them, who each has more than five times that volume. For years, Jeb and Don agreed on all issues. Now, however, Don has really been growing his book of business (which has more than doubled since he joined), and he is more demanding every month. A recent trend is for Don to push the owners into adopting his strategies by threatening to take his clients and leave. Thus far, the other owners have quickly gone along with Don in order to retain his $2.25 million practice. Even Jeb has put up with this because he is starting to worry about the risk of his retirement benefit if Don leaves (which would put almost $5.85 million in client volume at risk; Jeb's $3.6 million that has to be transitioned; and Don's $2.25 million that he would take with him). Gerald does not do much any more except during tax season because he has become very comfortable financially, especially given the amount of work he has done to earn it. Right now, only the two youngest owners have a smaller book of business than Gerald.

Because Jeb and Don only have one vote, they hoard their clients to ensure that they maintain the powerbase to get their way when they want it.

The Lessons Learned From Story 5

Rather than operate by strategy, the firm operates as a bunch of individuals sharing overhead. Because the superstar model is in full swing in this firm, conflict has been brewing between several owners that is starting to fracture the firm. Greed is the only thing holding them together. Jeb knows that the firm would be better off in the long term if Don was forced out, but Jeb also recognizes that, in the short term, his retirement payout will remain safe if Don is given free rein, which means the firm will be run profitably, and probably tyrannically. Don stays because he knows he will be able to do whatever he wants once Jeb retires, which will definitely mean that he takes home a lot more money. Gerald does not protest much because he is earning almost everything he bills, even though he believes he has earned this privilege. Gerald is a little concerned, however, because he has always felt safe with his brother in command, and that could change dramatically when his brother leaves. The four younger owners anticipate a horrible experience in the near future, but also figure that enduring the short-term stress and chaos of the next five or six years will be repaid by the end result: The big three owners will be retired and they will be in charge of a $9-million-and-growing firm.

So, reflecting on all that we have covered thus far, here is what needs to happen for this firm to flourish and for the owner group to remain together over the next 10 years.

First, Jeb needs to pull the owners together and develop a strategy for the firm, with succession being a top priority. The succession plan needs to focus on the transition of the client relationships to the younger owners and managers. This may require redefining the roles of various positions within the firm. It also may require them to reverse the pyramid so that the younger owners and managers have ample time to manage the new client relationships assigned. Jeb needs to be turning over clients at a rate of about $1 million in volume per year, with his biggest clients being first on the list, in order for him to be ready to retire around 65. Don should begin putting his transition plan into effect too, but fortunately, he can proceed at a pace of only about $500,000 a year.

Agreements must be reached immediately that will freeze the retirement calculations and terms of both Jeb and Don, in order to make each of them willing to transfer client relationships. In order to justify the risk that Jeb and Don will be taking in the transition of clients, the remaining owners must enter an agreement to pay a large premium for any clients they take with them if they leave. As part of this process, the firm must set mandatory retirement dates, including clearly identified options for ongoing relationships between retirees and the firms, and all other retirement benefits. Without these measures in place, Jeb and Don will pay only lip service to any effort to transition their client relationships, because they know that giving up these relationships will weaken their positions. On the other hand, Jeb and Don will be motivated to comply with the firm's plans if they know that their retirement benefits are appropriate, their salaries are not in jeopardy, and that there are financial protections in place for the transitions they are about to make. In return for all this, they need to agree that if either of them fails to act in accordance with their transition plan, the annual fees of any clients lost within 18 months after their retirement will automatically be deducted from their agreed-to payout.

Although WWS has an owner agreement that identifies the details of the retirement payout, it has not been discussed in years. When Jeb, Gerald, and Don set this up originally, the situation was different. Neither Jeb nor Don have wanted to change the payout formula because it seemed to work for all the other owners, however, they have always assumed they would negotiate a special payout for themselves when their time came (another reason they have hoarded clients). This is a common position for senior owners to take (and if they do not, it is probably because the payout is so skewed in their favor that as soon as they retire, the rest of the owners will change it for everyone else.). So, do not become lulled into complacency by your legal agreements, and make sure you are proactively addressing the reality of the issues.

Second, decision-making authority needs to be implemented within the firm, creating a separation between board functions and CEO/MP functions. The firm needs to set strategy and a budget and then allow the CEO/MP the room to implement. As a result of the approaching retirements of Jeb, Gerald, and Don, the new CEO/MP should be chosen from among the remaining owners. This will give the big three a chance to coach and mentor that person and gain confidence that the firm is in good hands. Additionally, the departing owners need to stay out of management and focus their attention as board members on creating a policy and procedure framework that will likely endure long after they leave.

Third, if Don does not fall in line with these changes (the transition of clients to younger CEO/MPs, setting the retirement amounts now), then he needs to be forced out of the firm. And even if he does seem to go along, the next time he threatens to leave, let him go. You cannot develop a successful firm succession strategy by constantly putting an individual's short-term preferences ahead of the long-term profitability and stability requirements of the firm. As long as Don chooses to be a boat anchor on every issue in order to impose his personal choice, the firm will suffer. Assuming Don maintains his current strategy of intimidation, the firm's long-term future is in doubt, and will continue to be a firm of individuals and in all probability will split into factions later anyway.

Fourth, the compensation plan needs to be tied to strategy, with the CEO/MP having the ability to shift clients around as needed to ensure that (1) no one is building their own personal empire and (2) the clients are being properly served. Although the book of business managed should remain some part of the formula, it should not be the main driver or everyone will continue to hoard business and underserve clients for the sake of internal power. Gerald's pay needs to be brought into line with his performance. If the group decides that Gerald should receive a special stipend because he founded the firm, then so be it. But his performance needs to dictate his pay from that point forward.

Fifth, the firm should put major pressure on the owners and managers to maintain regular visibility for those clients for whom they have relationship responsibility. All *A* and *B* clients should be assigned to firm members with a specific quarterly contact schedule. Monthly marketing committee meetings need to revolve around discussing the findings of those conversations and developing appropriate strategies to better serve those clients. *A* and *B* clients that only subscribe to one service (like tax) need to be targeted for other services to enhance their loyalty. If a CPA will only promote one type of service to his or her clients (like the one he or she specializes in), that person needs to be removed from client relationship management. All of these marketing processes need to be tied into the compensation system by using both lead and lag measures.

The steps used to address this situation have been drawn from each of the preceding chapters in this book. A solution that will suit Jeb, Don, and Gerald rests on the accomplishment and integration of all of these steps, not just one or two of them. In some variations of this situation, I have seen the owners in Don's position resign or be fired. In some cases, the group has decided to make the effort of putting the necessary foundation processes in place to maximize the chance of everyone staying together.

Merger And Acquisition Plans

Now we have covered a variety of situations that concern firm value. Next is a general review of the topic and the quality of leadership and organizational processes within the firm that will drive additional premiums or discounts.

As you either know or would guess, typical deals found in the marketplace for buying and selling or merging practices vary widely and almost without limit, based on the unique circumstances of the firms involved. But for the sake of this book, I want to at least cover some of the more common alternatives that I have either been involved with or heard about. The following section will discuss typical deals made to acquire CPA firms, typical deals made to merge CPA firms, what the seller looks for, and how candidates are identified.

Typical Acquisitions of CPA Firms

This section will cover typical multipliers, what purchasers look for, deal structures, and networks.

Acquisition Multipliers

Most acquisition stories have a multiplier of revenue in common. Over the past 25 years, I have observed multipliers anything from 50 percent (.5) or less to about 225 percent (2.25). A multiplier of 1 or 100 percent is the most often given as an example. However, in today's marketplace, the multiplier of 1 pertaining to all firm revenue is difficult to obtain in an arm's-length transaction. Nevertheless, it (or something else) is still regularly used for internal purchases, a "rule-of-thumb" value considered when one owner is selling his or her partial share of the business to the existing and remaining owners.

Acquisition Purchasers

In the past, there have been several times in our history when various firms would go on a buying frenzy, acquiring as many firms that met their criteria as they could. This activity temporarily created a supply and demand anomaly that drove up market prices, especially when the criteria for acquisition were loosely defined. We saw this phenomenon when firms such as American Express's Tax and Business Services, H&R Block, and Century Services Group were extremely active. Today, the deal action in the marketplace is not from big consolidators, but rather from local and regional firms looking to expand geographically, or in terms of services, industries, or volume.

> **O─¬ Key Point**
>
> For the most part, the firms in the market today are not willing to buy just anyone. On the contrary, they are looking for firms that will add synergistic value to their current offerings and strategy at minimal reorganizational costs.

This more constrained and conservative approach to acquisition and merger is the result of years of experience in this area. Lead firms (a lead firm being one which is either acquiring another firm or one into which the merged firm will be folded) have found that when diverse cultures collide, the result is often a terrible explosion with casualties on all sides. Firms have discovered that owner competencies, roles, and responsibilities can be extremely different from one firm to the next. Unfortunately, the widely embraced idea that all owners can easily be reshaped is about as sensible as believing that one can herd cats. The philosophy that two firms will be far better off by uniting their superstars has over and over yielded friction and annulment as power struggles fragment the firm. The misguided belief that any client can be converted to a good client has led to the purchase followed by the fairly immediate firing or loss of clients who raised issues of price sensitivity, profitability, and/or negligible opportunity for service expansion. The presumption that two well-run firms with strong process and methodology will seamlessly combine together has too often led to a loss in accountability; organizational chaos; and controversy over hierarchy, procedure, and policy. All of this has generated the recognition and observance of a critical success factor in the merger and acquisition process. Once the lead firm has found a synergistic target firm (those firms of interest to the lead firms) with seemingly compatible cultures, comparable personnel expectations, and a fair price, any transaction that takes place will come with the following caveat from the lead firm:

> Although we will listen to your ideas, and we are willing to consider your suggestions, there can only be one firm in charge. By agreeing to join us, you need to be clear that everyone in your organization will be forced to conform to our way of operating the firm.

Without clear communication on this important point, the entire organization becomes confused by the politics and power struggles that begin to rip the fabric of the institution. It is this reorganizational cost that has been the most damaging to the firms that have sustained it. The most frequent response from CEO/MPs on this topic is, "It wasn't the money we spent that was so detrimental. What was most destructive was the internal chaos, the loss in organizational direction, and the time and pain required to unravel the parts of the deal that did not work." The best way to minimize reorganization cost is make it clear which firm's infrastructure will drive the new organization forward from the date of execution.

Acquisition Structures

This merger and acquisition experience has also led to a much more complex and comprehensive investigation process pertaining to the characteristics discussed above. Let's take a simple example regarding client makeup alone. Years ago, a buying firm might have offered the seller a simple deal of 80 cents on the dollar based on gross revenue. Today, you might hear someone express a willingness to pay that amount, but with the caveats that:

1. The price is a rough prediction of a weighted average paying different values for different segments of business (and therefore, an exact average cannot be determined until a formal client analysis has been done).
2. The clients would transition to and stay with the new firm.

So, a $2-million firm buying a $300,000 local sole proprietor might break down the transaction as follows:

	Revenues	Value Given	Extension	Weighted Average
Individual tax practice	$120,000	50%	$ 60,000	20.0%
Corporate tax practice	$100,000	110%	110,000	36.7%
Bookkeeping work	$ 30,000	75%	15,000	7.5%
Reviews/Assurance work	$ 50,000	100%	50,000	16.7%
Total price proposed			$235,000	80.9%

Then, assuming this approach is acceptable, rather than guarantee that amount or pay it up front, the payments would in all probability be made over multiple years. Frequently, this is done over a three-year period at a rate of a third per year, or over four years at 25 percent per year. Given the standard modus operandi that buyers only pay for those clients retained, these payout arrangements might be augmented:

- By being capped for each client based on their prior year's fees at date of acquisition,
- By being capped at a specific total for the entire client base regardless of fees charged, or
- To reflect a premium in the purchase by applying the weighted average percentage to all fees charged to those clients, including new fees, during that payoff period.

The point is that in yesterday's market, you might have commonly heard of a multiple of 1.25 or 1.50. Today, that multiple is more likely to be .75. And this is assuming your client mix is what the lead firm is looking for and your organization can easily be assimilated into theirs. If not, the offer is almost certainly going to be little-to-nothing because the soft costs are too high to make nonstrategic acquisitions.

Acquisition Networks

Another marketplace mechanism, which is often a precursor to acquisition, is for small firms to band together through strategic alliances, networks of firms, and overhead and office-sharing arrangements. Because it has become increasingly more difficult for sole proprietors and small firms to handle the vast array of work their clients are demanding, more and more small firms are coming together to assist each other. Although these arrangements run the gamut from just sharing specific overhead while keeping the businesses totally separate to combining the businesses but splitting profits on an eat-what-you-kill basis, the arrangements are providing these small firms with advantages. They include access to additional staff when needed, reductions in operating costs, quick access to peers to exchange ideas, and groups to sell their clients to when the time comes. I not only believe that this option will continue to build momentum on its own, but it will exponentially explode when for-profit groups and CPA societies put together localized networks seeded with agreements, talent-sharing policies, billing procedures, practice continuation agreements, and succession plans. Note, however, that these networks will flourish only when they will have built quality SOP foundations for these firms to operate within and leverage.

Typical Mergers of CPA Firms

This section will cover the goals of sellers and purchasers, deal structures, and a hybrid strategy.

Merger Sellers and Purchasers

The primary driver for most of the merger transactions is to create an exit strategy for one or more of the senior owners of the target firm. Small firms are joining larger ones to ensure that their clients can continue to receive quality services while the owners are simultaneously being assured that their retirement benefits are financially secure. As you can guess, the snag in these deals usually concerns answers to the following questions:

1. How long do the senior owners have to work for the merged firm?
2. What is the owners' base salary, and how will their annual compensation be derived?

3. What guarantees exist? Are there any? Is there a one- or two-year guaranteed salary or a minimum retirement benefit?

4. Most important, how is the retirement benefit calculated, what will it likely be, and when are the owners eligible to start drawing it?

Besides providing an exit strategy for owners, there are other common reasons to enter into mergers and acquisitions. Most often, the lead firm has one or more of the following motives:

- Wants access to a well-run needed niche specialty service
- Wants access to a well-run needed industry-specific group of services
- Needs to prop up a marginally profitable small office in a specific area
- Desires a quick buildup of talented staff
- Decides to move into a new geographic area and believes acceptance will be highest by the local community if a local office is brought into the fold
- Has built an administrative and organizational infrastructure that is capable of managing far more business at negligible additional costs, and therefore is looking for additional volume

Obviously, the reasons for one firm to want to acquire or merge with another are all over the board, but between the bullet points above and the need for an exit strategy, you will likely capture more than 90 percent of the situations.

Merger Structures

Currently, the merger deals being made are minimal-to-no cash. They are more of a pooling of assets more than anything else. Although the target firm might get to keep its cash in the bank (partially to pay the payables), typically the receivables, work in process (WIP), and whatever fixed assets are considered valuable to the new firm form the basis of the new owner's capital accounts. If those amounts fall short of the firm's minimums, then a negotiated time frame will be set for the new owners to bring their balances up to expectations.

Once the target firms have been identified in a merger, the deals typically develop around two variables. The first is gross revenues, and the second is profitability. Logically, both of these variables will have either a positive or negative effect on the adjustments that will be proposed. If the profit margin on revenue billed is lower in the lead firm than in the target firm, then a positive adjustment is reasonable. If the reverse is true, then, logically, the reverse would apply to the adjustment. Some lead firms will ignore lower profit margins (assuming they are not substantially lower) because they assume the numbers will work themselves out once the target firm becomes assimilated into the lead firm's operating systems and processes.

Adjustments that are ordinarily considered to offset the various identified inequities, either pro or con, would be:

- *Minimum salary guarantees.*
- *Fixing the retirement formulas.* For owners who will be retiring soon, the lead firm might establish a minimum annual salary as well as freeze the retirement amount so that these owners can focus their time on transitioning their clients.

- *Adjustment to the variables.* A number of retirement systems have both a years-of-service component and an age component, which affect the retirement calculation. Most firms will tinker, either making positive or negative adjustments, to these variables to reflect the exceptional or marginal characteristics of the target firm. For example, adding years of service, or years to age, or years to both are examples of trying to reflect a premium value for the unique niche or profitability of the target firm when being incorporated into a fixed retirement system.

- *Revenue adjustments.* A number of mergers will freeze the gross income of the firm at the time of merger while others will consider changes to revenue for some period of time after the merger for ownership/benefit allocation purposes. For example, a firm might make negative adjustments against owners for key clients lost during transition if those clients were an impetus to the deal. Or, to satisfy a different situation, that same firm might allow the allocated revenue numbers to upwardly adjust and be credited to the target firm's owners to reflect new services sold during a window of time.

- *Ownership percentages.* A number of firms ascribe ownership percentages (ownership interest or shares in the firm) directly proportional to the comparable revenue/profitability of the two firms while others might assign equal units to all owners. Depending on which is used, different adjustments might be made. For instance, for a marginally profitable firm, the lead firm might discount the equity allocated to the target firm's owners in comparison to what the direct calculation would have dictated. Or, if this same firm was merging with an organization that only had equal unit owners, the lead firm might penalize the target firm owners through salary, years of service or age adjustments to the retirement formula.

Regardless of the adjustments made at the time of merger, most of these arrangements, except for those affecting retirement, will quickly default to treating all owners the same. For example, most guarantees, if given, are for a year, occasionally two, but few are for more than that. After that protected period, owners will have to earn their money based on whatever performance system is in place. In years past, some firms made the terrible mistake of cutting special compensation long-term contracts not only with each merged firm, but with different owners within that firm. This backfired big-time because rather than having a united owner group working to achieve the firm's strategy, the lead firms ended up with multiple owner groups managing their own disconnected compensation strategy. Silos appeared everywhere with the owners' personal interests in direct conflict with firm interests. Until these owners had their contracts renegotiated, were paid off, or were retired, the lead firm was trapped within its own expansion success. Firms learned very painfully that adjustments to compensation or retirement had to be made within one existing framework or its theoretical step forward through merger would actually become a couple steps backward.

As an added strategy to avoid dissatisfaction, a number of firms will offer a "no-fault-out" agreement as part of their merger package. This allows a new owner a window of time (often no more than a year) to determine whether he or she can operate within the lead firm's organization. If the owner cannot, he or she has the right to leave, taking his or her clients, assuming the identified financial issues have been resolved. (This is commonly a process of adjusting the leaving owner's total payments during this trial period to be commensurate with some percentage of the money he or she directly generated during this time.)

Merger Hybrid Strategy

Finally, there is a hybrid merger and acquisition strategy that you are likely to encounter more and more frequently. Rather than buying or merging with an entire organization, firms are soliciting niche, industry, or specialized teams of people to join them. For instance, if a firm needs additional support for one of its niches, or is interested in building a new service or industry specialization, it might go out and find a small team within a competitive firm and "make an offer they can't refuse." Although these firms might pay a nice bounty to their new employees for a niche-specific group of clients to transition with them, many are more interested in acquiring the expertise and are happy to pay their new employees to rebuild the niche from scratch. Who would have thought that a group of CPAs with no clients but a strong specialty expertise would be considered a good merger target? Logically, most firms have not put anything in place to address this possibility because the traditional thinking is that owner groups merge as a whole. So, buckle up and get ready as the stage is set for some very interesting deals in the decade to come.

What Sellers Look for

If you have been wondering whether some of our earlier discussions have been more about the best practices of running a CPA firm rather than succession issues, here are some litmus tests to think about. First, exclude the instance of a firm that is selling its practice for cash up front, because its key criterion is simply to find a buyer foolish enough to make an offer (unless the firm is going for a fire sale price of pennies on the dollar). Therefore, we are basing this conversation on the assumption that transactions of this type are paid out over time. With this in mind, if a sole proprietor decides to create a practice continuation agreement, or any sized firm decides to consider selling or merging with another firm, certain situations and circumstances are likely to affect the value.

First, consider some of the previous information drawn from the Succession Survey regarding practice continuation agreements. Owners that were selling were concerned about:

- Continued client service
- Client responsiveness
- Quality of service
- Competence of the new owner (experience of the new owner)
- Employee retention and ongoing employment

Although price and terms are deal breakers, there is also substantial concern about the operating practices, values, and competencies of the new firm that will take over the client and employee relationships.

Think of it this way: When CPAs enter into transactions to buy that are (1) not solely about the money or (2) triggered due to the seller's death or unexpected heath impairment or disability, then it makes sense that money is even less of a driver when owners are considering merger and having a long-term relationship with this firm. For example, if owners anticipate that future retirement benefits earned after years of service will be the source of most of the value of the merger, then other criteria take center stage. Unsurprisingly, "confidence in the lead firm's ability to manage," is a decisive, if seldom talked about, factor. Such confidence includes many variables that range from reputation, to perceived values and ethics, to trust. Simply put, target firms will rarely allow a takeover by lead firms that demonstrate poor management practices, have weak leadership, or operate without clear decision-making authority. Why? Because the target firms are not interested in being bought or merged with firms just like themselves (or as they see themselves becoming as soon as the controlling owners retire). If they were, the senior owners would be happy to sell to the junior owners. The target firms are looking for a lead firm that, unlike them, has developed the necessary leadership, authority, systems, processes, and training to endure over a long period of time. Target firms are looking for sell or merge candidates that have proven their stability though changes in leadership, or have a young leadership group in place, meaning that succession will not be an issue during the soon-to-retire senior owners' retirement payment period. The irony is that target firms place a very high value on decision-making authority and SOP foundation in the lead firm, the very things that they refused to implement themselves.

So, what factors, besides leadership and management, affect value? Let us consider a senior owner rainmaker who is looking for a lead firm to acquire or assimilate his or her firm. What excites this person? You guessed it—a firm that does not have a weakness in the business development area. What excites the walking tax library owner when looking for a firm? Once again, it is a firm that has strength in the areas in which he or she is a superstar. What motivates a group of young owners to refrain from splitting off on their own to join a firm where they will have less say in operations? The answer is often a firm that has accountability backed by defined process, procedure, support, training, technology (overall SOP foundation) because the younger owners can see the value of trading control in return for growth of their personal income. If you want to test the importance of decision-making authority and SOP foundation to succession, just reflect on what you as well as everyone else seems to be looking for in a lead firm. No one wants to walk into organizational chaos; people want to (1) work in a proven organization, (2) that will be stable over time, and (3) is supported by strong processes and systems.

For those firms that want to take over, decision-making authority and SOP foundation will allow the assimilation of other firms more easily, quickly, and at a lower reorganizational cost. On the other hand, firms with poor decision-making authority and undocumented or marginally accountable SOP foundation have found that mergers and acquisitions only create more confusion, turmoil, and anarchy. When the target firm being acquired or merged can clearly see that the lead firm's organizational structures and processes are in flux, it promotes the addition of their personal operating preferences to the mix of considered alternatives. Opening this "Pandora's box" creates significant and unnecessary internal conflict and controversy.

My personal experience has shown that, at a time of major change, e.g., merging into a new firm, the target firm members are the most open to accepting new ways of doing business. As with any change of this magnitude, someone will test the boundaries of conformity with those systems. It must be clear that "resistance is futile." Noncompliance by those with influence must be answered with swift reprimands or firing. As a result, very quickly, the remaining members of the target firm will embrace the processes of the new organization. In contrast, if it is clear that the anticipated boundaries do not exist, the resulting power struggles and organizational confusion will stifle the firm for years to come. So, it is not just about which firm is in control, but whether that controlling firm has decision-making authority and SOP foundation, including maintaining accountability for adherence to those systems.

How Sellers Identify Purchasers

Identifying a purchaser can be very difficult, especially if a target firm wants to find candidates for acquisition or merger. Target firms do not want the local community to know that they are looking for exit strategies. This information might trigger current clients to leave them or competitors to use this information to sell against them. So, often, target firms put the word out that they are looking—but only to a few discrete consultants and very close friends to determine whether any possibilities exist. Usually, this is a very slow and ineffective process because it is difficult to find buyers for sellers who want to remain anonymous.

Firm Associations

Many target firms join networks or associations to develop close personal relationships with potential buyers and sellers. CPA firm associations are growing quickly as an excellent source of information, including tools, checklists, guides, and other such support. Firms also use these organizations to access specialty talent and to avail themselves of best practices. Several large firms create small-firm networks to motivate referrals, to provide technical support to their network firms, develop a way to serve smaller markets, and provide some of those firms with exit strategies.

Personal Contacts

Personal contacts are the most common way to find a firm, or for a firm to be found. The most frequently exploited technique is for a firm that wants to buy, sell, or merge with another firm to pick up the phone and schedule a meeting to talk. As we discussed above, this transaction is not just about money, so the starting point is to contact the firms that you come to respect in the many encounters you have had with their personnel over the years.

CPA state societies find themselves making a few introductions and helping firms open a dialogue.

Many times, the identification of the target firm is based on a lead firm's strategic objectives, such as opening or augmenting an office in a specific location, or adding an industry or niche service specialty. Therefore, the lead firm will use the contacts they already have to learn which firms best fit their criteria. If little is known about the firms in a specific area, various state-wide or national contacts may be approached for references, suggestions, and introductions.

Brokers

Just as there are business brokers in the corporate world, there are CPA firm consultants that act as brokers in the CPA community. Normally, a firm informs a consultant that they are in the acquisition or merger market. The next step is typically to either pay a retainer or pay for the consultant's time to become familiar with the lead firm's operation. During this initial phase, the consultant usually performs the following:

- Either helps the lead firm define an acquisition strategy or becomes familiar with one that has already developed.
- Constructs a list of negotiating points (ranging from those that are deal breakers to those with extreme flexibility).
- Determines what the characteristics of the target firm should look like in order to develop a target firm profile.
- Ascertains the size of the market to solicit (geographic limitations, numbers of firms).
- Calls candidates that might be a good fit; and/or puts together a marketing campaign to solicit firms that seem to meet the profile and invites them to call for a confidential screening discussion.

The fees for this service vary, with retainers that start at about $5,000 and go up based on the amount of work that needs to be done up front. In addition, a percentage from 3 to 10 percent is commonly charged at the completion of the acquisition or merger. Just as it is with business brokers, the smaller or larger the deal, the more the fees are specifically negotiated. For instance, for a small half-million dollar acquisition, consultants will shy away from percentages and set fixed fees (maybe with a total for all the work of about $50,000). On the other hand, lead firms will negotiate fee ceilings if percentages are expected to generate about $300,000 or more.

The disadvantage of bringing in a consultant is cost, but the advantages are that consultants:

- Are familiar with the industry and can quickly rule out firms outside of the established profile.
- Can create an active and anonymous marketing campaign to reach a number of firms that would have been missed through an informal contact network.
- Can prequalify the candidate firms and thus minimize the number of first-round review evaluations.
- Act as middlemen, thus keeping conversations with the target firms more on point and impersonal.

- Act as middlemen, thus more easily withholding certain information. Often, if owners are confronted by target firms and asked for semiconfidential information, they provide specifics whereas consultants will provide industry generalizations.
- Can be gatekeepers, providing another level of protection against tire-kickers or firms that are using the invitation to do some competitive intelligence work.
- Can provide an objective view of the two firms in question and offer insights regarding potential clashes in culture, owner expectation, internal organization, and systems.

All in all, the soft costs of completing this kind of transaction can be up to twice the hard costs. Consequently, involving an outside consultant can improve the chances of success, as well as the seamlessness of the integration, and may actually be the most prudent use of money.

Retirement Plans

As you would guess, if you looked over 20 different CPA firms' retirement plans and calculations, you would likely come up with almost that many variations. Although many of the plans might have components in common, each would be tailored to satisfy the specific personalities of the firm. To illustrate, here are a few deviations that I have run into recently:

- Calculated retirement pay (one-times-annual-firm-gross-revenue times ownership percentage) paid out over a period of time (seven to ten years)
- Total firm value (tangible plus intangible capital times percentage of ownership)
- A fixed percentage of salary per year for life
- The buyout price, frozen for existing owners at percentage of ownership times gross revenues at the time a new owner joins the firm (Added to that amount is any additional growth above the frozen revenues times the newly calculated ownership percentages.)
- The total of the individual's compensation for the three previous complete calendar years, plus 80 percent of the total WIP and accounts receivables (A/R) multiplied by their ownership percentage, paid out over 10 years
- Cash-basis capital accounts, paid out immediately (The value of the remaining ownership interest is equal to that owner's share of ownership profit times firm revenues, A/R, and WIP paid over a period of 10 years without interest.)
- Highest earnings in the last 10 years times 3, paid out over 10 years plus the capital account, paid immediately
- Fifty percent of the prior year's gross billings plus hard assets, including A/R and WIP, times the percentage of ownership (Payments are spread over four to ten years with no interest.)
- Excluding the high and low salary of the last five years, the total of the three remaining years, paid out over 10 years
- The accrual basis capital account plus 75 percent of the average of the last two years' gross fees times ownership interest

- One-third of average salary over the last five years for the first 10 years of retirement, then 25 percent of that salary for the next five years
- Average of the last five years' salaries, multiplied by 65 percent and paid for 10 years

Regardless of the formulas used to calculate the retirement benefit amount, the determination of when, what percentage of that amount is owed, and how much will be received per year is usually based on three variables: years of service to the firm, the age of owner, and a retirement payout maximum. The first two attributes are the hurdles of when someone becomes entitled to these privileges (vests), when someone can retire, and the percentage of benefit they are entitled to (partial to full). The third variable, retirement payout maximum, sets a ceiling on the annual payments to retirees (usually as a percentage of profits or gross revenues) to ensure that retirement obligations do not cripple the cash flow of the organization. Alternatively, sometimes this limit is accomplished through a formula whereby the total annual retirement benefit is reduced if certain minimum salary amounts for the remaining owners cannot be met. Regardless, if one of these situations arises, the retirement benefit is not reduced permanently because any shortfall is either made up in future periods or by extending the number of years payment is to be made.

This section will discuss the goals of retirement plans, updating retirement plans, overselling in retirement plans, maximum retirement ages, and a rule-of-thumb value test for retirement.

Retirement Plan Goals

There is no perfect retirement formula for all firms, and quite frankly, there rarely seems to be a perfect formula for the same firm across generations of owners. Each formula is developed according to the particular set of expectations of the current group of owners. As firms grow, as their business changes to mirror the marketplace, and as new owners come on board with different personal and professional goals, the retirement plan should be updated to reflect evolving needs. At a minimum, the retirement plan should always:

- Provide the retiring owners with financial benefits that reward them for their years of quality service to the firm.
- Recognize the retiring owners' contribution to the overall value of the firm.
- Motivate the owners to always do the right thing for the firm because if the firm benefits, so do they.
- Motivate the owners to stay with the firm and work hard until retirement.
- Encourage owners to schedule their retirements in a planned and orderly way to minimize the impact on the firm for the loss of their talent and expertise.
- Motivate retiring owners to transition their clients as well as otherwise support the firm so that their departure will be as seamless as possible.
- Demand that when that time comes, owners retire gracefully and honorably.
- Require that the retired owners continue to be a positive influence in the community supporting the firm.
- Compel the retired owners to never publicly disparage the firm, emphasizing that they are ambassadors of the firm for life.

Retirement Plan Updating

Often, slowly, and over time, the balance is lost between the retirement formula and the value of the firm, or the benefits provided drift out of sync with the needs of the firm.

> ⇄ **Sample Scenario**
>
> Consider a firm that has successfully retired two or three owners over the past 10 years, but about five other owners (say, 60 percent of the remaining owners) potentially all fall inside the same retirement window. The formula that worked well for the first few owners might fail with this next generation because the firm might be able to handle the financial burden of the retirements, but is unlikely to be able to handle the exponentially negative decline that will occur in owner competency, talent availability, and client account management responsibility.

In this case, here are some steps that might ensure the smooth and successful succession of this next generation of owners:

- Revise the retirement plan to limit early retirement.
- Allow the CEO/MP some temporary flexibility in mandatory retirement age if conflicts over scheduled departure exist.
- Demand at least three years' notice of retirement.
- Require the retiring owners to stagger their departures (for example, owners might have to allow a minimum 12-month window between departures.

Obviously, once this large group of similarly aged owners has been retired, these modifications to the retirement plan should most likely be revoked. The point is that management has to recognize that important policies have to be updated all the time to address possible future conflicts and protect the viability of the firm.

Retirement Plan Potential Disconnects

Another goal is to, as much as possible, disconnect various compensation systems. Consider the following:

> ⇄ **Sample Scenario**
>
> A firm with annual gross revenue of $3 million has four owners; one is 64, another is 59, the third is 58, and the youngest is 52. Their annual salaries are $350,000, $300,000, $300,000, and $275,000, respectively. The retirement formula pays retirees three times each owner's highest salary earned during their last 10 years, paid out over 10 years. Assume that the salary averages are fairly constant. An arm's-length firm wants to buy the above firm and retire all of the owners creating a 10-year obligation totaling $3,675,000, with a present value at 6-percent interest of around $2.7 million. The formula, in this situation, is within a reasonable tolerance.

However, say this firm has wanted to significantly alter its owner compensation formulas to motivate and reward specific behaviors each year. Seven years ago, there was a big push to cross-sell additional services. As a result of his stellar performance, the owner who normally makes around $275,000 made $375,000 that year. Five years ago, the strategic issue of focus was to develop staff and push work down. That year, an owner who normally makes $300,000 earned $425,000, and so on. Now, assume that by using the 10-year history, the owners have high salary years of $515,000, $440,000, $425,000, and $375,000. This gives gross retirement benefits of $5,265,000 with a present value of almost $3.9 million. This number could work for the younger owners if the firm's growth and profits consistently increase, but one always has to confirm that these formulas do not grossly oversell the value of the firm. A firm is only worth so much, and if the junior owners believe they are being charged an unjustifiable markup, they will revolt and leave to find a fairer deal elsewhere. And there is a growing likelihood of a "more than fair" deal being made to junior partners given the hybrid strategy in play to merge-in niches or departments rather than entire firms. So, disconnects between a firm's retirement plan formula and value can easily run off a great deal of scarce talent.

> **O— Key Point**
>
> Any time you tie multiple systems together (like annual compensation and retirement benefits), you have to constantly monitor to avoid unfavorable outcomes, such as the following:
>
> 1. One system handcuffs the other (preventing the firm from making needed corrections).
>
> 2. One system is forcing the other system out of balance with reality (such as significantly overcharging firm value).
>
> 3. One or both systems fail to independently support the firm's objectives.

Retirement Plan Maximum Age Requirements

The reason so many firms, especially larger ones, have established maximum ages (mandatory retirement) for owners to continue serving in their management roles is because of past privilege abuse. As we discussed in Chapter 3, "Management and Operations: Extending the Life and Culture of the Firm," most owners gain the advantage of benefit creep the longer they stay with the firm. Many firms will defend benefit creep as a valued mechanism for protecting their senior owners from burning out since they know that during the latter years of their careers, they will be able to maintain good salaries while slowing down. Nevertheless, this approach creates a situation of high pay, reduced expected intensity of effort, salaries strongly influenced by years of service and ownership, little accountability for daily effort, and virtually no disincentive to maintaining the status quo. It is no wonder that so many CPAs are motivated to maintain their active status as long as they can. Consequently, firms have been forced to put in mandatory retirement to ensure that senior owners, so disposed, have a limit to the number of years they can effectively "retire in place."

The Problem

Owners who retire in place impose a financial burden on firms but also trigger economic and leadership conflicts as well. For example, the major incentives for a CPA becoming an owner are to:

1. Eventually take over the leadership of the firm.
2. Gain the salary advantages and advances realized through benefit creep.

3. Enjoy retirement benefits earned partially through the growth of the firm and partially through benefit creep.

These premiums mostly accrue to the younger owners as senior owners retire. Unfortunately, this system collapses under its own weight if one senior owner group chooses to remain active an extra 10 years or so. Such a choice is predictable, given the gradually rising retirement age mandated by Social Security retirement dates as well as the fact that people are living longer. Consider this situation.

💲 Sample Scenario

A firm has six owners. Two are 63, two are 55, and two are 46. The firm does not have mandatory retirement. The two senior owners own 50 percent of the firm combined. Neither plans to retire any time soon.

Let us assume that both senior owners want to work until they are at least 75. The other owners cannot force them out because they do not have the votes required to do so. Fast forward 12 years, to a point at which the mix of owners has become two owners, aged 75, two aged 67, and two who are 58.

First, as discussed earlier, a general rule is that senior owners will be the most conservative in their approach to running the firm, in order to maintain the status quo. Therefore, the odds are reasonable that this firm has been dying a slow death for at least 10 years. The senior owners are not likely to be as active as they once were. Additionally, they are probably not as effective at bringing in new business because their personal contacts and networks have either retired around them or have turned the control of their businesses over to younger management.

Second, it is reasonable to predict that at least one or both of the middle owners are contemplating retirement. Given this situation, the firm is looking at the possibility that two-thirds of its owners will be retiring within a three- to five-year period, creating an incredible burden on the two remaining owners.

Third, throughout all of this, the youngest owners have suffered financially because of the high salaries being paid to the older owners and the continually escalating retirement benefit that now all four of the older owners will soon enjoy. Also, given that the younger owners are themselves each 58 years old, it is unlikely that they want to dramatically increase their work effort to assume new leadership roles, ensure that all clients are transitioned properly, and maintain the retiring owners' debt service.

Finally, the firm has almost certainly had difficulty recruiting owners during this period because no clear benefits would accrue to them except for the privilege of paying off everyone else. The refusing-to-retire owners:

- Ate up important salary dollars that could be shared.
- Caused the stagnation of the firm by minimizing risk and maintaining the status quo until their own departures.
- Clung to their leadership roles in the firm.

- Guaranteed themselves a more generous retirement benefit through the continued growth of the firm.

In many situations around the country, without mandatory retirement in place, it is difficult for potential young owners to assess the value of becoming an owner as well as determine when they should be able to reap the benefits seniority usually brings. Because of all the issues discussed above, implementing mandatory retirement becomes an important cog in the wheel of a firm's life.

The Solution

Can the dilemma described in the preceding be solved by any means other than mandatory retirement? Yes, though a different solution requires a different view of retirement systems. Given the current shortage of talent in our profession, one good idea is to allow owners that can pull their own weight to continue to work, especially in firms that have mandatory retirement ages that are very low (55 or even 60). If you want to maintain the value and integrity of the premium for becoming an owner, create an owner cycle through SOP foundation. For example, rather than forcing owners that want to work to leave, create polices that require owners over a certain age to:

- Remove themselves from leadership so that the changing of the leadership guard can occur.
- Shift from an ownership-based salary to a pay-for-performance salary to free up some part of the firm's likely largest salaries to be reapportioned to the younger owners.
- Freeze the retirement benefit to which the owners will be entitled to reflect the value of the firm at that point in time so that value gained by the new leadership can be used to pay their [new leadership's] retirement. Transition the vast majority of the client management responsibility to younger owners so that younger owners will be put in the position of managing the firm's top accounts and looking for additional ways to serve them.

This is meant to give you ideas, without being an all-inclusive list of steps to take in maintaining the current environmental shifts that mandatory retirement facilitates. As always, the key is balance. If the retirement option is too rich, senior owners will retire early and junior owners will want to also leave to avoid the burden of overpaying for the retirements of others. Alternatively, if the deal is too lean, owners will postpone retirement, and hang on for as long as they can in order to provide "a proportionate value to their pay" that will make their financial situation work. Regardless of your approach, you have to maintain the premium for becoming an owner by forcing transitions though whatever mechanisms are most appropriate for your firm.

Retirement Plan Test on Value

For this reason, whenever an owner is getting ready to retire, I do a quick rule-of-thumb test to verify that the retirement policy still makes sense. The approach I am about to share certainly can be applied most effectively to smaller firms, but the theory should have some resonance for any sized firm. My quick rule-of-thumb test of a retirement scenario is as follows.

Step 1. Multiply the firm's gross revenue by one dollar.

Step 2. Add back the owners' educated guess as to the current market value of the assets, the unbilled billable WIP, and collectable A/R.

Step 3. Subtract from that amount the outstanding notes, lines of credit, and accounts payable. The result is my rule-of-thumb value for existing owners.

Step 4. Take this "existing owners' rule-of-thumb value of the firm" and subtract the present value of all outstanding retirement benefit amounts due, including the obligation to pay the next retirement candidate. I call this result the remaining value of the firm.

Step 5. Next, multiply the ownership percentage of the remaining owners (excluding the next retirement candidate) times the existing owners' rule-of-thumb value of the firm to arrive at the *remaining equity in the firm.*

Step 6. Compare the remaining value of the firm to the remaining equity in the firm. Generally speaking, the remaining value of the firm should be greater than or equal to the remaining equity in the firm for the current policy to make sense. You can take a similar approach by assuming the immediate retirement of all but the youngest owner and see how the numbers add up. Usually, this latter calculation is more skewed, which is acceptable as long as the gap is not too big and both the firm's top and bottom lines are expected to continue to grow.

The following scenario demonstrates this approach:

Sample Scenario

Paul is 60-percent owner of a $1.5-million firm. They currently have $200,000 collectable in A/R, $110,000 in unbilled, good WIP, and the market value of the firm's assets is $90,000. Outstanding payables are around $50,000, with a line of credit of $200,000 and a long-term note of $175,000. Using my rule-of-thumb test, I would get the following result:

Step 1—$1.5 million in revenues × $1 dollar =	$1,500,000
Step 2—Adjusted receivables + WIP + assets =	400,000
Step 3—Payables + notes + line of credit =	425,000
My rule-of-thumb value for existing owners:	$1,475,000

Step 4—To reflect the soon to be retiring owner's impact on value:

Rule-of-thumb value for existing owners:	$1,475,000
Present value of the 10-year, $100,000 per year payout at 5% discounted rate	772,174
Remaining value of the firm:	$ 702,826

Step 5—To reflect the value of the firm that the remaining owners should be left with:

Rule-of-thumb value for existing owners:	$1,475,000
Remaining owners' ownership of the firm:	40%
Remaining equity in the firm:	$ 590,000

Since my simple calculation shows that the remaining value of the firm is greater than the remaining equity, then the owners remaining have more to gain by paying off the retiring owner than taking a drastic action, such as splitting up. However, if the retiring owner was to receive $125,000 a year for 10 years, this situation starts to become very marginal because the remaining value is less than the remaining equity.

To reflect the soon to be retiring owner's impact on value:

Rule-of-thumb value for existing owners:	$1,475,000
Present value of the 10-year, $125,000 per year payout at 5% discounted rate	965,217
Remaining value of the firm:	$ 509,783

The greater the negative balance between the firm's value and its equity, the more likely it becomes that the remaining owners will either demand adjustments or create ultimatums for change, such as starting their own firm or leaving to join a firm with a more reasonable plan. Nevertheless, there are extenuating circumstances that create more flexibility in this formula. These might include, on one side, creating very favorable purchase terms, maximum payout protections, remaining owner salary guarantees. On the other hand, the formula could be influenced by provisions to reduce the retirement benefits for poorly transitioned clients, or by taking into account the efforts by retired owners to maintain an active public relations role after retirement, or serve in visible community service volunteer roles.

One of the dangers of discussing a simple rule of thumb such as mine is that it is just a point of departure in testing a situation. You have to consider all factors before you can determine what is really fair. You will not be surprised to learn that I also have a rule of thumb for what is fair, too. Usually, *fair is a place where* both sides believe they have compromised more than they wish. Logically, it is easy for each of us to evaluate what we are giving up or the effort we have to make. It is just as easy for us to minimize what the other side is giving up and overlook the effort they have to make. Remember, we live our own lives and we merely view the lives of others. The result is the probability of drawing boundaries that favor ourselves, whether we mean to or not.

Succession Plans

Succession is not an isolated issue; developing a succession plan requires an examination of the entire business strategy. Consequently, succession can become an important catalyst that compels firms to finally make changes that previously never got beyond being topics for discussion at planning meetings.

Succession, more than any other issue, can be the catalyst for the owners in a firm to reach a consensus. Addressing succession is compelling because the senior owners understand that the time is drawing near for them to let go of the firm's reins, and yet they simultaneously want to reduce their risk of nonpayment of retirement benefits. The younger owners are ready to take over the firm, but recognize that they lack important skills and experience needed to ensure a successful transition. Therefore, all parties involved are almost certainly more open to change than at any time in the past. But most important, given the looming transition to the next generation of leaders, all the owners are likely willing to give up some privileges and powers in exchange for things that are becoming more important in light of this changing environment.

Some of the many issues that are open for change are:
- Who is going to take over the firm, and what skills do they need to develop?
- How can the firm's decision-making process be established to ensure a viable and enduring chain of command?
- What processes are needed to ensure the consistency of operations among leadership groups?
- What systems should be adopted to reward and promote the behaviors the firm desires?
- How will everyone in the firm be held accountable for his or her actions and inactions?
- How do we leverage both our people with extraordinary business development capability, as well as those with a similar level of technical competence, to be of maximum benefit to the firm?
- What are the roles, responsibilities, and expectations of owners, managers, and staff?
- How can the firm make the transition from operating like a group of individuals to a group supporting one firm (i.e., putting the firm first)?
- How can the firm's clients be transitioned, what is the order of the transition, and when do we start the transition process?
- What and when should the firm communicate about the transition plan to both employees and clients?

- What roles, responsibilities, and expectations as well as corresponding benefits and privileges have been identified for the retiring owners?

Succession Plan Steps

By addressing each of the preceding questions, you have traveled a long way down the road to developing your firm's succession plan. In drafting the plan, do not get caught up writing a novel when a series of outline notes will most likely do just as well:

- Agree to the concepts of a general plan. Everyone needs to understand that no one can give final approval until the details of each issue have been laid out because "the devil is always in the details." On the other hand, do not let this become a loose commitment; the owners need to conceptually agree that they will work hard to find a way to embrace the spirit of the general plan.
- For each issue deemed important, draft a strawman plan that outlines the details of the proposed implementation. The best approach is to empower your CEO/MP to develop the plans for presentation, modification, and approval by the board (or other such designated group).
- Always start with strategy, not personality. As much as possible, create foundation by looking to processes, technology, and systems—not to individuals who will want create their own boundaries and interpretations. Establish frameworks that identify boundaries to work within. Most important, give the responsibility for critical activities (technical competence, pushing work down, marketing), to the entire firm, not to just an individual or two.

Succession, if the right processes are in place, is actually fairly simple. One person replaces another. In most firms, however, the team is built around the person. This means that when a key individual leaves, the entire operation needs to be reshuffled, a new person or two chosen, and a strategy devised about how to rebuild a team that will leverage the talents and skills of new personnel. However, if positions are finely defined by clear powers and limitations, and supported by processes (natural checks, balances, and oversight), then replacement is not a big deal.

Succession Plan as a Catalyst

In terms of adding value to the firm, succession should be the impetus to implement processes and practices that should have been in place all along, which will have a long-term positive impact on the firm. Here are just a few ideas addressed in previous chapters:

1. Start charging clients a fair fee for the work being done.
2. Expect everyone in the firm to perform and be rewarded by reaching an established set of objective criteria.
3. Take steps to either convert your *D* clients to *C* clients, or let them go.
4. Stop supporting marginally profitable, nonstrategic island services.
5. Refuse to take work that theoretically provides income during the slow months.
6. Staff your firm for normal rather than peak operations, and use part-time staff to help to fill the gaps, rather than the other way around.
7. Do not allow part-time staff to take on key management responsibilities. Part-time staff should relieve work overloads, but not become central cogs in the machinery.

8. Reverse the pyramid, force work down, and emphasize client management.

9. Stop allowing owners to do manager-level work because it is an easy way for them to stay busy.

10. Start paying managers (supervisory managers) to develop and train their people.

11. Eliminate or modify any policy or procedure for which there is no willingness to hold people accountable.

12. Adjust billing rates and total billing expectations to give everyone an opportunity to be of value to the firm; to do this, consider, for each individual, the type of work he or she does, his or her likely realization, and his or her probable utilization.

13. Pass client and billing responsibility down to managers, at a minimum, for all *C* clients, in order to free up owners to stay in front of their *A* and *B* clients.

This baker's dozen summarizes just a few of the ideas found throughout this book. So, with the intent to "fix what has been broken for too long," list all the issues that rang true about your firm when you read about them and start addressing them one at a time. The few years leading up to succession is a great time to clean house and eliminate the burden of excess baggage for the firm's new leadership.

Succession Plan Transitions

As promised in the last chapter, I have included a nine-step approach to transitioning clients to ensure continued loyalty and retention. It is very simple and straightforward. I can hear you ask, "If this is so easy, why do so few firms do it well?" Firm-value transitions are done poorly in most firms because there is no system in place to force the senior owners to do them well. Therefore, owners continue doing what they have always done until it is time for them to go, because doing so maximizes their internal power, compensation, and flexibility.

Transition Steps

All there is to client transition is the following:

1. The CEO/MP should be in charge of developing the transition plan. This is not a job for the board unless it needs to provide some high-level guidance to the client redistribution process.

2. The retiring owner's current compensation and future retirement benefit should be conditioned on following the plan, with emphasis away from billable hours, to one of transition, business development, community visibility, and mentoring. Sizable penalties to the retirement benefit should be imposed for lack of compliance with the plan.

3. A minimum of about three years should be allowed for this process. Some owners may need five years because of the size of their client base.

4. A list of clients that need to be transitioned should be created.

5. People taking over account responsibility should be identified for each account.

6. A calendar should be created that depicts the order and timing of initial contacts for each client.

7. The largest and most important firm clients should be transitioned first. This gives the retiring owner more time to support the transition because he or she is still active in the firm.

8. Some firms, regarding their largest clients, create a team approach to serving those clients so people being moved in or out of the account seems to be less about transition and more about better client service.

9. SOPs are established that outline the allowable follow-up and involvement from retiring owners once transition begins. As an example, a firm might set up a process such as the following:

    a. In the first year of transition, any time service reporting or follow-up occurs with a transitioning client, the retiring owner will not conduct those discussions without the newly assigned account manager present.

    b. In the second year, the retiring owner might defer the presentation of all services to the new client manger.

    c. In the third year, the retiring owner will find excuses not to be present at most of the client meetings. In addition, that owner will issue constant reminders to his or her friend and client that the new client manager is the one who knows what is going on and has been taking care of them.

As indicated above, what makes transition problematic is the failure to do it, not that the process is too complex.

> **O— Key Point**
>
> Transition is simply about giving clients more reasons to stay with a firm than to leave it when their long-standing relationship manager is retiring.

Although it should be expected that your top clients all know several other firms that would love to serve them, switching firms is not a decision made lightly. Clients develop a comfort zone in working with their CPAs, especially knowing that their financial situation and secrets will be kept confidential by the firm. Most clients will not leave if the newly assigned client account manager is given a couple of years to build on the trust, confidence, and confidentiality of the existing relationship. This assumes, of course, that the retiring owners do their part and deliberately fade into the background.

Will all transitions be successful? No! We are talking about people, not objects, which explains my suggestion to penalize senior owners who do not follow the agreed-to transition plan. There will always be some client casualties when key people leave an organization. The point is not to obtain specific results, but for the retiring owners to take thoughtful and logical precautionary steps that will maximize client retention. Part of the economic value that offsets the retirement benefit is the firm's ability to continue to serve those owners' past relationships. Transition plans are an important mechanism to hold owners accountable.

Transition Leadership Development

> **O— Key Point**
>
> Success in developing leadership requires understanding that "mistakes need to be proportionately in line with position."

Here is what I mean: Whether you are talking about the new leaders in training in a CPA firm or any business on the planet, essential life and business lessons are learned, most often, through mistakes. This issue is one of the biggest problems encountered in succession of family businesses.

Although sons and/or daughters may have worked in the business their whole lives, they rarely made an important decision that was not scrutinized and approved first by Mom or Dad. This means that incoming leaders may have always carried impressive titles, but they never really had the power or authority of those positions. Mom and Dad believed they were doing the kids a favor by being there to catch them before they fell on their face and hurt themselves. The reality is that, instead of building leaders who were developing and continually refining their own "gut instinct" about what might work or fail, these new leaders merely proposed ideas that were considered by those in power. Here is how the scenario typically plays out:

> **↻ Sample Scenario**
>
> Dad owns a manufacturing business. Daughter has worked in the business for 22 years. She has held positions in purchasing, accounting, administration, and manufacturing. She is now Vice President of Operations. Dad is a strong-willed, very controlling entrepreneur. He has run this business with an iron fist since he started it 25 years ago. He wanted to retire five years ago, but did not believe that his daughter was ready to take over, nor was he willing to risk his biggest asset by turning it over to her. Six months ago, Dad got very sick. The prognosis for full recovery is excellent, but his close encounter with death has changed his priorities. He now is ready to turn the business over to his daughter and walk away to pursue his new priorities.

This is a very common situation, both in businesses of all sizes as well as CPA firms. Just change the specific people and their relationships to each other and everyone reading this can think of similar situations. My latest reading of some statistics from the Small Business Administration showed that more than half of small businesses fail in the first five years, and the transition can be particularly challenging for businesses being passed from one generation to the next. My personal experience points to "mistakes proportional to position" being a root cause for this lack of success.

Considering the outcome of the story above, one might think, "The daughter will do fine ... Dad was holding on long after she was ready." Nevertheless, the key to my interpretation is the words "strong willed" and "with an iron hand." I have been involved with similar situations over and over. The outcome is that although the daughter has been active in the business and is knowledgeable about all aspects of it, she has almost never been held accountable for the decisions she made. When she made bad decisions, Dad intervened and killed them. If she made good decisions, Dad implemented them. But the daughter, all along, never developed a "gut" instinct that would give her an early warning sign about when and why something was likely to go wrong. So, when she was in purchasing and wanted to use multiple shippers to increase flexibility, she never had the experience of having to account for the added cost of dispersing the volume, or the added difficulty of tracking shipments, or the customer dissatisfaction resulting from shipping errors. When she was in accounting and wanted to integrate all the systems throughout the organization, she never got to see for herself the improved information and streamlining of operations that would have resulted from this investment in technology. Nor did she observe, first-hand, the political nightmare of obtaining compliance from each department, as would have been required under fully integrated systems. I could go on and on, but the point remains the same. Daughter needed the experience of making $5,000 and $10,000 mistakes in purchasing and $25,000 to $50,000 mistakes as head of manufacturing. Dad or Mom might have been making those same mistakes, but she was not. Now, she is the new head of the company with no "gut" in place, and instead of making mistakes that were proportional with her position years ago and learning important lessons from them, she now will be effectively "betting the company" every time she has a new idea. Typically, businesses can take no more than one or two big, high-level mistakes before going under. I believe this is why so many businesses fail from one generation to the next.

Now, let me draw an analogy to succession in a CPA firm. If a firm is going to transition to new leaders, the new group should be given enough rope to hurt themselves and fail along the way under the guidance but not the control of the older owners. Their mistakes will cost the firm money in the short term, but not nearly as much as the costs that will result if older owners simply retire and walk away. So, in preparing to retire, older owners should not veto the younger leaders' ideas. Even if the older owners dislike proposals, they should allow them to proceed in such as way that the consequences are blunted. For example, assume the new leadership wants to expand into three new industry niches and open a new office. Rather than carrying out these initiatives simultaneously, which is exactly what the new leadership would want to do, older owners should approve the plans but also set some limits. The new leadership should be told to pick their best alternative, develop a business plan with specific annual hurdles and investment requirements, and run with it. The resulting experience will allow them to be accountable for their actions, yet limit the firm's risk by narrowing the investment. The new leadership will have a chance to "learn what they did not know." The experience of planning, setting objectives, identifying criteria for discontinuance, and defining what success should look like, will help them do a better job the next time around. The best news of all is that this formalized process will likely also become an accepted SOP foundation best practice for incubating all future ideas.

I cannot tell you how many times senior owners, as they approach retirement, become so conservative that they force the firm to stagnate. Their favorite response to any proposed change is, "You can do whatever you want once we are gone, but as long as we are here, things will stay the same." This attitude and posture does nothing but frustrate the incoming leaders, making them even more impatient to act. Demands for change become pent up, to the point that once the seniors are gone, too many projects will be attempted too fast without the proper controls. The new leadership is then in danger of failing to:

- Take on only one or two projects at a time.
- Follow a formalized process to propose new projects.
- Monitor and report how those projects are meeting expectations.
- Methodically implement them.

Although the do-nothing strategy may have helped the senior owners manage their risk while they were around, the conservatism of their actions and attitudes actually puts the firm in greater jeopardy after their retirement. The firm would have been far better off if the senior owners had been wise enough to recognize that the younger owners were going to make changes as soon as they could. Rather than fight them, the senior owners should have created processes, expectations, formalized requirements, and an approval process that would form the foundation for all future firm investment proposals (niches, offices, technology upgrades). This way, risk can be minimized, advice and counsel can still be given and accepted, and the firm can sustain whatever mistakes are made. Otherwise, the same actions will be attempted later, outside of a process under circumstances in which the new leadership may be unwittingly "betting the firm" and the senior owners' retirement payout.

To summarize: Put new firm leaders in positions in which they *can* and are permitted to make mistakes from which they can learn while costing the firm relatively little. Do not wait until the retiring owners leave—the new leaders' mistakes, after that point, might be large enough to cost the firm everything.

Succession Plan Agreements Issues

Recall the earlier suggestions that an essential first step is to redo your owner, retirement, compensation, and other agreements, eliminate from them *all of the formulas and specific requirements that are likely to change over time*, and instead incorporate these as policies in an SOP manual. These policies and formulas can then be reviewed annually or biannually on a rotating schedule to ensure their relevance.

Agreements Points

Besides the heightened level of issue scrutiny and oversight that will occur as a result of reworking the agreements, there are additional, specific agreement points that should be addressed relative to retirement and succession. Some basic issues would include:

- What is the retirement age, and is it mandatory?
- Is early retirement allowed and, if so, what are the differences in benefits?
- What activities can a retired owner continue to perform after retirement? What authorization is required for those activities to continue?
- How are retired owners compensated for their continued activities, if any (e.g., percentage of collection, hourly fee)?
- Who is liable for the amount of outstanding retirement payout to the firm (the firm, and/or the owners personally)?
- What recourse or cures can retired owners invoke if they are not paid in full?
- What voting privileges do retired owners have during their payout period? For example, can they block mergers or sales of the business? Can they block a partial sale, like the sale of a niche service?
- If a merger or acquisition (full or partial) occurs, will the outstanding retirement payout amounts become due in full immediately?
- Is there insurance on key people in the firm that will pay off the retirement obligations to those people if they die or become totally disabled? Will this key-person insurance also cover outstanding retirement obligations to other retired shareholders?
- What acts can force the termination of an owner (e.g., illegal activities, misconduct such as harassment, lack of performance, bankruptcy)

- What acts can force the retirement of an owner (e.g., public embarrassment of the firm, lack of performance, owner disability, bankruptcy)
- What percentage of votes is required to remove an owner?
- What percentage of votes is required to force the retirement of an owner?
- What is the client transition plan for owners three to five years away from retirement?
- If an owner does not comply with the dates, deadlines, and responsibilities defined in the client transition plan, what impact will that have on the calculation of his or her retirement payout?
- How do uncollectible A/R or WIP affect the responsible owners' compensation?
- How do liabilities incurred after retirement based on work performed by a retired owner affect the remaining and outstanding retirement payout obligation?
- Do you require all retiring owners to sign a noncompete agreement with the firm as part of their retirement obligations? Assuming the firm does require these agreements, and assuming a retired owner continues to perform work as a CPA after retirement on his or her own, thereby competing with the firm, what recourse does the firm have? Can this act void the firm's requirement to pay retirement pay, or reduce obligations by the amount of work being performed?
- What responsibilities for their own conduct do retired owners have during the retirement payout period? For example, can the retired owners publicly criticize the firm? Can the owners refer business to competing CPA firms? Can the retired owner perform egregious acts of misconduct in the community? Should the retired owners violate their conduct responsibilities, what recourse can the firm take against them during the payout period?
- What is the maximum retirement payout to all retired owners that has to be paid annually as a percentage of gross or net income? If an annual retirement payout amount is reduced because the cash-flow percentage ceiling has been met, how is this resolved (e.g., by making it up in the following year or extending the payout period)?
- Does owner death or disability accelerate the payment of the retirement amount? If so, how?
- If the active owners' compensation falls below a specified amount, does that affect the annual retirement payout requirement?
- Is there a preretirement period, such as three years, during which the retiring owners are removed from the firmwide compensation plan and put on a retiring owner's plan to motivate them to complete their preretirement activities and not punish them for not performing the normal owner requirements?

These questions are not meant to be a list of all of the issues, but rather capture a number of the most common ones. In addition to addressing these, two other agreement areas might benefit from added examination. The first is an employment agreement for anyone who has regular contact with clients and the second is a severance agreement that outlines the compliance expected of terminated employees or owners.

Employment Agreements

Let us start with the employment agreement. Through working with several of my clients and their attorneys, it became obvious that the success of traditional noncompete agreements depends on specific circumstances. Therefore, we decided to take a different approach and consider the circumstances of the modern workforce, which seems especially prudent for workers in nonmetropolitan settings whose employment opportunities are limited outside a specific mile radius (such as 25 miles) from their residences. Rather than focusing on the noncompete aspect of employment agreements, which tends to mostly line the pockets of the opposing attorneys and provides little to the firms, we took the approach of being reimbursed for client losses incurred, which, during succession, is even more appropriate.

For any clients taken by a previous employee, we decided to charge multiples of the annual revenue earned, which declined over time (the highest multiple in the first 12 months, a reduction of the multiple in the second 12 months). This was put in place to account for the time, effort, training, expertise-building, and privilege of direct client contact that had been invested in this employee. Moreover, because these policies are based in the firm's standard employment agreement, we not only are obligating former employees to pay the firm for any clients that leave with them, we are also attempting to obligate any competitive firm that hires these former employees. In other words, if a competitor hires a former employee within the defined grace period, we will send them notice of that employee's existing employment agreement and notify them of their implied agreement to assume certain financial obligations if they elect to have their new employee solicit clients of their former employer. Given the current environment, in which firms are wooing away entire teams of specialized employees from competitors, this clause is important and necessary for the purpose of securing the value of your firm.

We also took this approach because in many smaller communities, instead of generating ill will and disputes about how former employees are making a living, the intent is to treat them as professional colleagues and simply charge them for any clients taken during a specific period of time after their departure from the firm. It may also be that they have a duty to disclose this agreement to any competitor they work for during the grace period, so that their new employer's first notice of the agreement is not a letter from the employee's previous firm. This employment agreement, properly drafted, can set the ground rules for any new relationships that involves providing services to clients of previous employers.

Severance Agreements

Let us discuss severance agreements. I bring this up now because as you start implementing strategies for succession, there will probably be employee and owner casualties. These typically are the people who immediately come under scrutiny when new performance systems are implemented, or those who refuse to be held accountable, or will not accept specifically defined roles and responsibilities. So, make sure you have an agreement in place that outlines what is expected from these employees in order to receive their final severance checks. Some of the standard issues that are important to address are:

- Return of property and what specific property that includes, tailored for each employee

- Notification of when such employee will get his or her final check, including the understanding that the amount stated is the full settlement of the firm's obligation
- The date of termination and benefits, and a specification of those benefits, such as COBRA, that will remain available
- A waiver of claims by accepting the severance sum, which could include claims of harassment or discrimination.
- Explanation that severance is not an admission by the firm of any violations
- Assurance that the employee will not disparage the firm for a specific period in any way
- Notification of the confidentiality requirement of the agreement
- Notification that any breach of the agreement will be settled through binding arbitration (and how that is specifically arranged)

Caveat

Obviously, it is essential to consult with your firm's attorney as to what strategies are permissible in your jurisdiction, as well as what will work best for the particular circumstances of your firm.

Additional Succession Plan Issues

Here are some of the remaining questions and responses we have yet to cover in full from the PCPS Succession Survey. These questions were only asked of those firms that have multiple owners.

How many owners plan to retire from your organization in the next five years? Of those that responded, the answers were:

- 63 percent of the firms had at least one person retiring in five years.
- 32 percent of the firms had more than two or more people retiring in five years.

What percentage ownership of the firm does each group represent? The ownership percentages are as follows:

- In multiowner firms, the average age of the most senior partner was 60 and their average ownership percentage was 35 percent.
- Among sole proprietors, the 65 percent were 55 or older.

Other responses mostly support hypotheses I have covered earlier in this book. For example, a number of conclusions would be that:

- A great number of owner-level CPAs will be retiring in the next 10 years.
- A large number of senior owners have no idea when they might retire.
- A number of firms do not have mandatory retirement ages.
- There will be a significant number of firm leadership changes during the next decade.
- CPA owners are continuing to work longer.
- A number of firms have senior owners who own a significant portion of their firms and who will be looking for low-risk exit strategies.
- Well-managed firms that have decision-making authority in place and are run by strong SOP foundation will be in a great position to exponentially grow their businesses at a very low cost during the next 10 to 15 years.

For the firms in the last item, a banquet of firms looking for low-risk exit strategies will lie before them. Additionally, firms that are aging without a planned exit strategy will find that a number of their clients, as they see their CPAs retiring in place, will look for a viable firm to which to take their business.

Succession Plan Potential Pitfalls

This book has been about the typical pitfalls encountered during succession and the support systems necessary to shore up weaknesses. Nevertheless, it seems appropriate to highlight some of them again in this section of our final chapter. These pitfalls are:

Pitfall 1. Lack of decision-making authority
Pitfall 2. Controlling owner
Pitfall 3. Continuing roles of retiring owners
Pitfall 4. Operational swings
Pitfall 5. Designated rainmaker
Pitfall 6. Transiting CEO/MP
Pitfall 7. Fragmenting the firm
Pitfall 8. Lack of interest in becoming an owner

The following sections discuss these eight potential pitfalls.

Pitfall 1. Lack of Decision-Making Authority

I start with lack of decision-making authority as one of the most prominent pitfalls. Decision-making authority either exists because the firm has an owner with a controlling interest in the firm, or because an established organizational hierarchy delineates the lines between board (owner group) responsibilities and CEO/MP responsibilities. For any organization, creating decision-making authority is the place to start. Without a strong level of command and control, all the procedures and agreements in the world will not matter because there is no authority that will consistently hold people accountable.

Pitfall 2. Controlling Owner

Interestingly enough, another pitfall comes as a direct result of command and control. In this case, we are talking about the controlling owner and why he or she often becomes the firm's biggest problem. The good news is that accountability can be implemented throughout the firm (most likely for everyone but the controlling owner, unless he or she is a benevolent dictator and subjects him- or herself to the same rules as everyone else). Unfortunately, what too often happens is the controlling owners will talk about retiring, but do not want to pin themselves to a specific date. They will maintain control of their client accounts until almost the last day of work. When they finally announce their retirement date, these leaders will not want to hang around for too long without remaining in control. Because they would not commit to a specific retirement date with plenty of advance notice, poor client transition and client book management result. This actually works in the controlling owners' favor, however. A number of them will be able to "double-dip," so to speak, and augment their retirement benefits by either keeping a certain number of clients after retirement and/ or requiring ongoing financial payments to compensate them to manage the activities they should have already performed. In addition, these owners will commonly ask for remuneration to carry on firm activities (such as marketing) which they did not transition, or for which they failed to create systems. In every case I have been involved with, the instant that these deals were finalized and the operational issues resolved, the remaining owners modified their agreements to ensure that the firm would never be put in this position again.

Pitfall 3. Continuing Roles of Retiring Owners

Another area of abuse is found with continuing roles of retiring owners. As I have said before, retired owners should not have *any* client management responsibilities. Firms' active owners should maintain all client relationships. Granted, retired owners will have numerous personal friendships with the firm's clients, and those clients may still call the retired owner first when problems arise. Nevertheless, the retired owner has an obligation to refrain from handling the issue and, instead, to immediately put the client in touch with the owner who currently holds responsibility for the account, thus helping to strengthen the new relationship. As long as the retired owner is allowed to act as an intermediary, full client transition cannot occur. Allowing retired owners to manage firm clients guarantees a future disconnect between the firm and the client regarding services offered and delivered, fees, or some other issues. Misunderstandings will arise because the retired owner is no longer privy to the firm's strategy or management conversations.

Pitfall 4. Operational Swings

Another common pitfall is extreme pendulum swings in the way the firm operates. The more a firm operates on the personal whims of the owners rather than on defined process, procedures, and policies, the more likely operations will shift from one extreme to another as ownership percentages are reshuffled. For example, a swing will almost certainly occur if a powerful controlling owner retires. The firm commonly will shift from that of dictator to committee-run operations. Although it is predictable that both of these extreme operating styles wreck havoc on organizations, assuming the dictator has reasonable business acumen, the presence of decision-making authority will almost always be better than operating without it. Another common swing occurs around work and life balance. Assume a workaholic controlling owner group. It is highly likely that once power shifts away from this group, the remaining owner group will want to do away with the pressure-cooker workplace and install a "low stress, no pressure" environment. I know I am going to take some heat for saying so, but both of these extremes are poor long-term choices. Workaholic firms tend to burn out their CPAs, leading to a very predictable end. Low stress, no pressure environments tend to create a positive work setting for the owners and employees, but these firms, time and again, are shown to be poorly managed because the owners refuse to focus enough attention on doing what is necessary to sustain the long-term value and viability of the firm. Often, low stress, no pressure firms rise in a second or third generation of leadership and slowly deteriorate as individual priorities supersede the need to put the firm first. Either extreme is a predictor that, as soon as older voters are retired, the new leadership will swing

180 degrees in the opposite direction. Successful succession is about consistency, not about setting the firm up for these kinds of dramatic swings.

Can a firm be successful swinging from one extreme operating style to another? Absolutely! But remember the discussion above about "keeping mistakes in proportion to position?" When you move from one known extreme operating mode to a new, unknown one, the new leadership is in uncharted waters about how to make this kind of organization run effectively. Therefore, the learning curve is more likely to include mistakes on the scale of "betting the business." Developing processes throughout the organization becomes a major selling point in the sense that new leadership can take over and smoothly begin to function in an environment that has been successful and will require only occasional minor alterations. Such environments offer a much higher likelihood of uninterrupted success.

Pitfall 5. Designated Rainmaker

Surviving the departure of a firm's designated rainmaker is another common stumbling block in succession. As we have discussed before, owners are apt to place too much emphasis on attracting new business when, in reality, a great deal of growth comes from the provision of additional services to existing clients. Moreover, analysis suggests that new clients are the byproduct of an active client and professional referral network more than anything else. A firmwide SOP foundation marketing engine coupled with regularly scheduled visits to the firm's top clients achieves results in these developmental areas much more consistently than reliance on a couple of superstars. This is not nearly as much about selling as it is about ensuring that everyone who works for your firm embraces the responsibility to live up to the profession's mantra of being clients' "most trusted adviser." You cannot become such an adviser if you are not genuinely interested in spending time with your clients, listening to them, and helping them find whatever resources they need to achieve their personal and professional goals and objectives.

Pitfall 6. Transiting CEO/MP

Choosing the best person for the top position in the firm poses many hazards. Most firms consider the CEO/MP position a way to honor seniority or satisfy an ego. The problem is that many CPAs are not well suited for this job. The CEO/MP position, in my view, should be filled by someone who takes a systems approach to running the firm. This is a person who enjoys achieving the defined mission of the organization, who likes working within the framework of a budget, who believes it is important to constantly communicate throughout the firm, who defaults to implementing support processes, procedures, and technology to create consistency of operations, and who wakes up every day thinking about how to make the firm run more efficiently and profitably. Although the CEO/MP is also a face in the community and will be involved in various networking activities, his or her primary job is to work on the business rather than just in it. Suppose an owner in your firm is a great project manager, loves working with clients, enjoys networking, and is happiest when challenged by new client situations. Do not make the mistake of making him or her your CEO/MP. The firm will always come second; this person's passion is working with clients, not managing the firm.

In addition, when making this transition in power, consider turning this job over to someone who could do it for 10 years or so, assuming he or she proves to be competent in the job. A three- to four-year tenure as a CEO/MP barely gives this owner enough time to get his or her hands around the job and implement anything significant. For example, going paperless is an initiative that has become a commonplace undertaking for firms. Experience shows that it takes at least three years to fully implement the efficiencies and new ways of managing projects that go with a paperless environment, not to mention being able to assess the economic payoff. Initiatives in planning, budgeting, operating framework, reversing the pyramid, marketing, performance pay, and employee motivation are even more complex, given the intricacies of how these systems are integrated and overlapping. Consequently, you must give your new CEO/MP a chance by giving him or her enough time to be able to make a difference. If you have someone who is best suited to take on the role of being the firm's face to the community but is not a good candidate to be CEO/MP, assign him or her a prestige role like chair of the board. Do not undermine your organizational hierarchy by naming this person as CEO/MP while assigning the real operations duties to chief operating officer or firm administrator. Whoever is making day-to-day decisions about how the firm operates must also hold the appropriate title, or there will be chaos and confusion among the staff as changes are being implemented.

Pitfall 7. Fragmenting the Firm

A significant pitfall is the fragmentation of the firm perpetuated by the model that allows owners to take the posture that, "I manage my own book of business." A corollary of this model is an "eat-what-you-kill" outlook that can be very satisfying and lucrative for some individuals, but it creates conflicts for firms undergoing growth, change, or succession. Simply, if there are three owners, and they all generally manage the same sized book of business, and each manages his or her book to about the same profit ratio, all will be well. But invariably, one owner's book will grow faster than another's. Conflict is imminent as soon as there are substantial differences in the book sizes within the firm because these differences often precipitate large discrepancies between personal income and voting rights.

This brings up an insurmountable obstacle for any CEO/MP. The job of CEO/MP is to primarily manage the firm (granting that the amount of time required to devote to this obviously varies based on the size of the firm). The first task for a new CEO/MP is to give him- or herself enough time to work on the firm by transitioning much of his or her client responsibilities to others. Note, however, that even in large firms, it is a good idea for the CEO/MP to do from 250 to 500 hours of client work annually, which will ensure a continuing perspective onto the demands clients constantly place on members of the firm. Given the assumption that the CEO/MP needs to free up time to devote to the firm, and given that client book size is often a primary source of power within firms, what protections are the rest of the owners willing to provide to minimize the CEO/MP's transitioning risk? In other words, if, over the course of the next few years, half or more of the CEO/MP's clients are transitioned to other owners, what assurance does the CEO/MP have that divesting client responsibilities will not hurt him or her in the long run, e.g., at the point in the future when a new CEO/MP is chosen? In many firms, a protection period covering total compensation is given. For example, an assurance package might be that the salary of the stepping-down CEO/MP will not decline more than 10 percent a year from the previous year for three years in order to provide enough time for this owner to regain a reasonable client base. It also might include, assuming this person is not going to retire in the very near future, the right to have selected clients transitioned back, or an understanding that new clients will be assigned to him or her so as to achieve an equal redistribution among the owners. Too often, however, *owners put their CEO/MPs in a no-win situation* by asking them to make managing the firm their priority even though it is clear that client-base managed is the only true source of power. Unless this conflict is addressed, you are ensuring that the CEO/MP will only provide lip service to running operations and doing what is best for the firm (planning for succession, increasing profitability, developing SOP foundation). He or she, driven by a healthy sense of self-interest, will continue to consider managing his or her client base the top priority.

Pitfall 8. Lack of Interest in Becoming an Owner

Sometimes succession is thwarted because qualified people are not interested in becoming owners. If this is occurring in your firm, step back and take a hard look at the deal that is being offered to these people. In many firms, new owners do not make much more money than they were already earning. Nevertheless, they have to meet higher expectations in performance; they have to personally assume the risk of the firm's debts and liabilities; they have little to no say in the company; and, most important, they see themselves as indentured servants paying the senior owners' retirement obligations. Existing owners who take the attitude that "It-was-good-enough-for-me-when-I-was-a-new-owner," are not rationalizing very well. Younger people who question the deal may be smarter than you were when you just accepted it. Remember, too, that the adage, "Trust me ... it will work out for you," is so overused and abused that it does not hold much water. And sometimes, there may be really good reasons why owner candidates are not interested in becoming owners. It might be that there is a potential lawsuit pending that could bankrupt the firm. It might be that there are no mandatory retirement policies in place for the senior owners, meaning that the new owners cannot assess how the economics will work for them. In any event, often, when I find managers resistant to becoming owners, it is less about their willingness to perform and more about a flawed deal. If you want to build a firm that has viability beyond the current generation of owners, and you are having trouble getting people to participate, make sure the "new-partner" deal is good enough.

This leads me to the next potential obstacle. Owner status should not be the predictable result of seniority. In other words, your people should not feel that if they do not become owners, there is no place for them. People choose different priorities and aspirations, and becoming an owner, and taking on the burden of owner responsibilities, may be very low on the list. However, do not confuse not wanting to become an owner with not believing that a career is important. In order to retain your key employees, it is essential to express to them that their expertise and contribution is valued. This means, at times, you must devise ways to keep your top performers engaged, including programs to reward them—and you must do this better than your competitors do. For example, you do not want your superstar senior manager(s) to leave in order take a nonequity position elsewhere that includes sharing in the firm's profits or having access to a special "time-off" reward for people who significantly exceed their incentive targets. In other words, show your employees that becoming an owner is not the only measure of their value to the firm, nor the only source of rewards for top performers, nor the only way for them to prove their loyalty to the firm.

Conclusion

In conclusion, succession is accomplished by taking the following steps:

1. Identify the firm's strategy.
2. Empower a management team (CEO/MP, COO or firm administrator) to implement the changes necessary to achieve the directives of the board of directors (decision-making authority) without constant micromanagement.
3. Establish firmwide SOP foundations that support your strategy (accountability, trained and motivated employees, reversing the pyramid, performance management, service synergy, marketing, business development, client retention and loyalty). Develop integrated systems that buttress SOP processes, incorporating performance measurement and monitoring (creating consistently followed process by utilizing technology, policies, procedures).
4. Tie compensation to the achievement of key objectives (using either lead or lag measures).

Identifying the Firm Strategy

This list of steps should not be surprising; they summarize basic concepts covered throughout this book, yet also are seldom accomplished by firms. Even firms that are considered exceptionally well run by our profession actually struggle to get their hands around one or more of these areas. Usually, there is lack of clarity (item 1, in the preceding list), following by a default into micromanaging (item 2). Although you can put a few systems in place to address most of the issues below owner without taking the first two steps, you cannot holistically implement anything throughout the firm or hold people accountable until these first two steps are complete.

Whether you are a sole proprietor or a senior owner in a large firm, you want to develop Step 2 around policy, responsibilities, powers, and limitations as much as possible. This helps everyone—even a sole owner—to hold up a mirror and continually verify how the organization was designed to work. This approach positions the firm as if it was a separate life that must be protected, nurtured and developed. At some point in a company's success, hierarchical decision-making authority will be needed to advance the firm to the next level. But why wait? Owners need to willingly trade in their individual powers and privileges for the greater good of organizational processes and accountability. Those firms that can accomplish this important transformation will position themselves to be able to leap past others in leveraging the consolidation that will be driven by succession in the coming decade.

Implementation

Regardless of the size of the firm, from two to two thousand employees, every one of the five steps listed above is the same. Issues like operating based on strategy, adhering to a budget, accountability, reversing the pyramid, service synergy, marketing, business development, and client retention or loyalty, are equally applicable. The difference comes in the complexity of implementation and the level of required formalization. When a sole proprietor can look beyond the income-hit he or she sustains today in order to build infrastructure everywhere possible, this operator model approach will return long-term efficiency, productivity, and profitability. Moreover, in the end, this investment also drives up the value of the firm while making it a prime target for acquisition or merger, even in a soft market.

A Final Word

There is no question that succession planning is one of the hottest topics of the day. Everyone is looking for a simple plan that will shore up firm value. The superstars are looking for a couple of ideas they can put in place before they retire that will pay huge dividends. For many of these firms, succession is being looked at as if it were merely a buy/sell transaction, where the cost of goods sold were pieces of inventory rather than human relationships. Obviously, it is a far more complicated transaction.

So, given this landscape, if you want to pass your firm's torch without getting burned, become one of the few that really applies the concepts in this book. Stop relying almost exclusively on people to carve their own unique paths, and start building roads that all employees can easily follow to eventually move ahead. Realize that although your clients have a value in the marketplace, firms gaining access to additional talent will likely be of equal value. So, stop looking at your clients as your only asset to sell, and instead, look at your firm, its SOP foundation, and the talented people you develop as assets of equal or greater value. In the coming years, new business will be pervasive because of the number of clients looking for new homes as their trusted CPAs retire. Those firms that build an infrastructure that will allow them to easily and seamlessly take on this potential abundance of new work will be mostly limited by their people. Therefore, it becomes imperative to establish processes that leverage people (the operator model) in order to be able to train them more quickly, interchange them more often, and manage them more effectively.

Succession is about working "on your business." Succession is about finally taking those steps you have known you needed to take for years. Succession is about making "you" less important by creating a self-running operational engine that cranks out satisfied and loyal clients as a byproduct of the consistently high-quality work performed. Succession is about developing a team of stars, not developing a team around superstars. And most important, succession is about leadership. New leaders cannot take over if the old leaders will not ever let go.

Take a good hard look at why your firm has been successful and continue to leverage the traits and characteristics that are good. But also start building bridges to traverse the chasms in strategy and operations that have occurred through constantly placating the firm's superstars. It is time to realize that a firm cannot achieve significant momentum by following everyone's navigation strategy. Pick a direction, put someone at the helm, and have everyone else get out of the way. It is time to invest in the construction of formalized methodology (SOP foundation) so that your superstars' strengths do not eventually define the firm's structural weaknesses. If you want to successfully pass the torch, start implementing whatever ideas rang true for you in this book while constantly trying to replace superstar ideology with an operator and interchangeability mentality.

I wish you the best of luck in your future succession. And regardless of the path you choose, it has been my honor and a privilege that you have allowed this book to be part of your process.